Instructor's Manual to Accompany

Psychology

Instructor's Manual to Accompany

PSYCHOLOGY

Henry L. Roediger III
J. Philippe Rushton
Elizabeth D. Capaldi
Scott G. Paris

PREPARED BY
Hiram E. Fitzgerald
Cathleen Erin McGreal
MICHIGAN STATE UNIVERSITY

LITTLE, BROWN AND COMPANY Boston Toronto

ISBN 0-316-75381-5

5 4 3 2 1

SEM

Published simultaneously in Canada
by Little, Brown & Company (Canada) Limited

Printed in the United States of America

OVERVIEW

Teaching introductory psychology is a demanding task. The instructor must have a working knowledge of almost every subfield of contemporary psychology and must have a broad understanding of psychology's philosophical and scientific history. Moreover, the instructor is expected to present this diverse information in a manner that will stimulate a student clientele that is at least as diverse as the field of psychology itself. Many students enroll in introductory psychology because they intend to major in psychology; others hope to gain personal insight into their own behavior and the behaviors of those around them; still others enroll only because the introductory psychology course fulfills a requirement of their degree program. This variety of students and subject matter will challenge even the most experienced instructor. This manual was prepared to help meet this challenge.

This manual is one component of a complete system of teaching resources designed specifically for PSYCHOLOGY. We included materials that should be helpful both to the experienced instructor and to the instructor who is teaching introductory psychology for the first time. The instructor's manual details specific issues that should be considered prior to teaching the course, such as lecture preparation, testing student performance, determining an evaluation criterion (grading), and planning for instructor and course evaluation.

The components of this instructional package have been integrated in order to provide a complete system of instructional aides. For example, the learning objectives listed in this manual also appear in the Student Study Guide. In turn, the test items have been written to correspond to the objectives. The strong integration among learning objectives, test items, student text, and instructor's manual, allows for easy adaptation of this teaching package to increasingly popular self-paced methods of instruction.

There are two parts to the instructor's manual. Part I corresponds directly to the textbook. Each chapter has specific guides and suggestions to help in lecture preparation for the corresponding text topic. Each chapter in Part I consists of the following sections:

(1) *Chapter Overview.* The major highlights and topics covered in the text are summarized to provide the instructor with a brief review of the chapter.

(2) *Learning Objectives.* This section lists the specific objectives for the chapter. Test items for PSYCHOLOGY are referenced to these objectives.

(3) *Attention Getters.* This section presents some questions and situations to stimulate and aid class discussion, or to use as essay items.

(4) *Lecture Suggestions and Class Demonstrations.* Hints for the preparation of lectures are given along with instructions for demonstrating many of the concepts discussed in the text. Where appropriate, reference is made to transparencies that have been developed for use with PSYCHOLOGY. Marginal notations refer the instructor to text headings and specific pages where the topic is discussed in more detail.

(5) *Audiovisual Aides.* This section lists audiovisual aides (including films, audiocassettes, filmstrips, and other media resources) that can be used to illustrate the points made in each particular chapter.

(6) *References and Annotated Sources.* References are provided for sources discussed in each particular chapter in the manual. In addition, brief descriptions are given of additional sources that may prove useful for lecture preparation.

Part I concludes with a section listing many sources for software programs developed for introductory psychology courses. We tried to include as many sources in this section as possible, but we recognize that computer assisted instruction is such a volatile field that new programs for use in introductory psychology courses appear almost daily.

In Part II, general issues related to teaching introductory psychology are raised as are matters pertaining to teaching in general. Among the topics covered are: various instructional methods (including contingency management methods), teaching graduate students how to teach, testing and evaluation of students, grading, evaluation of individual lectures, and evaluation of the course as a whole. In addition, a bibliography of teaching resources directs the instructor to the primary literature, including many references to articles published in *Teaching of Psychology*, the official journal of Division 2 of the American Psychological Association. The names and addresses of film suppliers are listed to facilitate the use of audiovisual materials. Finally, we note many books and guides pertaining to teaching that are available from the American Psychological Association.

We hope that this manual and all other components of the PSYCHOLOGY instructional system help instructors to prepare for teaching introductory psychology and help students to enjoy learning about this complex and fascinating discipline.

INSTRUCTIONAL COMPONENTS OF THE PSYCHOLOGY TEACHING SYSTEM

Student Text

PSYCHOLOGY offers students a comprehensive, integrated, and up-to-date introduction to the discipline. By emphasizing both fundamental principles and current developments, the text shows how the issues, methods and applications of psychological research contribute to psychology's growth.

The text is divided into 17 chapters, beginning with a broad overview of psychology's past and present, and leading systematically through the discipline's primary topics, from psychobiology, all the way to environmental psychology. The major approaches within psychology--physiological, cognitive, behavioral, psychoanalytic, and humanistic are introduced in Chapter 1 and integrated throughout the book, especially after Chapter 8. The chapter sequence in the book should fit many existing curriculum needs; however, the chapters are also designed to be used independently, and an instructor may assign them out of sequence, or omit certain chapters. The following outlines suggest possible alternatives:

A. Emphasis on Basic Processes (Experimental Emphasis)

Chapter
1 The Nature of Psychology
2 Biological Bases of Behavior
3 Sensory Processes
4 Perception
5 Consciousness and Attention
6 Conditioning and Learning
7 Memory

Chapter 8 Development
9 Language and Thought
10 Intelligence Tests and Mental Abilities
11 Motivation
Appendix Statistics

B. Emphasis on Application (Social-Personality Emphasis)

Chapter 1 The Nature of Psychology
5 Consciousness and Attention
8 Development
9 Language and Thought
10 Intelligence Tests and Mental Abilities
11 Motivation
12 Emotion and Stress
13 Personality
14 Abnormality and Deviance
15 Therapies
16 Social Psychology
17 Social Problems

PSYCHOLOGY combines clear writing and effective pedagogical features, including the following:

The Research Process: This chapter feature offers details and results of an important, provocative research issue. For example, in Chapter 5, the authors examine research surrounding subliminal perception.

Controversy: Another chapter feature looks at a particular, unresolved issue within psychology. For example, in Chapter 2, the authors consider the sociobiological approach to behavior.

Applying Psychology: A third chapter feature explores psychology's contemporary applications; for example in Chapter 11, the authors introduce the topic of anorexia nervosa.

Today's Psychologists: Interviews with eminent psychologists, including Bibb Latané, Stanley Schachter, Richard Gregory, and Hans Eysenck, appear at the end of each part.

Each chapter begins with an outline of topics and ends with a summary of key points and a list of suggested readings. Finally, at the back of the book, PSYCHOLOGY offers an appendix on statistics, a glossary of terms, a complete bibliography of research studies cited in the text, an index to authors cited, and a general index.

Study Guide

The student Study Guide to accompany PSYCHOLOGY, prepared by Barbara and David Basden of California State University at Fresno, is a unique selection of activities and exercises suitable for students of all abilities. The Study Guide offers the same Learning Objectives for the course found in the Instructor's Manual and the Test

Bank. It also contains a detailed completion outline for each chapter, numerous sample multiple-choice items, exercises on key terms, pen-and-paper experiments, plus a special feature, "Psychology in Everyday Life," a short reading which ties psychological research to familiar problems.

Test Bank

The Test Bank to accompany PSYCHOLOGY, prepared by Joseph Thompson of Washington and Lee University, in collaboration with the text authors, provides over 2,100 multiple-choice items, printed on tear-out cards. Each item is referenced to a Learning Objective, identified by chapter topic, indexed to text page, and labeled as either fact or comprehension-type.

Test Generation Program

The Test Bank to accompany PSYCHOLOGY is also available on software for the micro- or mainframe computer. Either program enables the instructor to generate tests according to precise specifications--by item, by chapter, by learning objective, or by question-type. Answers to test items are printed on a separate sheet. The microcomputer program is compatible with most major microcomputers, including the Apple II, the IBM PC, and the TRS 80 models.

The Transparency/Slide Package

This unique selection of two-color visual aides, many of which are not found in the textbook, was prepared by Joseph Stokes of the University of Illinois at Chicago. Over seventy figures, tables, anatomical drawings, and photographs tie closely with the text and with the lecture suggestions found in the Instructor's Manual. The package, which includes complete lecture notes detailing the content of each aid, is available in two formats: either as 8½ x 11 acetate transparencies for overhead projection or as 35 mm slides.

Transparency		Description	Text Source
(1)	1-1	How Psychologists Divide Their Field	Figure 1-3
(2)	1-2	Examples of Positive and Negative Correlations	
(3)	1-3	A Simple Experimental Design	
(4)	2-1	The Neuron	
(5)	2-2	Outline of the Nervous System	
(6)	2-3	Hypothalamus and Thalamus	Figure 2-10
(7)	2-4	The Endocrine Glands	Figure 2-11
(8)	2-5	Map of the Brain	Figure 2-12

(9)	2-6	How Information Travels from the Eye to the Brain	Figure 2-16
(10)	2-7	Genetic Control of Eye Color	
(11)	3-1	Structure of the Human Eye	Figure 3-4
(12)	3-2	Cross Section of the Human Retina	Figure 3-5
(13)	3-3	Structure of the Human Ear	Figure 3-14
(14)	3-4	Psychophysical Function	Figure 3-17
(15)	3-5	The Psychophysical Function for Brightness	Figure 3-18
(16)	4-1	A Gestalt Demonstration	Figure 4-1
(17)	4-2	Top Down and Bottom Up Processing	
(18)	4-3	Visual Illusions	Figures 4-25; 4-26b
(19)	4-4	Explanation for the Muller-Lyer Illusion	Figure 4-28
(20)	5-1	Two Models of Selective Attention	Figure 5-4
(21)	5-2	Recordings from the Sleeping Brain	Figure 5-7
(22)	5-3	Three Nights of Sleep	Figure 5-8
(23)	5-4	Action of LSD in Blocking Neural Transmission	
(24)	6-1	Classical Conditioning Procedures	Figure 6-3
(25)	6-2	Relationships between CS and UCS in Classical Conditioning	Figure 6-7
(26)	6-3	Extinction and Spontaneous Recovery of a Classically Conditioned Response	
(27)	6-4	Resistance to Extinction of an Instrumental Response	Figure 6-15
(28)	6-5	Types of Instrumental Conditioning	
(29)	6-6	Latent Learning Results	Figure 6-19
(30)	7-1	Model of Memory Storage	Figure 7-2

(31)	7-2	Retroactive and Proactive Interference	Figure 7-9
(32)	7-3	Results of an Experiment on State Dependent Retrieval	Table 7-2
(33)	7-4	A Fragment of Semantic Memory	Figure 7-16
(34)	8-1	Piaget's Stages of Cognitive Development	Table 8-
(35)	8-2	Conservation	Figure 8-10
(36)	8-3	The Pendulum Problem	Figure 8-13
(37)	9-1	Labels' Influence on Recall of Pictures	Figure 9-1
(38)	9-2	Tree Diagram of a Simple Sentence	
(39)	9-3	The Wugs Tests	Figure 9-6
(40)	9-4	Plastic Shapes Used by Sarah the Chimp	Figure 9-8
(41)	9-5	Luchins Water Jar Problem	Figure 9-14
(42)	10-1	Items like those from the Wechsler Adult Intelligence Scale	
(43)	10-2	The Distribution of Intelligence	Figure 10-1
(44)	10-3	Test-Retest Reliability	
(45)	10-4	Items used in Culture-Free Tests of Fluid Intelligence	
(46)	10-5	Items Used to Test Creativity in Children	
(47)	11-1	The Liver's Role in Feeding	Figure 11-1
(48)	11-2	Samples from the Eating Restraint Scale	
(49)	11-3	Thematic Appreception Test	
(50)	11-4	Maslow's Hierachy of Needs	Figure 11-9
(51)	11-5	An Experiment Supporting Arousal Theory	Figure 11-10
(52)	12-1	The Autonomic Nervous System	Figure 12-4

(53)	12-2	Three Different Kinds of Conflict	Figure 12-8
(54)	12-3	The General Adaptation Syndrome	Figure 12-10
(55)	13-1	Items Like Those on the MMPI	
(56)	13-2	Freud's Three Types of Mental Activity	
(57)	13-3	Freud's Structure of the Personality	
(58)	13-4	The Oedipal Complex	
(59)	13-5	A Rorschach Ink Blot	Figure 13-5
(60)	13-6	The Heritability of Personality	Table 13-4
(61)	14-1	Major Categories of Mental Disorders according to DSM III	
(62)	14-2	Organization of Mental Disorders	
(63)	14-3	Percentage of Adopted Males with Criminal Records	Table 14-7
(64)	14-4	Frequency of Schizophrenic Behavior in Relatives of a Schizophrenic	
(65)	15-1	Revolutions in Mental Health	
(66)	15-2	Different Types of Psychotherapists	
(67)	15-3	Patient Populations in Mental Hospitals	
(68)	15-4	Improvement Percentages for "stage fright" after Different Treatments	Table 15-2
(69)	15-5	Examples of Therapeutic Psychoactive Drugs	
(70)	16-1	Kelly's Attribution of Causality	Table 16-1
(71)	16-2	Balance Theory	
(72)	16-3	Cognitive Dissonance	
(73)	16-4	Asch's Conformity Experiment	Figure 16-6
(74)	16-5	Milgram's Results	Figure 16-9

(75)	17-1	Motivational Determinants of Aggression	Figure 17-7
(76)	17-2	Changes in Racial Attitudes	
(77)	17-3	Cultural Differences in Sex Roles	
(78)	A-1	Two Distributions with Different Standard Deviations	
(79)	A-2	The Normal Curve	A-3
(80)	A-3	Scattergrams	A-5
(81)	A-4	The Exaggerated Graph	A-6

CONTENTS

PART I: TEACHING PSYCHOLOGY

CHAPTER 1 The Nature of Psychology 3

CHAPTER 2 Biological Bases of Behavior 9

CHAPTER 3 Sensory Processes 17

CHAPTER 4 Perception 23

CHAPTER 5 Consciousness and Attention 31

CHAPTER 6 Conditioning and Learning 39

CHAPTER 7 Memory 47

CHAPTER 7 Development 55

CHAPTER 9 Language and Thought 65

CHAPTER 10 Intelligence and Mental Abilities 75

CHAPTER 11 Motivation 83

CHAPTER 12 Emotion and Stress 91

CHAPTER 13 Personality 99

CHAPTER 14 Abnormal Psychology 109

CHAPTER 15 Therapies 117

CHAPTER 16 Social Psychology 127

CHAPTER 17 Social Problems 135

APPENDIX 145

Computer Assisted Instruction 151

Software Programs 151

Computer Software Sources 154

PART II: TEACHING THE INTRODUCTORY COURSE: GENERAL INFORMATION AND RESOURCES

Instructional Methods 159

Approaches to Education 159

Learning Objectives 161

Instructional Methods 163

Preparation for Teaching 172

Testing and Evaluation 179

Objective Tests 179

Essay Examinations 185

Feedback 186

Grading 187

Evaluation of Instructor Performance 188

Course Evaluations 194

Teaching Resources 197

Bibliography on Teaching 197

Film Suppliers 201

Instructional Materials from the American Psychological Association 203

Instructor's Manual to Accompany

Psychology

PART I.

TEACHING PSYCHOLOGY

Chapter 1

THE NATURE OF PSYCHOLOGY

CHAPTER OVERVIEW

The text opens by defining psychology as the systematic study of behavior and mental life. An historical overview notes that humans have long been interested in the issues that intrigue modern psychologists, but it is only during the past 100 years that a scientific discipline has emerged. Contrary to the belief of many college freshmen, scientific psychology did not have its origins in the work of Sigmund Freud. European physicists and physiologists such as von Helmholtz, Fechner, and Wundt were especially important individuals for the fledgling field. The text then compares the subject matter, research goals, and research methods of each of five early schools of psychology: structuralism, functionalism, behaviorism, Gestalt psychology, and psychoanalysis.

The authors then shift to a consideration of six contemporary approaches to psychology: psychobiology, ethology, behaviorism, cognitive psychology, humanistic psychology, and psychoanalytic psychology. The text specifies the goals of each approach, rates each along a molar-to-molecular continuum of preferred explanation, and points out similarities and differences among the approaches. Obesity is used as a focal issue in a discussion of levels of explanation. Stressing the fact that there is no absolute level of explanation, the authors show how genetic, physiological, learning, cognitive, psychoanalytic, and/or cultural factors can be used to "explain" obesity.

Having pointed out the diversity of explanation, the authors consider the diversity of the field of psychology itself. The text highlights six subfields within psychology: experimental, social-personality, developmental, clinical and counseling, organizational and industrial, educational and school psychology. The text then describes the divisional structure of the American Psychological Association and relative distribution of membership within each division.

Research methods: naturalistic observation, case study, correlation, and experiment are described. Bystander apathy becomes a focal topic to explain how each of these methods can be used to study the same phenomenon.

The next section examines five general research issues: Research with animals as subjects, internal and external validity, ecological validity of research settings, distinctions between basic and applied research, and ethical issues related to research with animals and humans.

LEARNING OBJECTIVES

01-1. State the definition of psychology given in the text, and explain how that definition has changed over the years.

01-2. What was the basis for Ebbinghaus's statement that psychology has had a long past but a short history? Name three scientists who were pioneers of psychological research. What were their contributions?

01-3. List and define the five historical schools or movements in the history of psychology. Your definitions should specify the subject matter, research goals, and research methods for each school.

01-4. Name the six contemporary approaches to the study of psychology. Identify the goals for each of these approaches.

01-5. Describe a hierarchy for explaining psychological phenomena. Your description should proceed from molecular to molar events. Define reductionism.

01-6. List the six subfields of psychology. What activities do psychologists in these subfields perform?

01-7. Distinguish among the four major types of research methods and be able to specify the strengths and weaknesses of each of them.

01-8. Define the following terms and describe their importance to understanding experimental research: independent variable, dependent variable, control variable, confounding. Specify some techniques for avoiding confounding.

01-9. List five issues regarding the conduct of experimental research. Distinguish between internal and external validity and be able to relate these concepts to laboratory and field research. What three guidelines should be followed in protecting the rights of human subjects?

ATTENTION GETTERS

History of Psychology 6-13

The authors quote Ebbinghaus who said that psychology has a long past but a short history. They point out that many of the issues explored by psychologists came from philosophy. What approaches to the study of the issues led psychology to be considered a science? What is science? What methods must be used for an approach to be called scientific?

The Humanistic Approach 15-16

The text notes that some humanistic psychologists feel that a scientific approach to the study of humans is inappropriate and therefore they reject scientific values. Do you feel humans can be studied in a scientific manner? Explain your opinion.

Levels of Explanation 16-18

The same phenomenon can be explained in many "correct" ways. How can anorexia nervosa (see Chapter 11) be explained at several different levels (example: genetic factors, physiological factors, learning, cognitive factors, psychodynamic factors, social factors, cultural factors).

Research Methods 21-31

As an expert in the field of psychology you are asked to determine whether frequent playing of video games causes problems in school children. Which of the research methods discussed in Chapter 1 would you rely on? How would you begin to plan a study to investigate this issue?

LECTURE SUGGESTIONS AND CLASS DEMONSTRATIONS

Most students probably have heard of Freud, Pavlov, and Skinner, but few are likely to be familiar with Helmholtz or Wundt. E. G. Boring (1950) believed that Fechner's *Elements of Psychophysics* (1860) marked the founding of psychology as a science, whereas others, including the authors of the text, note Wundt's founding of a research laboratory in 1879 as the seminal event. A review of the Zeitgeist prevailing in Europe and the United States in the late 1800s can help students understand why a pioneer country like the United States favored a functionalist psychology rather than Wundt's structuralism.

Historical Sketch 6-13

Historical schools of psychology. The APA suggests a demonstration to help students understand the various historical schools of psychology. Ask a student to volunteer to be the subject for the demonstration. The subject's task is to eat a piece of candy. After the candy is eaten, ask the class to describe how a structuralist would study this behavior. Record their responses on the board. Then point out why a functionalist would object to this method and engage the class in an analysis of the behavior from the functionalist perspective. The instructor, in turn, becomes a behaviorist, Gestaltist, and psychoanalyst. When methods from all the schools are summarized on the board, the class can compare each method. (For more details see pages 139-140 in the *Psychology Teacher's Resource Book: First Course*, 1973. Prepared by the American Psychological Association, Washington, D.C.)

Current Approaches 13-16

A review of the historical origins of psychology can serve as a lead into current approaches in psychology. Students often want to know which approach is right and which is wrong. A lecture that focuses on how each approach may look at and attempt to explain different behaviors or different aspects of the same behavior may help students understand the role of theory and hypothesis testing in scientific inquiry. At the very least it will help point out that there rarely is one correct and enduring answer to a question. Indeed, Leahey (1980) suggests that the work of any scientist is "transcended in time," thereby making science distinct from art.

Range of Psychology 18-21

What do psychologists do? Many students equate psychology with therapy. Stapp and Fulcher (1981) provide an up-to-date review of the employment picture in psychology. Their data indicate that 60 percent of the members of the American Psychological Association specialize in the combined areas of clinical, counseling, and school psychology. However, most of these individuals are not in private practice but rather are employed in institutional settings such as universities (43%) or hospitals (24%). On the other hand, division 42 of the American Psychological Association (Psychologists in

Private Practice) is by far the largest division in the association. The fact that there are 42 divisions attests to the diversity of psychology. Students generally are surprised to learn that there is a division of military psychology or a division of psychologists interested in religious issues. Selecting five or six divisions and providing descriptions of the type of work members of the division may be engaged in can give students a sound sampling of the kinds of endeavors individual psychologists engage in. Transparency 1-1, "How psychologists divide their field" will serve as a good attention-getter for this topic.

Lecture material emphasizing research methods is especially important since a complete understanding of the remainder of the text is dependent upon understanding how research is conducted.

Research Methods 21-27

Designing an experiment. A class project involving experimental design can be a useful supplement to a formal lecture. Since students often have difficulty distinguishing among independent, dependent and confounding variables, designing an experiment in class may help clarify these points. Ask the students to select a topic which they would like to use in designing their experiment. If they choose a topic that is inappropriate for an experimental study use this opportunity to discuss alternate methods (case study, naturalistic observation, correlational study). Transparency 1-2 illustrates positive and negative correlations and Transparency 1-3 provides an example of a simple experimental design. Review of each of these will help students design their experiment. When an appropriate topic is selected help the class determine the independent and dependent variables. Discuss any possible confounding factors, the need for random assignment, and the problems of subject and experimenter bias. Single-blind and double-blind techniques can be mentioned in this context. If students fail to generate an appropriate topic for research, be sure to have one of your own to fall back on!

Ethics in Research 31

Research ethics. Another topic that students will find of interest concerns ethical issues in research. The principles set forth by the American Psychological Association can be incorporated into a lecture. "Ethical Principles in the Conduct of Research with Human Participants" (APA, 1973), provides examples of research involving ethical issues. These can be presented in lecture format or used in a lecture-discussion class. The classic studies on obedience by Stanley Milgram can serve as a focal issue. The film "Obedience" can be shown first and then the class can address issues relating to ethics. It should be noted that contemporary practices do not necessarily rule out research that has risk for participants. Rather, such studies must be submitted to a review committee which attempts to determine whether the scientific benefits outweigh potential risks to the participants. There are many examples of this review process and undoubtedly each instructor has his or her favorites. Sometimes the ethical issues are more subtle than students may realize. Consider, for example, the following:

The subjects were informed correctly regarding the basic procedures that would be used, but they were misinformed about the purpose of the experiment. They were told the experiment was designed to test the speed of the visual system. Actually, the experimenter was interested in testing long-term memory. The subjects were not told the real purpose because the investigator was afraid this knowledge would influence their performance. The experimenter reasoned that a subject who would participate for the stated reason would also participate for the real reason. Is this an acceptable procedure? (Wood, 1981, pp. 19-20).

AUDIOVISUAL AIDES

Films

The Skinner Revolution. 16mm or 3/4" video, color, 23 minutes. Research Press. A comprehensive look at the life and work of B. F. Skinner. Interviews and conversations with Skinner and demonstrations of operant conditioning including behavior modification with a retarded, non-ambulatory child.

Methodology: The Psychologist and the Experiment. CRM/McGraw Hill Films, 31 minutes, color, 16 mm. Use of animation and special effects help illustrate the essential features of experimental research. Schachter's "fear and affiliation" experiment and Riesen's experiment in the development of visual coordination in kittens serve to illustrate basic research issues.

Aspects of Behavior. CRM/McGraw-Hill, 31 minutes, color. A brief presentation of topics currently being investigated by psychologists. Ethical considerations in research are discussed.

Obedience. 16mm, B & W, 44 minutes. A graphic presentation of Stanley Milgram's famous experiments on obedience. The film is sure to provoke class discussion about conformity behavior and obedience to authority, but is also likely to arouse interest in the use of deception in psychological research.

Ultimate Experimental Animal: Man. NBC Films Incorporated. 37 min, color. Human experimentation and the risk/benefit ratio. Are subjects fully informed of risks? Should convicts and the mentally retarded carry the burden of experimentation?

Audio Cassettes

Bronfenbrenner, U. Reality and research in the ecology of human development. APA Tape 11/11, 1975. A leading advocate for "ecologically valid" research defines the ecology of human development. Bronfenbrenner contrasts the ecological approach with other research approaches, particularly those associated with the study of environmental influences.

Eichorn, D. H. Longitudinal research: Alternative methods and major findings. APA Tape 11/13, 1975.

Audio Colloquies. 45-60 minutes each. Harper and Row Media. 46 distinguished behavioral and social scientists discuss their research. Included are: Judith Bardwick, Frank Beach, D. E. Berlyne, Charles Cofer, Sir John Eccles, Ernest Hilgard, David Krech, Stanley Milgram, Paul Mussen, J. B. Rhine, Muzafer Sherif, B. F. Skinner, Philip Zimbardo.

Film Strips

Landmarks in Psychology. Human Relations Media, color/sound filmstrip. This 3-part filmstrip examines the origins of the study of human behavior beginning with folklore concerning human behavior. Psychoanalytic, behaviorist, humanistic, and existential views on human behavior are compared and contrasted.

New Patterns in Psychology. 3-part filmstrip, color/sound, Instructor's Guides. Human Relation Media.

Other Instructional Aides

Freud: The Man and His Work. 24 minutes. A music and slide presentation that explores Sigmund Freud's life, friendships, professional influences, and family life. Produced by Dennis C. Gold, Department of Psychology, King's College, Wilkes-Barre, PA 18711.

REFERENCES AND ANNOTATED SOURCES

Boring, E. G. (1950). *A history of experimental psychology.* New York: Appleton-Century-Crofts.

Isaac, S. (1971). *Handbook in research and evaluation.* San Diego, CA: Editors Publishers. This book provides a concise description of various research methods. Each method is discussed in terms of its purpose, strengths and weaknesses, and basic characteristics. It contains many examples that will be useful when preparing lectures on research methods.

Leahey, T. (1980). *A history of psychology.* Englewood Cliffs, NJ: Prentice-Hall. Leahey notes that most definitions of psychology assert that psychology is a science, but vary in what psychology is a science of. Some definitions restrict psychology to the study of behavior, whereas others include mind or mental processes as well. You will find many good lecture ideas in this book. Leahey's answer to whether psychology qualifies as a science is a qualified yes!

Stapp, J., & Fulcher, R. (1981). The employment of APA members. *American Psychologist, 36,* 1263-1314.

Wood, G. (1981). *Fundamentals of psychological research.* Boston: Little, Brown, and Co. This introductory level text in experimental design discusses the four basic methods of psychological inquiry: observation, correlation, experiment, and quasi-experiment. Examples are presented at a level appropriate for most introductory psychology students.

Chapter 2

BIOLOGICAL BASES OF BEHAVIOR

CHAPTER OVERVIEW

In this chapter the authors review nerve physiology, the structure and function of the nervous system, and evolution, genetics and behavior. The chapter opens with a review of nerve transmission and differentiation of sensory neuron, motor neurons and interneurons. Neural transmission of information begins with ionic exchange processes and electrical triggering. The discussion of synaptic transmission focuses on the role of chemical neurotransmitters such as acetylcholine, norepinephrine, dopamine, and GABA. In *Applying Psychology* the authors highlight the relationship among neuro-transmitters and depression. This section proceeds with a discussion of recent and exciting work with brain endorphins, or opioid peptides, with special reference made to the role that endorphins play in regulation of pain and stress. The section closes with a brief discussion of the blood-brain barrier.

The second major section of the chapter discusses the structure and function of the central and peripheral nervous systems, and the spinal cord and brain stem.

Then the authors review current knowledge with respect to functions of the thalamus, hypothalamus, endocrine system, and limbic system. In addition to pointing out the role that each plays in regulating human behavior, special attention is given to James Olds' research involving the "pleasure centers" of the hypothalamus in *The Research Process: Brain Stimulation.*

The fourth section of the chapter details the organization of the cerebral cortex with separate sections devoted to the sensory cortex and the motor cortex. The work of Roger Sperry and his colleagues leads to an extensive discussion of hemispheric specialization, including a review of current evidence for hemispheric specialization for language, spatial-pattern-perception, emotionality, and cognitive organization.

The final section of the chapter notes the contributions of Charles Darwin and Gregor Mendel to our understanding of evolutionary theory, and then procedes to a discussion of ethology and sociobiology. Ethological concepts include fixed action patterns, sign stimuli, critical periods, and imprinting. Altruistic behavior serves as a background for introducing the field of sociobiology. In addition, *Controversy* addresses one of the central themes of sociobiology, inclusive fitness. This section, and the chapter as a whole, concludes with a detailed presentation of behavior genetics and the strategy of studying fraternal and identical twins in order to tease out the genetic influence on behavior.

LEARNING OBJECTIVES

02-1. Name the major parts and functions of a neuron and a microneuron. What are the three different types of neurons? What other type of cell is present in the brain?

02-2. Describe the process of neural transmission. Be able to define resting potential, action potential, all-or-none law, synaptic transmission, deactivation, and re-uptake.

02-3. Name and describe the role of four transmitter substances. Define the role of endorphins. Define the blood-brain barrier.

02-4. Name and describe the functions of the two main devisions of the central nervous system and of the peripheral nervous system. What are the two major subdivisions of the autonomic nervous system?

02-5. Name the five major regions of the brain stem. Briefly describe the functions of each of these regions.

02-6. Be able to discuss the influence that each of the following has on behavior: thalamus, hypothalamus, endocrine system and limbic system.

02-7. Identify the cerebral cortex, cerebral hemispheres, and name the four sections of each hemisphere. Name and locate the three sensory areas of the cortex. Describe the functions of the motor cortex and the association areas. Be able to describe how scientists "map" the functions of the brain.

02-8. Be able to discuss how scientists carry out experiments with split brain patients. Identify the three areas in the left hemisphere which are associated with speech production, reception and conduction. Name five capabilities of the right hemisphere.

02-9. Be able to summarize the theory of natural selection, genetics, and the modern synthesis of the two. Name the two fields of study which are concerned with the study of the evolution of behavior and be able to distinguish each field. Why is one field controversial?

02-10. State the goal of the field of behavior genetics. List some of the methods that are employed to study genetic influences on behavior.

ATTENTION GETTERS

Applying Psychology 46-47

Why is a basic understanding of human physiology necessary to study psychology? What examples can you cite showing the relationship between some mental disorders and disorders in the brain?

Evolution and Behavior 67-78

What evidence can you cite to support the suggestion that the body may have evolved mechanisms to deal with pain or stress?

Hemispheric Specialization 57-65

In the past it was often believed that the left side of the brain was dominant. It has been shown recently, however, that each side of the brain is superior in certain activities. For what activities would you expect left hemispheric superiority? For what activities would you expect right hemispheric superiority?

Sociobiology 71-73

As a sociobiologist you are asked to explain the increase in parent-child conflict as children get older. How can you explain this behavior based on the concept of inclusive fitness?

LECTURE SUGGESTIONS AND CLASS DEMONSTRATIONS

Neural Transmission 36-42

Many students find lectures on the anatomy and physiology of the nervous system tedious. Nevertheless, it is important for students to understand the physical and chemical events that regulate transmission of information in the nervous system. Recent discoveries in brain chemistry can put some excitement and purpose into the study of nervous system activity. Neurotransmitters are chemicals that are located at the synaptic junction of nerves which function to transmit information from one nerve to another. Within a nerve, transmission is an electrical event. Thus, nerve transmission involves both electrical and chemical activity.

Transparencies 2-1 and 2-2 will give students a visual frame of reference for discussion of the structure and function of the neuron and the overall organization of the nervous system. Transparency 2-3 illustrates the functions of the thalamus and hypothalamus, and Transparency 2-4 shows the major sections and areas of the brain.

Synaptic Transmission 42-47

Want a high? Go to the brain pharmacy. Neurotransmitters found in the brain are different from neurotransmitters conveying information from one nerve to another. Brain neurotransmitters, or peptides, are larger, more complicated, and remain active for considerably longer periods of time than do other transmitters. In fact, some peptides may remain active for hours (Gurin, 1980). Among the peptides of the brain are a group called endorphins, which are opiate-like chemicals. As Joel Gurin (1980) points out, more than 20 peptides have been identified and prospects are high for discovery of many more. What do peptides do? One, called LRF, is thought to function as an aphrodisiac. Rats given LRF mate and impotent men given LRF regain their sexual function. Another peptide, Beta-endorphin seems to play a role in the suppression of pain, as do enkephalins. On the other hand even small doses of bradykinin cause intense pain. Other peptides have been linked to body weight regulation, memory and learning, blood pressure regulation, and the regulation of thirst. Just where research in brain peptides will lead is difficult to predict. It is clear, however, that their many potential beneficial effects could be offset by equally harmful effects, if abused. One suspects that the brain pharmacy has only just begun to reveal its many secret compounds. Students may want to discuss this kind of research, particularly with respect to values in society for drug management of behavior. They could consider, for example, the alternatives to deinstitutionalization of the mentally ill which in large measure was made possible by drugs. (for additional information see J. Gurin, 1979, Nov/Dec. Chemical feelings. *Science 80.*)

Hemispheric Specialization 57-65

Finger localization and finger graphesthesia. Two tests that are components of many neuropsychological examinations are sure bets for getting students actively involved in the topic of central and peripheral nervous system structure, function, and interaction. The first test is sometimes called finger agnosia and is sometimes called finger localization. The second test also has several names, two of which are finger writing and finger graphesthesia. Each of these tests involves tactile sensitivity (peripheral nervous system) and each is thought to provide information about structural and/or functional deficits in the brain (central nervous system). Some clinicians suggest that each test can be used as a screening tool for evaluation of learning disabilities in preschool age children, albeit a highly subjective screening test. The versions described here are adapted from Aaron Smith's *Michigan Neuropsychological Test Battery.* Students must understand that these tests are not standardized tests, but are useful to the clinician as part of a much more extensive neuropsychological evaluation.

Finger localization. Have students pair up. One student of each pair will act as tester and one will act as client. The client is instructed to keep his or her eyes closed throughout the test. The test requires the tester to touch the client's fingers, one at a time, according to a predetermined sequence. The client must report which finger was touched by stating the number assigned to the finger. The fingers of each hand are numbered in sequence, with the thumb as number 1 and the little finger as number 5. For Part A of the test, fingers are touched one at a time. There are 10 trials per hand so the instructor must have 2 sets of number sequences listed on the chalkboard or on the overhead projector so the tester can touch the correct fingers. Do not list them, however, until the client's eyes are closed. Testers must keep mental track of incorrect responses.

In Part B, two fingers on one hand are touched simultaneously. The client must indicate by numbers which two fingers were touched. Again, a mental count of incorrect responses is made (one wrong identification makes the pair wrong). All combinations of two fingers must be given, with each combination used twice. Finger pairs should be touched in random orders so that the client cannot benefit from any clearly obvious pattern. After parts A and B are done, have testers and clients switch roles and report the tests using new number sequences.

Finger graphesthesia. In this test the tester writes a number on the client's fingertips, one finger at a time. The client must identify the number--eyes closed, of course. The numbers 3, 4, 5, and 6 are used in Reitan's modification of Halstead's neuropsychological examination. A ballpoint pen makes an excellent writing stylus (with the point retracted). When writing the symbols, do not press hard on the client's skin. The number sequences to be used should be prepared in advance so they can be posted on the overhead projector or on the chalkboard. Have students count mentally the number of errors.

After completing these demonstrations discuss the ways in which assessment of peripheral nerve function can provide information about lesions or function of the cerebral hemispheres, particularly the parietal region which is thought to be involved in both language function and motor control. Transparency 2-5 shows the routes involved in information transmission from eye to brain and also illustrates the role played by the corpus callosum in interhemispheric communication.

Handedness. In recent years the study of handedness has been revived, because it plays an important role in identifying subjects in cerebral lateral specialization research and because its development is an important topic in its own right. Approximately 90% of the human population is right-handed, the remaining being left-handed. One fact that handedness research is pointing out is that most individuals are not as strongly right- or left-handed as they think. To demonstrate this point, have students complete the following handedness questionnaire, which is an adaptation of a questionnaire used in a longitudinal research project at Michigan State University. For each of the following statements have students rate their hand preference on a 5-point scale: (1) Always left, (2) Usually left, (3) Equally right and left, (4) Usually right, and (5) Always right.

1) To write a letter legibly.
2) To throw a ball at a target.
3) To hold scissors to cut paper.
4) To deal playing cards.
5) To hold a toothbrush while cleaning teeth.
6) To unscrew the lid of a jar.

Now have students perform a different measure of handedness. Distribute a sheet of paper that contains two separate sets of boxes arranged sequentially; about 100 little ¼" boxes in each set. Have one set of boxes on the top of the page, and one set on the bottom. Now have them take their pencil in hand. At the word "go" students are to tap each box in sequence from left to right using their right hand. After 30 seconds, signal "stop!" Give a 30 second rest period. Now have students tap the boxes on the bottom of the page using their left hand, again for 30 seconds. Have students exchange papers and score the taps--pencil point marks must appear in the square; on the line does not count! The hand with the higher score is defined as the dominant hand. Students can now compare the two measures of handedness and discuss the degree of consistency between the two. If the two measures differ, which measure do they believe gives the most accurate assessment of their handedness? Why? One measure is a self-report questionnaire, whereas the other involves skilled performance.

Evolution, Genetics, and, Behavior
67-78

Expression of eye color: Genotypes and phenotypes. The authors explain that recessive characteristics are not expressed in the phenotype unless both parents contribute the recessive gene. In the exercise below, students determine the probability of two parents producing a blue-eyed child (a recessive trait). The instructor can put a series of charts on the board indicating parents' eye color and their particular dominant or recessive characteristics (alleles). Students can be asked to fill in the boxes with the children's expected eye color. Transparency 2-6 can be shown first to illustrate simple genetic control of eye color and then more complicated examples can be worked out by the class.

In example 1 below, both parents have brown eyes. The father, however, has a recessive characteristic for blue eyes whereas the mother does not. Although all the children will have brown eyes, it is probable that two children out of four will have a recessive allele for blue eye-color. In example 2, both parents have a recessive allele for blue eye color. In this example the two brown-eyed parents could be expected to have one brown-eyed child with both dominant alleles, two brown-eyed children with a recessive allele for blue eyes, and one blue-eyed child. The instructor should point out that genetic variations do occur leading to other eye-colors (green, hazel, etc.).

Example 1

Mother's Eye Color Brown (BR BR)	Father's Eye Color Brown (BR BL): BR	BL
BR	BR BR Brown	BR BL Brown
BR	BR BR Brown	BR BL Brown

Example 2

Mother's Eye Color Brown (BR BL)	Father's Eye Color Brown (BR BL): BR	BL
BR	BR BR Brown	BR BL Brown
BL	BR BL Brown	BL BL Blue

FIGURE 1. Mendalian Ratios for Inheritance of Eye Color. (See text for additional explanation.)

AUDIOVISUAL AIDES

Films

Biology and Behavior. Harper & Row Pub., Inc., 21 minutes, color. Discusses the questions of nature vs. nurture and of biology vs. learning. Presents research on taste aversion, instinctive drift, and imprinting.

Imprinting. Appleton-Century-Crofts. Film Library, 37 minutes, color (1968). Laboratory studies of imprinting. Illustrations of critical periods and innate releasing mechanisms.

The Hidden Universe: The Brain. CRM/McGraw-Hill Films, 2 parts, total 48 minutes, color. Part 1 opens with a operating room scene showing a craniotomy. Discussion focuses on cerebral specialization of function and the "split brain." Part 2 presents topics as diverse as visual perception, infant cognitive behavior, aphasia, and brain malfunctions. David Janssen narrates.

Classic Experiments in Behavioral Neuropsychology. Harper & Row Media, 22 minutes, color. Seven classic experiments in behavioral neuropsychology are shown. Investigators shown are Paul Weiss, Roger W. Sperry, Vincent G. Dethier, Bartley G. Hoebel, and Jose M. R. Delgado. In addition, research on brain localization also is demonstrated.

The Brain: Creating a Mental Elite. Document Associates, Inc., 20 minutes, color. This film examines recent developments in brain research. Researchers include Wilder Penfield, Roy John, and scientists at the University of California at Berkeley. Arthur C. Clarke speculates on the possibility of imprinting knowledge directly on the brain.

Audio Cassettes

Schlesinger, Kurt. Behavior genetics: Current status and perspective. APA Master Lecture on physiology. APA Tape 10-16, 1974. This lecture traces the history of behavior genetics back to Galton's work on hereditary genius. Tyson's selective breeding experiments and other genetic experiments are discussed.

Lacey, J. I. Psychophysiology of the ANS. APA Tape 10-12, 1974. Lacey presents evidence contrary to the idea that the state of arousal can be specified by the physiological events that occur when the organism is aroused. ECG, EDA, & EEG functions are related to arousal states.

Teuber, Hans-Lukas. Brain function: Key questions in the study of the brain and human behavior. APA Tape 10-17, 1974. Teuber's lecture includes both clinical and experimental studies with animals. Working on the premise that injury or disease reveals much about normal function, Teuber describes the relationship between behavior and neurologic abnormality offering exciting insight into the function of the nervous system.

Film Strips

Exploring the Brain. Human Relations Media, 5 filmstrips, color audiocassettes 13-15 minutes each and Instructors Guide. Five filmstrips present data from current brain research and raise philosophical and ethical issues related to study of the human mind and personality. The Geography of the Mind; Memory; Split Brain Research; Electrical Stimulation of the Brain; and Biofeedback.

REFERENCES AND ANNOTATED SOURCES

Bennett, T. L. (1977). *Brain and behavior.* Monterrey, CA: Brooks/Cole Publishing Co. A crisp, clear presentation of the brain and its role in arousal, sleep, dreaming, emotions, motivation, and memory.

Brobeck, J. R. (Ed.) (1973). *Neural control systems.* Baltimore: Williams & Wilkins. The analyses of neural control systems, including organization of the CNS, control of smooth muscle, posture, and locomotion.

Gardner, H. (1974). *The shattered mind.* New York: Vintage Books. Discussion and examples of aphasia, left-right hemispheric function, memory, etc.

Luria, A. R. (1973). *The working brain.* New York: Basic Books. Summarizes nearly 50 years of research and includes examples of drawings by individuals with aphasia, left-side spatial agnosia, and other dysfunctions.

Plomin, R. DeFries, J. C., & McClearn, G. E. (1980). *Behavioral genetics: A primer.* San Francisco: W. H. Freeman & Co. Excellent review of behavioral genetics--especially the section on heritability.

Chapter 3

SENSORY PROCESSES

CHAPTER OVERVIEW

Recognizing the difficulties involved in making a clear distinction between sensation and perception, the authors suggest that they be treated as two points along a continuum. Heuristically, one can think of sensation as stimulus reception and perception as stimulus interpretation and understanding. Although Aristotle's 5-way classification of the basic senses--vision, audition, taste, smell, touch--fails to encompass all of the basic senses, the authors employ the 5-way scheme as an organizational basis for the chapter. Aristotle's omissions, such as the kinesthetic sense and vestibular sense, are handled within this general framework.

Discussion of vision opens with a review of the physics of light, light intensity, wave length, and subjective colors. The text then discusses the structural characteristics of the eye focusing on the rods and cones of the retinal neural pathways mediating our visual experience, and various alterations in the lens which require correction with glasses. In each case, illustrative figures support text discussion. The authors conclude the section on vision by discussing spatial and temporal context, simultaneous contrast, and dark and light adaptation.

Having discussed the basic features of the eye and vision, the authors then discuss color vision beginning with concepts of hue, brightness and saturation.

The authors then consider two prominant theories of color perception; a modern version of the Young-Helmhotz trichromatic theory, and the opponent-process theory originally proposed by Hering. In particular, the opponent-process theory accounts for color-blindness and after-images and so in *Applying Psychology,* the authors examine the topic of color-blindness, distinguishing among trichromats, dichromats, and monochromats.

At this point the text turns its attention to hearing. The authors review the physics of sound and then define the structural characteristics of the ear. Place and frequency theories are explained, and both are suggested to play a role in pitch perception: frequency theory for low frequency sounds, place theory for high frequency sounds. Discussion of audition closes with a review of work on sound localization.

From their discussion of the ear and hearing, the authors move to the so-called minor senses. Smell, touch, the skin senses, pain, kinesthesis, and equilibration (balance) are discussed briefly and changes in taste over the life span are highlighted in *The Research Process.*

The chapter ends with issues involving measurement of sensory abilities, or, what is called psychophysics. Discussion focuses on thresholds, psychophysical methods, scaling, and signal detection theory. *Controversy* addresses speculations as to the existance of extrasensory perception.

LEARNING OBJECTIVES

03-1. Distinguish between sensation and perception. Briefly describe the difference between naive and critical realism. List Aristotle's five-way classification of the senses and name two senses not covered in that classification.

03-2. Describe light as a physical stimulus. How do variations in wave length and intensity affect vision?

03-3. Be able to describe the passage of a pattern of light through the eyeball and retina to the optic nerve and trace the neural signals through the brain, from the lateral geniculate nucleus to the striate cortex. Summarize the current research regarding brain cells called feature detectors.

03-4. Define context effects in vision. Be able to give examples of spatial context and temporal contrast.

03-5. Be able to define hue, brightness, and saturation. Be able to distinguish additive and subtractive mixture in color vision.

03-6. Summarize the Young-Hemholtz trichromatic theory and the opponent-process theory of color vision. Define the two types of color blindness.

03-7. Describe sound as a physical stimulus. How do variations in amplitude and frequency affect hearing? Be able to describe the passage of a sound wave through the structures in the ear to the auditory nerve. Summarize place theory and frequency theory. Define auditory localization.

03-8. Describe the physical stimuli and receptors associated with the other senses: smell, taste, the skin senses, kinesthesis and equilibration.

03-9. Define the goal of psychophysics. Describe the methods employed in determining sensory thresholds and be familiar with Weber's law. How does signal detection theory improve upon earlier techniques of threshold determination?

03-10. Be able to define psychokinesis and the three types of ESP. Summarize types of research used to study ESP and list reasons why psychologists are skeptical about the research findings.

ATTENTION GETTERS

Realism 90

Define naive realism and critical realism. Which do you feel most accurately describes the manner by which humans evaluate sensory information?

The Eye 92-97

Sometimes the visual image is not focused sharply on the retina and so a person has difficulty seeing the world properly. What optical defects occur in myopia, heropia, presbyopia and astigmatism?

Color Vision
98-102

Scientists who study color vision find that evidence supports both the trichromatic theory and the opponent-process theory. What evidence suggests that two mechanisms may be used to perceive color? What are the strengths and limitations of each of these theories?

ESP
118-119

The topic of extrasensory perception is both fascinating and controversial. Do you believe in ESP? What experiences have led you to this opinion? How could you support or test your view in a scientific manner?

LECTURE SUGGESTIONS AND CLASS DEMONSTRATIONS

Instructors who choose to lecture on the structural components of the eye and ear will find transparencies 3-1, 3-2, and 3-3 useful. Transparency 3-1 shows the structure of the eye and light transmission. Transparency 3-2 illustrates a cross-section of the retina and can be shown when discussing the functions of the rods and cones. Transparency 3-3 illustrates the structure of the ear, including the semicircular canals which are part of the vestibular system. Each of these transparencies also are figures in the text.

Color Vision
98-103

Color vision: A demonstration of after-images. The text provides several illustrations concerning sensation that can be used for class demonstrations. For example, by staring at color plate 10 for 60 seconds and then looking at a blank classroom wall, students should experience a negative after-image. What colors are seen in this after-image? How would this support the opponent-process theory? Students can experiment with patches of different colors (they should be brightly colored) and record the after-image colors following each color viewed.

The Other
Senses
107-108

The link between smell and taste. The authors discuss the close link between taste and smell noting that we lose our taste when we have colds. Similarly, when the nose is blocked it is difficult to identify an object placed in the mouth by its taste (smell). To demonstrate this prepare a bowl of apple slices and a bowl of onion slices. Ask volunteers to block their noses and attempt to determine which slice has been placed in their mouths. Be sure to blindfold volunteers so that visual cues are eliminated.

Taste adaptation can be demonstrated by having students hold a piece of hard candy in their mouths for a few minutes. Do not allow them to move the candy around the mouth or to move their tongues. Is there a point at which the candy's taste actually disappears? Demonstrate cross adaptation by giving a student a glass of orange juice followed by a slice of grapefruit. The grapefruit should seem like an unusually sour one to this student because the taste buds have adapted to the sweetness of the orange juice. Give another section of the grapefruit to a second student. The grapefruit should be judged to have a moderate amount of sourness that one would expect from a grapefruit. (The instructor may want to taste a segment before class to make sure the particular grapefruit isn't unusually sour!) Finally, salt a grapefruit segment and give it to another student. This should reduce its sourness.

The Skin Senses 108-109

Hot or cold??? Students can test the effects of temperature adaptation using John Locke's experimental method. First, they can fill three bowls with hot, cold, and lukewarm water. Person A should put her left hand in the hot water and Person B should put her left hand in the cold water. They should be asked to check off their estimates of the water temperatures using their right hand (see sample data chart below).

Temperature Estimate	Condition A	Condition B
120°	____	____
115°	____	____
110°	____	____
105°	____	____
.	.	.
.	.	.
.	.	.
.	.	.
35°	____	____

After 60 seconds they should place their left hands in the bowl of lukewarm water and once again estimate the temperature (they should not be able to see one another's chart). Person A should think the water is cool whereas Person B should report that it is warm. Each student should test several pairs of subjects and then the class results can be combined.

Estimating temperatures is a form of scaling. Of course, the study of psychophysical scaling was extremely important to the historical development of psychology. Transparency 3-4 illustrates a psychophysical function and defines the absolute threshold, whereas Transparency 3-5 depicts Stevens' magnitude estimation method as applied to the psychophysics of brightness. Ask students how the exercise involving estimation of temperatures would have to change in order to fit the requirements of magnitude estimation scaling.

Pain 109-111

Protopathic pain. There are several topics involving sensations other than vision and audition that can be of interest to students. One of these is pain. For example, Geldard (1972) devotes 26 pages to a discussion of pain including thresholds, sensitivity, adaptation, mechanoreception, and protopathic pain. Henry Head's experiment on protopathic pain is sure to catch student attention inasmuch as Head was his own subject in an experiment which involved cutting the radial and external cutaneous nerves in the forearm in order to study sensory loss! Head was able to record the return of his sensation as the nerves slowly regenerated. Immediately after the surgery, there was an area of complete lack of sensation surrounded by an intermediate zone. Not only could pain sensations be felt in the intermediate zone, but they were more painful than in his normal skin. Extremes of temperature were sensed, but moderate temperatures were not. Moreover, adaptation to temperature extremes did not occur. Head concluded that the unusual sensations in the intermediate zone were caused by a phylogenetically primitive neural system which had been disconnected from a phylogenetically more advanced neural system. Head called the primitive system, protopathetic, and the advanced system, epicritic. Surgery interfered with the epicritic system's ability to inhibit the action of the protopathic system, thereby producing the unusual sensory reactions in the intermediate zone.

According to Geldard, although empirical studies of nerve supply fail to support Head's contention that two nerve mechanisms are involved in pain sensation, the theoretical distinction has persisted. Geldard also describes two attempts to repeat Head's experiment, one by Lanier and one by Boring, with rather long-term consequences in each case. In addition to discussion of pain and the controversy over the protopathic-epicritic distinction, students may wish to examine the motivation of scientists who would submit themselves to such invasive procedures, in the name of scientific inquiry!

Controversy
118-119

ESP. Experiments on ESP are quite easy to demonstrate and usually provoke high student interest. Four different tasks can be used. First, in the telepathy task a "sender" concentrates on a card and the "receiver" decides which symbol is on the card. Prepare twenty-five 4 x 6 inch cards by placing one of the following symbols on each of five cards: star, diamond, circle, cross, and square. Thoroughly mix the cards. Send the receiver out of the room along with a volunteer research assistant. Every fifteen seconds the sender will concentrate on one of the cards. The assistant records the symbol named by the receiver on a data sheet every 15 seconds. Obviously, times will have to be synchronized quite closely. In order to demonstrate telepathy the receiver's correct identifications must exceed chance. For clairvoyance, neither the sender nor the receiver looks at the symbols on the cards. After 15 seconds the receiver decides what symbol is on the card and then it is turned over and the correct symbol is recorded. Again, above chance performance must occur in order to support the presence of clairvoyance. For precognition, cards can be replaced by dice. The subject rolls a die and predicts what number will be rolled. Finally, in the psychokinesis task the experimenter suspends a needle into a bottle. The subject must make the needle sway solely through concentration.

AUDIOVISUAL AIDES

Films

The Sensory World. CRM/McGraw-Hill, Inc., 33 minutes, color. Environment and human sensory functioning. Includes discussions by Jerome Lettvin on optic fibers and W. Penfield on electrical stimulation of the human brain and memory. Excellent film, includes animation, experiments, and interviews.

How Much Do You Smell? Films Incorporated, 50 minutes, color. Recent studies in nonhuman animals indicate that smell signals are used to communicate much information. In humans, smell may be more important than we think it is.

A Touch of Sensitivity. Films Incorporated, 50 minutes, color. Touch deprivation has been linked to abnormal and violent behavior, to brain damage, heart disease, and lack of resistance to infection. Touch is important for premature infants and adults as well. This film examines the importance of touch for development of various age levels.

What Time is Your Body? Films Incorporated, 50 minutes, color. Internal timing mechanisms known as circadian rhythms regulate much of our behavior. Will people eventually be able to detect the onset of disease by noting changes in normal rhythms. Long-term isolation experiments are shown.

The Senses of Man. Indiana University, 18 min., B & W. Shows how light, sound, odor, touch, and taste sensations are converted into nerve impulses by sense receptors. Contains animation.

Sense Perception. Moody Institute of Science, 28 min., color. Illustrates how the senses of sight, hearing, taste, touch, and smell are adapted to make life possible on earth. Shows inverted vision experiments.

REFERENCES AND ANNOTATED SOURCES

Geldard, F. A. (1972). *The human senses.* New York: John Wiley & Sons.

Harlow, H. F. (1971). *Learning to love.* San Francisco, CA: Albion Publishing Co. An overview of his work on the development of affectional systems and the importance of contact comfort.

Hubel, D. H., & Wiesel, T. N. (1965). Receptive fields and functional architecture in two nonstriate visual areas (18 and 19) of the cat. *Journal of Neurophysiology, 28,* 228-229. Describes their work on feature detectors for which they were awarded the Nobel Prize.

Montagu, A. (1971). *Touching.* New York: Columbia University Press. A popular review of the role that touch plays in human sensory experience.

Stevens, S. S. (1962). The surprising simplicity of sensory metrics. *American Psychologist, 17,* 29-39. Describes power law of sensory intensity as major revision of the classic Weber and Fechner Laws from psychophysics.

Chapter 4

PERCEPTION

CHAPTER OVERVIEW

Chapter 4 focuses on perception, or the interpretation of sensory information. Two key problems in perception are posed: "Why (does) the world look as it does?" and, "How can pattern recognition be explained?"

The authors begin their exploration of the first problem by considering perceptual organization. Gestalt principles of grouping (similarity, proximity, good continuation and figure-ground segregation) are described and illustrated in figures.

To explain pattern recognition the authors present two categories, bottom-up and top-down theories. The authors note that both types of theory involve feature detection and that bottom-up theories are popular. However, top-down theories posit a more active perceptual process than do bottom-up theories. They argue that top-down theories do a better job of explaining the speed and contextual aspects of pattern recognition, but note that perception is best understood by considering the operations implied by both sets of theories.

In the next section the authors review current knowledge involving depth, size, and shape perception. The role that binocular and monocular cues play in depth perception is explained and such cues as disparity, texture gradient, linear perspective, interposition, and motion parallex are defined and illustrated. Discussion of perceptual constancies focuses on size and shape. The difference between proximal and distal stimuli is explained and it is noted that distal or distant stimuli are more intimately tied to constancies than are proximal stimuli.

Next the authors address the age-old nativist-empiricist controversy pointing out that current knowledge favors a blend of the nativist and empiricist positions. Studies of visual deprivation give more support to empiricist arguments than to nativist arguments but some data also support the nativist position. Nonetheless, the use of lenses to distort visual perception clearly indicates the importance of experience. *The Research Process* highlights classic studies using goggles to distort perception.

One way to study the effects of learning on visual perception is to study immature organisms. Fantz's work on pattern perception in infants is reviewed. Alternatives to the visual fixation method that have been developed include visual scanning, habituation, and the visual cliff. Gibson and Walk's pioneering research on depth perception leans toward the conclusion that it is an innate property of the visual system.

To help sum up the discussion of perception, *Controversy* examines the distinction between direct and indirect perception. Apparent motion is cited as an example of indirect perception and von Helmhotz's theory is cited and contrasted with James Gibson's emphasis on direct perception. Research involving the Necker cube suggests that both theorists may, in part, be correct.

The chapter concludes by discussing research with visual, spatial, and retinal illusions. Gregory's theory that spatial illusions are linked to size constancy also is supported by the theory of indirect perception.

Applying Psychology deals with illusions in the "real" world as distinct from laboratory studies. The Doppler effect, moon illusion, and waterfall illusion are described as illusions of the everyday world.

LEARNING OBJECTIVES

04-1. Be able to give an example of how perception differs from sensation. Distinguish vertical and illusory perception, and be able to give examples of each.

04-2. State the Gestalt position regarding the relationship between perceptions and sensations. Name and briefly describe the two Gestalt principles of perceptual organization.

04-3. Be able to define pattern recognition and to distinguish between bottom-up and top-down theories of pattern recognition.

04-4. List the major types of cues to depth perception. Distinguish proximal and distal stimuli. Define perceptual constancy and give examples of perceptual constancy in size and shape perception.

04-5. State the nature/nurture controversy regarding perception and be able to identify four types of investigations that bear on this controversy. Assess the research on restored vision in humans and visual deprivation in animals.

04-6. Describe experiments on adaptation to visual distortion in humans and be able to discuss the findings from these experiments.

04-7. Describe the perceptual capabilities of infants and how these capabilities are measured.

04-8. Distinguish between direct and indirect perception. Under what circumstances does the direct or indirect model best explain perception?

04-9. Distinguish retinal and spatial illusions and be able to give examples of each.

04-10. Describe four illusions that occur in everyday life.

ATTENTION GETTERS

Pattern Recognition 127-129

Two types of theories of pattern recognition (bottom-up theories and top-down theories) are discussed in the text. Which do you feel most accurately describes the process of human perception? Which circumstances would lead to a top-down explanation? Would other situational factors be better described by a bottom-up theory?

Perceptual Constancies 131-133

The authors point out that we often see objects as remaining constant even in situations where the retinal image is changing continuously. What are some examples of perceptual constancy that you have encountered in your everyday life? In what circumstances has this phenomenon "broken down" (e.g., people seem ant-size from a tall building)?

Learning and Perception 137-146

Which plays the greater role in perception, nature or nurture? Which evidence supports your view? Which evidence is inconsistent with your view? How can you incorporate information about the restoration of vision in the blind and about visual deprivation into your view?

Visual Illusions 146-152

How do visual illusions provide clues about how the perceptual system operates in normal circumstances? Give specific examples based on the illusions discussed in the text.

LECTURE SUGGESTIONS AND CLASS DEMONSTRATIONS

A Gestalt Demonstration 125-127

The organization of perception. The Gestalt principles for the organization of perception provide demonstrations that students find appealing. After reading Chapter 4, students can be asked to bring in a figure that illustrates one of the principles mentioned in the text. For example, the principle of good continuation could be illustrated by the figures below.

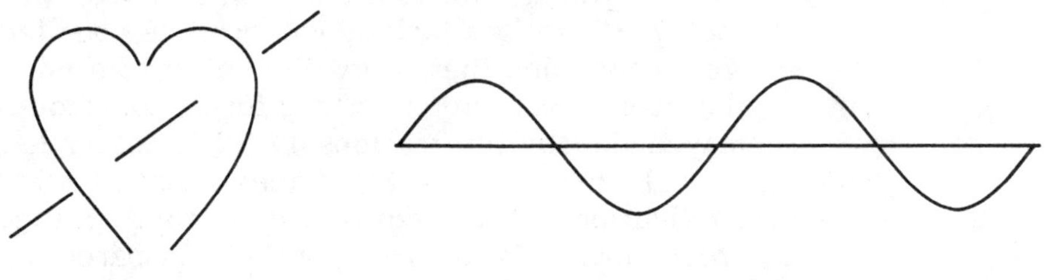

FIGURE 2 FIGURE 3

Students should report seeing an arrow piercing a heart in Figure 2 and a wavy line crossing over a straight line in Figure 3. It would be unusual for a student to report seeing four half-circles in Figure 3! The text contains a picture of a woodcut by the artist, M. C. Escher that is an excellent illustration of the relationship between figure and ground. Other examples of Escher's art also are based on manipulations of figure-ground relationships. For example, in *Mosaic II.* (reproduced in Freedman, 1982, p. 74) one sees either a group of black creatures on a white background or a group of white creatures on a black background. Escher's art contains many unusual perceptual cues that would be interesting to discuss. Most libraries and bookstores have collections of this art. Transparencies can be made on xerox machines and used on overhead projectors. Transparency 4-1 illustrates the Gestalt dictum that the whole is different from the sum of its parts by showing what happens when a light is attached to a wheel and then is rolled across a dark room.

Pattern Recognition 127-129

Pandemonium. An excellent source for lecture material is Lindsay and Norman (1977). Their book is exceptionally well illustrated, with nearly every principle of perceptual organization, illusion, depth cue, and anatomical structure presented in figures large enough to make good transparencies for class use. Indeed, one can organize several lectures solely by showing transparencies as attention-getters. Students respond especially well to discussion of pattern recognition when lecture material is supplemented by overhead transparencies of Selfridge's "pandemonium demons." Six figures of the little fellows at work are included in Chapter 7 of the book. Pandemonium is a scheme applied to an analysis of pattern recognition and selective attention. As noted by Lindsay and Norman, it is similar to a template matching model except that it matches features rather than specific lines or angles. Thus, "Pandemonium systems will recognize letters despite changes in size, orientation, and despite a number of other distortions. Pandemonium, then, describes the sequence of events needed for a feature analysis of patterns" (Lindsay & Norman, 1977, p. 261). That sequence involves image demons (record the input image), feature demons (analyze specific aspects of the image), cognitive demons (recognize patterns), and a decision demon ("....selects the cognitive demon who is yelling the loudest as the pattern that is most likely occuring in the environment"--Lindsay & Norman, p. 260). If you are not familiar with this book we strongly recommend that you give it a look as you prepare your lectures on perception. We do not think that you will be disappointed. In fact, inasmuch as the book deals with human information processing in general, you may find many illustrations useful for other lecture topics as well.

Transparency 4-2 provides a fun illustration of the different implications of top-down and bottom-up theories of information processing. In addition, this transparency illustrates the importance of ambiguity.

Learning in Perception 137-142

Perception in everyday life. S. Howard Bartley has been a student of perception for nearly 50 years, and during that time has contributed enormously to the scientific investigation of perceptual phenomena. The material that follows is from his book, *Perception in Everyday Life* (1972), and illustrates the linkage between causality and vision.

Applying Psychology 151-152

> Our purpose here is to describe briefly an investigation made some years ago by the well-known Belgian psychologist Michotte (1946) in his book, *La Perception de la causalite.* In general, when we see an object A move up against an object B, if B, without delay, moves away in a direction that is the continuation of A's prior movement, it looks as though A has set B into motion. In other words, it appears that A caused B's motion. This need not be the case at all even though the whole event is perfectly convincing as a visual experience.

> Michotte had an arrangement consisting of a blank perpendicular screen bearing a narrow slot. What was to be seen to move acted behind the screen and appeared through the slot. The observer was made to see a colored "block" (A) move along the slot on the screen. The rate of motion of this block could be varied by the experimenter. A could be made to move from left to right and stop midway along the slot. At that point B, another item seen as a block behind the slot, had been motionlessly waiting. As A moves up alongside B, B is made to move, not by A having actually bumped it, but by the experimenter starting the device carrying B to the right. Visually, A is seen to *cause* B to move. While most people might be amused and simply say that this is an illusion, we do not stop there for it does not clarify the matter one bit. Michotte and I (Bartley) both see causality as something to be studied.
>
> ...
>
> Michotte announced several factors necessary for the cause-effect impressions: (1) There must be two objects, for when there is only one object, cause and effect are not distinguished (isolated). (2) The movement of one object must visually dominate, as is the case when one object moves first. (3) The "impact" of one object on the other must be seen in foveal vision. (4) Fixation on B is best for the impression of causality. (5) For the clearest causal impression, there must be sufficient unity (continuity) in space, time, and direction (Bartley, 1972, pp. 226-227).

Bartley then links Michotte's demonstration of visual causality to intersensory causality; the case where information from one sensory modality is connected to information from another sensory modality. To illustrate the connection Bartley offers the following anecdote:

> ....Frequently, I go down to the basement and pass by an ironing board on which an electric iron is standing in the usual nose-upright position as when left after ironing. Being a very cautious person, I am habitually concerned as to whether the iron has actually been turned off. On the evening in question, as I saw the iron I chanced to pass under the ceiling register which was putting out considerable heat from the furnace, and this struck me in the face. The very realistic impression I received was that the iron had been left on and I was feeling the heat from it. Momentarily the iron looked hot. Of course, I walked over to the iron to test it. By that time, I had passed from under the blast of heat and no longer felt it. Although I reached out my fingers cautiously to check the iron, it no longer convincingly *looked* hot. I then realized where the heat had actually come from.

In this illustration we have the requirements stated by Michotte, that there be two objects or two separate sensory experiences and that they are not seen as unitary. One seems to cause the other. Furthermore, in this case, the one experience was mediated by one sensory mechanism (temperature sense), while the other was visual. The heat was felt on the face, the causal item seen at a distance. This was a cause-effect perception that had been learned.... (Bartley, 1972, pp. 230-231).

From S. Howard Bartley. (1972). *Perception in Everyday Life.* New York: Harper & Row Publishers. Copyright 1972 by S. Howard Bartley. Reprinted by permission of the author.

After reviewing Michotte's criteria for causal inferencing and Bartley's example of intersensory causal inferencing, the instructor either can give additional examples of such perceptions of everyday life or can ask students to try to think of similar experiences from instances in their own lives.

Experience certainly affects our causal inferencing about sensory events and analyses of these effects helps us to understand normal perception. We also gain important information about perception by analyzing "things that aren't really there." Transparencies 4-3 and 4-4 illustrate some of the illustions used in the scientific study of perception. Transparency 4-3 shows the Muller-Lyer and Poggendorf illusions, and Transparency 4-4 illustrates how the Muller-Lyer illusion can be explained by size constancy.

Perception in Infants 142-146

Infant perception. Developmental changes in perceptual tasks can be demonstrated if the instructor has access to infants! Bower (1977, pp. 34 to 38) reports a study he performed with infants that is similar to the visual distortion experiments performed on adults. A 5-month-old baby is fitted with wedge prisms that make objects seem like they are to the side of where they are actually located. When the baby reaches for an attractive object, she will miss because she is reaching toward the "distorted" location rather than the actual location. The baby will continue to miss the object on successive tries. The prisms can then be put on a 7-month-old infant. Although the older baby will make a mistake on the first part of the reach, he will correct the aim once the hand is also in the visual field. Bower suggests that younger infants have difficulty monitoring their hand's position while simultaneously attending to the object. This may be a difficult demonstration to pull off but if it works it can be quite dramatic.

AUDIOVISUAL AIDES

Films

The Mind's Eye. Films Incorporated, 50 minutes, color. A review of much recent research in visual perception including distance perception, circuitry of the visual centex, feature defectors, color-specific cells. The mystery of how we see.

Perception. CRM/McGraw-Hill, 28 minutes, color. This film shows how perception is an individual and subjective way to view reality influenced by our social upbringing, culture and media.

The Amazing Newborn. 25 minutes, color. Case Western Reserve University. Portrays the sensory-perceptual development, organization, and abilities for interaction present in the infant's first few days of life.

Theories of Perception. Ohio State University, 6 min., B & W. Kenneth Norberg relates theories of perception to applications in industry training programs, intercultural programs, and programs for the culturally deprived.

Motor Perception I: Two-dimensional Motion Perception. Houghton Mifflin, 7 min., color. Gunnar Johansson uses computer generated stimuli, and movements of human subjects, to show how motions are seen and analyzed in terms of groups and subgroups. Illustrates Gestalt laws of perception.

Motion Perception II: Three-dimensional Motion Perception. Houghton-Mifflin, 11 min., color. Computer generated stimuli are used to show information necessary for perception of three-dimensionality. Motion patterns, changes of size, and changes of length are illustrated.

REFERENCES AND ANNOTATED SOURCES

Bartley, S. H. (1972). *Perception in everyday life.* New York: Harper & Row. A collection of essays illustrating how perception operates in everyday life.

Bartley, S. H. (1969). *Principles of perception.* New York: Harper & Row. Reviews thirteen theories of perception and devotes a full chapter to perceptual constancies.

Bower, T. G. R. (1977). *The perceptual world of the child.* Cambridge, MA: Harvard University Press.

Cornsweet, T. N. (1970). *Visual perception.* New York: Academic Press. A comprehensive review of visual perception, including structural and functional aspects.

Fredman, J. L. (1982). *Introductory psychology,* (2nd ed.). Reading, MA: Addison-Wesley Publishing Co.

Gibson, E. J. (1969). *Principles of perceptual learning and development.* New York: Appleton-Century Crofts. A comprehensive review of perceptual theory and research, loaded with potential illustrations for lecture.

Haith, M. M. (1980). *Rules that babies look by.* Hillsdale, NJ: Lawrence Erlbaum Associates. A fascinating review of programmatic research on newborn perception including a provocative information-acquisition, rule-based interpretation of newborn visual behavior.

Lindsay, P. H., & Norman, D. A. (1977). *Human information processing.* New York: Academic Press.

Chapter 5

CONSCIOUSNESS AND ATTENTION

CHAPTER OVERVIEW

The authors point out that spatial metaphors are generally used to describe the conscious mind. One key aspect of consciousness is that it is limited in capacity. A second aspect of consciousness is that psychologists have heuristically divided it into different levels or states: conscious, preconscious, unconscious, and nonconscious. Nonconscious processes cannot be moved into consciousness, whereas unconscious processes can be, albeit with great difficulty. Attention is a process which affects movement of information within and across the various levels of consciousness.

Specifically, the authors define attention as "focusing of perception (leading) to a greater awareness of a limited number of stimuli." They indicate that the systematic study of selective attention received impetus in the 1950s as psychologists attempted to solve a practical problem facing air-traffic controllers: How to attend to one message and ignore others. The technique of speech shadowing developed to solve this problem. Various models of attention have been proposed in order to account for such phenomenon including Broadbent's filter theory and Norman's (and others) response selection theory. *The Research Process* focuses on subliminal perception and illustrates the use of speech shadowing.

Next the authors consider the relationship between hemispheric specialization and consciousness. Do we have two brains? Two types of consciousness? They review evidence suggesting that culture and/or language may play a far more important role in structuring consciousness than previously thought. *Controversy* examines Jaynes' hypothesis that humans achieved consciousness only a few thousand years ago. Jaynes argues that prior to the achievement of consciousness, people were like automatons directed by "gods" which were in actuality commands from the right hemisphere to the left hemisphere.

The remainder of the chapter reviews states in which consciousness is changed, as for example, during sleep or hypnosis, or by drugs. The electrophysiology of sleeping is detailed and the various stages of sleep are described both physiologically and behaviorally. The authors point out several contextual and individual difference variables that may be important in varying the effects of sleep deprivation. On the other hand, we do seem to need to dream and when deprived of dreaming (REM sleep periods) often spend time attempting to catch up (REM rebound). In *Applying Psychology* the authors examine various sleep disorders including situational, benign, arrhythmic, and drug-related insomnias; apnea; and narcolepsy.

Altered states of consciousness--hypnosis, meditation, and effects of psychoactive drugs--are reviewed as are studies of hypnotic states by Ernest Hilgard and T. X. Barber. Drugs singled out for specific discussion include depressants (alcohol, barbiturates, opiate narcotics), stimulants (caffeine, nicotine, amphetamines, cocaine), and hallucinogens (marijuana, LSD).

LEARNING OBJECTIVES

05-1. Give two metaphors commonly used to describe consciousness. Distinguish among conscious, preconscious, unconscious, and nonconscious mental states.

05-2. Define selective attention and briefly describe how it is studied in the laboratory. Distinguish between early selection and late selection models of attention. Describe how subliminal perception is tested in the laboratory.

05-3. Distinguish controlled and automatic processing and briefly describe how each type of processing is tested in the laboratory.

05-4. Define hemispheric specialization and be able to discuss some of the implications of split-brain research. Outline Julian Jaynes' theory of the bicameral mind.

05-5. Describe a night of sleep, including the stages of sleep and the phenomenon of REM sleep. How are the brain waves of sleepers measured?

05-6. Summarize the effects of sleep deprivation including the effects of REM sleep deprivation.

05-7. Outline the difference in causes and treatments for various types of insomnias, sleep apnea, and narcolepsy.

05-8. Describe briefly how a person is put under hypnosis and what suggestions a hypnotized person would be likely to follow. Describe the process of meditation.

05-9. List the major categories of drugs, and be able to give examples of drugs in each category, and how these drugs affect conscious experience.

ATTENTION GETTERS

Consciousness 156-157

It is often pointed out that the topic of consciousness has been neglected for much of this century. Many behaviorists felt that it was an inappropriate area to study (either because it did not exist or because it was an epiphenomenon). In psychoanalytic theory the unconscious was emphasized much more than the conscious. How do *you* define consciousness? How do you think it can be studied in a scientific manner that will fit your definition?

Attention 158-159

What evidence suggests that during a selective attention task the ignored message is *not* filtered out only at a sensory level? Given this evidence would you argue for an early selection or late selection model of attention?

Sleep 172-180

The authors point out that most people assume that we sleep because it has a restorative effect. But actually science has no firm answers as to whether this is true. Why do you think we sleep? How can you support your view based on the information on the text?

LECTURE SUGGESTIONS AND CLASS DEMONSTRATIONS

Selective Attention 159-163

Speech shadowing and selective attention. Selective attention can be demonstrated by asking for a student volunteer to participate in a speech shadowing experiment. The instructor and a teaching assistant (or another student volunteer) should read aloud from books about two different subjects. The subject should try to repeat the message being delivered by the teaching assistant. In the middle of the reading the instructor should begin reading in another language or reading from another source (e.g., nursery rhymes). Toward the end the instructor should switch back to the original material. (To be maximally effective the passages should be written and timed *before* the class meets!) The subject should then be asked questions about both passages. Subjects should do well when remembering the accepted message but poorly when they try to recall information from the unattended ear. In fact, the class may be amused to find that the subject was not aware that the instructor had begun speaking in Spanish or reciting "There was an old woman who lived in a shoe..."!

Transparency 5-1 illustrates an early selection and a late selection model of selective attention. After performing the demonstration above, show Transparency 5-1 and ask students to determine whether early selection or late selection model best explains the phenomenon demonstrated.

Hemispheric Specialization 168-171

Batter up! For the average person, cerebral specialization reduces to handedness, which in turn, generally is defined by the hand used in writing. By this criterion, about 90 percent of the human population is right-handed and 10 percent is left-handed. Throughout history, left handedness has been discouraged, even linked to demonic possession. Hence the term "sinistrality" to refer to left-hand preference. In baseball, however, left-handedness has advantages and disadvantages as pointed out in the following:

> "In the case of the batter, as Grantland Rice once pointed out, the left-hander stands on the near side of first base and is thus one or two steps closer to it than the right-handed batter is. Also, when the left-hander hits the ball, his swing turns him toward first base, giving him a positional advantage that enables him to get under way more quickly. The right-hander, by contrast, turns away from first base after completing his swing, and so must reverse his position before he can start his run toward first base.
>
> The left-handed batter would enjoy yet another advantage because, for the greater part, he faces a right-handed pitcher, who finds it difficult to curve the pitched ball away from the left-handed batter. Of course, the right-handed batter has a similar advantage when facing a left-handed pitcher, but since many more major-league pitchers are right-handed than left-handed (3:1 ratio in 1951 survey), the left-handed batter is facing a right-handed pitcher far more often than the right-handed batter faces a left-handed

pitcher. Of course, batting from the left side does not always help. Perhaps we can illustrate the point with a story told by a player named Davy Jones about an incident when he was with the Cubs in 1902. (From Ritter's book, *The Glory of Their Times*).

'We had a young pitcher on that club named Jimmy St. Vrain. He was a left-handed pitcher and a right-handed batter. But an absolutely terrible hitter--never even got a loud foul off anybody.

Well, one day we were playing the Pittsburgh Pirates and Jimmy was pitching for us. The first two times he went up to bat that day he looked simply awful. So when he came back after striking out the second time, Frank Selee, our manager, said, "Jimmy, you're a left-handed pitcher, why don't you turn around and bat from the left side, too? Why not try it?"

Actually, Frank was half kidding, but Jimmy took him seriously. So the next time he went up he batted left-handed. Turned around and stood on the opposite side of the plate from where he was used to, you know. And darned if he didn't actually hit the ball. He tapped a slow roller down to Honus Wagner at shortstop and took off as fast as he could go...but instead of running to first base, he headed for *third*!

Oh, my God! What bedlam! Everybody yelling and screaming at poor Jimmy as he raced to third base, head down, spikes flying, determined to get there ahead of the throw. Later on, Honus told us that as a matter of fact he almost *did* throw the ball to third.

"I'm standing there with the ball in my hand," Honus said, "looking at this guy running from home to third, and for an instant there I swear I didn't know *where* to throw the damn ball. And when I finally did throw to first, I wasn't at all sure it was the right thing to do!"' (Ritter, 1966, p. 46).

Clearly, right-handed baseball players recognize the advantage to be gained from left-handed batting. Lehmann and Webb showed this very dramatically in an examination of over 5,000 major-league players listed over a 29-year-long period, in *Who's Who in Baseball.* (This report was published in *Motor Skills Research Exchange* in 1951, so it would cover the period from 1931 to 1950.) Among right-handed throwers, 24 percent adopted a left-handed batting stance, whereas among left-handed throwers, only 0.5 percent adopted a right-handed batting stance. In other words, there were about 48 times as many right-handed throwers who used a left-handed batting stance as there were left-handed throwers who used a right-handed batting stance.

Evidently, these proportions have not changed appreciably since 1951. Last year, in a letter to the *New England Journal of Medicine*, McLean and Churczak (1982) reported a new survey that showed that among 569 current major-league players (excluding pitchers), 91 (16%) threw right and batted left, and *none* threw left and batted right. Of the remaining players, 324 (57%) threw right and batted right and 85 (15%) threw left and batted left. McLean and Churczak also considered the 41 best hitters of all time and found a similar distribution" (From Ritter, L. S. (1966). *The glory of their times: The story of the early days of baseball told by the men who played it.* New York: Macmillan. Copyright 1966 by Lawrence S. Ritter. Reprinted by permission of the author. Cited in L. J. Harris, D. F. Carlson, & H. E. Fitzgerald, Current theories and research on manual asymmetry. Paper presented at the annual meeting of the North American Society for the Psychology of Sport and Physical Activity, East Lansing, Michigan, May 31, 1983 with permission of the authors.)

Sleep learning. The text describes characteristics of sleep in sufficient detail for students to be able to design an experiment to study "sleep learning".

Study of Sleep 172-177

However to set the stage, review Transparencies 5-2 and 5-3, both of which also appear in the text. Transparency 5-2 shows EEG stages of sleep, and Transparency 5-3 illustrates differences among the stages in three samples of nightly sleep recordings obtained from the same individual. Periodically, claims are made that the time spent asleep can be used in learning new material. Students should be asked to form small groups in order to plan a study testing this hypothesis. The example below provides a sample experiment.

> HYPOTHESIS: If information is played to a person while s/he is sleeping then they will be able to repeat what they have learned when awake.
>
> METHOD: Subjects will be asked to come to the laboratory so that their EEG's can be recorded while the taped information is being played. Stage of sleep during which information is presented will be recorded. Each piece of information (question and answer) will be presented only once. When the subject awakens in the morning s/he will be asked all the questions that were presented during sleep.

After each group has formed an experimental plan the instructor can reveal the results of a 1956 study by C. W. Simon and W. H. Emmons (cited by Bransford, 1979, page 23). They presented questions (such as "In what kind of store did Ulysses S. Grant work before the war?") followed by answers ("Before the war, Ulysses S. Grant worked in a hardware store.") to sleeping subjects. Whether a subject could recall the answer later depended on his/her level of sleep during the presentation of the material.

> "Participants could answer 80 percent of the questions when the EEG indicated a state of being awake but relaxed, 50

percent when the EEG indicated a drowsy state, and only 5 percent when the EEG suggested a transition state between drowsiness and light sleep. For the actual states of sleep, light, deep, and very deep, there was essentially no evidence that learning had occurred" (Bransford, 1979, p. 23).

Why Do We Dream 178-180

Pick your dream. Dreaming is a topic that is intrinsically interesting to almost everyone. The following activity can set the stage for an interesting class discussion or lecture on dreaming. The Senoi people of Malaysia not only teach children to report dreams each morning, but they teach them to control frightening dreams (Cartwright, 1978). Cartwright describes an experiment conducted by Foulkes and Griffin. Select five students to serve as judges. Ask each remaining student to prepare a list of topics for dreaming and to select one as the target topic. Before going to sleep each night for ten consecutive nights, students must instruct themselves to dream about the target topic each selected. Upon awakening, students are to write a description of their dreams and turn them in at class time. Each student should have an identity code to place on their dream list and dream description so the two can be matched. After each student turns in five dream descriptions, give all descriptions to the panel of judges and ask them to identify which topic the dreams represent. (Recall, each student selects only one topic from their dream list.) Foulkes and Griffins' judges did not reliably deduce target topics. Even if laboratory studies suggest that the dream content cannot be controlled, it does not mean that it cannot occur in everyday life. For example, the Senoi children receive daily training over a period of years, not a period of days. Is it possible that children find it easier to control dream content than do adults? How would students design an experiment to test out this question? (See Cartwright, R. D. (1978). Happy endings for our dreams. *Psychology Today*, pp. 66-76.)

Meditation 182-183

Count your breaths. The text points out that the mystique that surrounds meditation is not necessary for meditation to lead to deep relaxation. Ornstein (1977) reports that some of his friends went to India to learn the mysteries of meditation from a famous guru. After a very difficult journey they met with the guru who told them to "Sit facing the wall and count your breaths. This is all" (Ornstein, 1977, p. 157). Ornstein reports that his friends were crestfallen. Students may also be disappointed to find that there is little "magic" in meditation. However, they may be surprised to find how difficult meditation is for the beginner. Have the class try the exercise outlined in the text on pages 182-183. They may repeat a word or count as mentioned in the story above. Whenever they find that their focus drifts from the word or counting, they should concentrate on the word (count) again. With practice this exercise is done for 30 minutes. In class, students may find 5 minutes difficult. After this exercise students can discuss the experience. Was it difficult? Ask the students to try a

30-minute session that evening. Do they experience the changes described in the text?

Drugs also affect our level of consciousness as illustrated in Transparency 5-4. This transparency shows how LSD acts to block the action of inhibitor neurotransmitters such as serotonin. This transparency can be used to stimulate discussion of the effects of such drugs as nicotine and caffeine on levels of consciousness. Anyone for caffeine free cola!

AUDIOVISUAL AIDES

Films

Left Brain, Right Brain. Filmmakers Library, 56 minutes, color. Examines the nature and function of the two hemispheres of the human brain. Discusses the evolutionary history of the brain and the localization of language and other skills.

Mind of Man. Indiana University, 119 min., color. Research in the United States, Soviet Union, India, Western Europe and Canada. Wide variety of topics including chemical changes in the brain, the brain and sexuality, mental development in children, effects of drugs, dreams, reasoning, and mental control of bodily functions. Star-studded cast of researchers.

Sleeping Brain. Houghton Mifflin, 23 min., color. Michel Jouvel discusses the neuropsychology and neurophysiology of sleep and dreaming. Good illustration of the importance of animal research for advancing our understanding of human behavior.

Sleep and Dreaming in Humans. Houghton Mifflin, 14 min., color. William Dement demonstrates research techniques used to study sleep stages and dreaming.

Darkness, Darkness. Nolan, Wilton, and Wootten, Inc., 37 min., color. Interviews with young people who are or have been, admitted addicts. Gives a realistic view of people who inhabit the drug would. Should be used only if class discussion time follows.

Audio Cassettes

Webb, Wilse B. Current sleep research: Methods and findings. APA Tape 10-18, 1974. Sleep has received little attention in terms of its character or its effects on all other behaviors. Webb traces the history of sleep research and describes the various stages of sleep and the major variables affecting those stages including drugs, shift work, travel, enureses, sleep deprivation, sleep disturbances, and sleep learning.

Film Strips

Charting the Unconscious Mind. Human Relations Media, 2 part filmstrip program.

REFERENCES AND ANNOTATED SOURCES

Bransford, J. D. (1979). *Human cognition: Learning, understanding and remembering.* Belmont, CA: Wadsworth Publishing Co.

Orstein, R. W. (1977). *The psychology of consciousness* (2nd ed.). New York: Harcourt, Brace, Jovanovich, Inc.

Pope, K. S., & Singer, J. L. (Eds.) (1978). *The stream of consciousness.* New York: Plenum Press. This volume contains a lead chapter by Strange which gives an historical sketch of consciousness in American psychology.

Springer, S. P., & Deutsch, G. (1981). *Left-brain, right-brain.* San Francisco: W. H. Freeman & Company. A thorough but readable review of cerebral lateralization touching on nearly every aspect of the topic including handedness, sex differences, reading problems, stuttering, and what paw your dog shakes with!

Webb, W. B. (1975). *Sleep, the gentle tyrant.* Englewood Cliffs, NJ: Prentice-Hall. An excellent and readable review of sleep research touching on all aspects of the topic.

Young, G., Segalowitz, S., Corter, C., & Trehub, S. (Eds.) (1983). *Manual specialization and the developing brain.* New York: Academic Press. Twenty-three chapters collectively deal with nearly every aspect of early lateral differentiation, and include researchers using cross-sectional and longitudinal approaches.

Chapter 6

CONDITIONING AND LEARNING

CHAPTER OVERVIEW

In their definition of learning the authors allow for changes in knowledge as well as behavior. Learning reflects "a relatively permanent change in behavior or knowledge that occurs as a result of experience." The major portion of the chapter is devoted to careful examination of classical and instrumental conditioning procedures. The chapter concludes with a discussion of observational learning and cognitive aspects of learning.

Following a careful description of Pavlov's original studies with conditioned salivation in dogs, the authors define the key components of the conditioning procedure (UCS, UCR, CS, CR) and provide many examples of classical conditioning in everyday life.

The authors then review a variety of factors that influence classical conditioning including UCS intensity, CS-UCS relevance and CS-UCS interval (delayed, simultaneous, trace, backward procedures), in the process highlighting Garcia's research on taste aversion. From factors, the authors move to classical conditioning phenomena, including extinction (linked to the therapeutic technique known as systematic desensitization), stimulus generalization, discrimination, and higher order conditioning. *The Research Process* highlights the procedure referred to as "blocking" in which the pairing of CS and UCS is inadequate to elicit conditioning.

The second section of this chapter focuses on instrumental conditioning. Beginning with Thorndike's classic puzzle-box experiment, the definition of the law of effect, Skinner's operant conditioning variation, and his famous "Skinner box," the authors move to discussion of shaping and reinforcement. Magnitude and delay of positive reinforcement are cited as two key aspects of performance, and the authors note that reinforcer effectiveness depends in part on the organism's prior experience with a particular reinforcer. Basic distinctions between continuous and partial reinforcement and among the various reinforcement schedules are described as is the relationship between acquisition schedule and resistance to extinction.

Discussion of negative reinforcement includes procedures for demonstrating escape learning, active avoidance learning, and passive avoidance learning (punishment). Stimulus generalization and discrimination learning using instrumental procedures also are described. In *Applying Psychology* the authors discuss how attention-getting can reinforce undesireable behavior, and how behavioral rehearsal can enhance assertiveness.

Next the authors discuss similarities and differences between classical and instrumental conditioning. One account links classical conditioning to UCS elicited responses (autonomic responses and reflexes) and instrumental conditioning to skeletal responses. However, such simple dichotomies fail to encompass the many exceptions to the rule as is illustrated by autoshaping (classical conditioning of a skeletal response) and biofeedback (instrumental conditioning). In *Controversy* the authors provide an overview of research offered as support for instrumental conditioning of autonomic responses.

The chapter concludes with discussion of observational learning and of cognitive processes in learning. Bandura's research demonstrating modeled aggression in children leads into the broader issues of cognitive processes in learning, a topic pioneered by E. C. Tolman early in this century. Tolman's early demonstrations of cognitive mapping (spatial relationships) and latent learning have stood the test of time as has Hunter's early demonstrations of delayed responding, which appears in modern form--though varied--in the delayed-match to sample technique. These techniques have enabled researchers to study such basic processes as short and long term storage, interference effects, and retrieval processes in animals thus opening broad speculation as to the meaning of animal consciousness. The chapter closes with a discussion of expectancy (temporal relationship) and Seligman's work on learned helplessness.

LEARNING OBJECTIVES

06-1. Define learning. Be able to give examples that distinguish learning from other processes, such as fatigue and motivation.

06-2. Outline Pavlov's experiment and define classical conditioning. Be able to distinguish between conditioned stimulus, unconditioned stimulus, conditioned response, and unconditioned response. Be able to give examples of classical conditioning in everyday life.

06-3. Define extinction, spontaneous recovery, stimulus generalization, discrimination training, higher order conditioning and acquisition, in classical conditioning.

06-4. Be able to discuss the four variables that affect acquisition in classical conditioning: UCS intensity, CS-UCS relevance, CS-UCS interval, and the relative validity of the CS.

06-5. Be able to describe how blocking is produced in classical conditioning and to discuss the significance of blocking.

06-6. Define instrumental conditioning and distinguish it from classical conditioning. Be familiar with the Skinner box and the process called shaping.

06-7. State the principle of reinforcement and be able to distinguish between a positive and negative reinforcer. Describe the effects of varying the size and schedule of reinforcement in instrumental conditioning. Relate escape conditioning and active avoidance, distinguish punishment from negative reinforcement. Relate stimulus generalization and discrimination training to instrumental conditioning.

06-8. Be able to discuss the relationship between instrumental conditioning and classical conditioning by identifying the types of responses each procedure brings under control.

06-9. Define observational learning and describe the major research techniques used to show how it occurs.

06-10. Describe the cognitive approach to learning. Define insight, latent learning, expectancies, learned helplessness and relate these concepts to cognitive processes in nonhuman animals.

ATTENTION GETTERS

Classical Conditioning 197-208

As a therapist you are called upon to treat a person who has an intense fear of open areas. How could you use the principles of classical conditioning described in Chapter 6 in your therapy?

Instrumental Conditioning 208-217

During a visit to the circus you see a pigeon "dance" to the music played by its trainer. What principles discussed in Chapter 6 can help you explain the pigeon's ability to learn this behavior?

Applying Psychology 218

Once stimuli have been associated with primary reinforcers repeatedly they often become conditioned reinforcers themselves. What are some examples of conditioned reinforcers (both positive and negative) in your everyday life?

Reinforcement Schedules 211-212

A friend states that he doesn't know why his young child is constantly begging for toys in the supermarket because most of the time he doesn't give in. What explanations can you give for this type of behavior based on the information in the text on schedules of reinforcement?

LECTURE SUGGESTIONS AND CLASS DEMONSTRATIONS

Many students find lectures on classical conditioning and operant conditioning dry. One way to spice them up a bit is to use a good attention-getter to open the lecture and then to fill the lecture with examples of how these types of learning occur in the everyday world.

Pavlov's Experiment 198-200

Pavlov: scientist and eccentric. One good attention-getter is to introduce students to some of the key historical figures in the area of learning. Fancher (1979) is a good source. Fancher describes Pavlov as a worldly eccentric who was completely opposite in character when in his laboratory. A number of amusing anecdotes are given about Pavlov's life. Students especially should find Fancher's account of Pavlov's work with gastric fistulas interesting, not only because it lead to his being awarded the Nobel Prize in physiology, but because it also illustrates the precision Pavlov expected in his laboratory. Equally interesting is Fancher's description of the scientific duel fought between Pavlov and his chief rival, Bekhterev, as well as his account of Pavlov's interactions with his wife. Fancher also includes biographical information about Watson and Skinner.

"Two types" of learning. Students always seem to have difficulty grasping the procedural components of classical and instrumental

conditioning. Therefore, after using some of the above as attention-getters, we advise moving immediately into a slow and detailed description of classical conditioning and the factors that influence elaboration of conditional reflexes. If only one lecture is devoted to learning, then move right along with instrumental conditioning. Ideally, the two "types" of learning should be presented in separate lectures. Use of the overhead projector, chalkboard, or slides is a must. When one is certain that students understand the basic paradigms, they may be ready to consider the question as to whether they represent two different types of learning or are merely variations of the same theme.

Examples of Classical Conditioning 200-

Classical Conditioning. To demonstrate classical conditioning bring a large book to class and place it at the edge of a table or desk. During the lecture on classical conditioning gesture periodically and when gesturing knock the book off the desk. After four gesture-knock pairings, gesture but do *not* knock the book off the table. At that point ask the class to evaluate their reactions. Did conditioning occur? What was the UCS? (loud noise caused by book). What was the UCR? (wincing, startle response). What was the CS? (gesture). What was the CR? (wincing, startle). The class can use this demonstration as a basis for discussing the details of classical conditioning described in the text. At this point it may be helpful to show Transparency 6-1 which illustrates classical conditoning procedures. A brief review of the procedures will provide a context for considering aspects of the demonstration. For example, was the CR the same as the UCR (stimulus substitution view) or was it different (expectancy view)? What time interval was there between the CS and the UCS--would this demonstration be an example of delayed conditioning, simultaneous conditioning, trace conditioning, or backward conditioning? After students seem to understand these concepts they can be asked to discuss examples of classical conditioning that occur in their daily lives. For example, many students will have noticed that pets which are fed canned food will come running into the kitchen at the sound of a can opener. The class can decide how this behavior can be explained by classical conditioning.

Conditioning the Eyeblink Response. Another possible demonstration (adapted from Gardner, 1980) involves the classical conditioning of an eyeblink response. The class divides into groups of four students. Each group has an observer who records whether or not an eyeblink occurs, a subject, and two experimenters (one to deliver the CS and the other to deliver the UCS). Each group is provided with a bell and a straw. The UCS is a puff of air aimed just above the eye; the CS is the sound of the bell; the CR and UCR will be an eyeblink. Subjects should place their elbows on their desks and place their chins in their hands. One experimenter should ring the bell while the observer records whether there are any orienting responses to the sound. This should be repeated until the subject does not show a regular response to the bell. Then the training procedure can begin. The following procedure should be used:

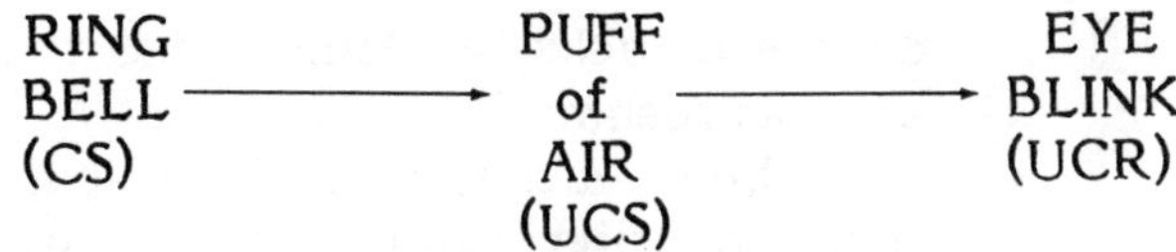

Adapted from Rick M. Gardner, *Exercises for General Psychology.* Copyright 1980 by Burgess Publishing Company. By permission of Burgess Publishing Company, Minneapolis, Minnesota.

The text points out that the timing between the CS and UCS is important and that to condition an eyeblink the optimum interval is .5 of a second (500 milliseconds). (Transparency 6-2 illustrates differences in the CS-UCS relationship among simultaneous, delayed, trace, and backward conditioning procedures.) The training procedure should be repeated five times. Then for a test trial, no puff of air will be delivered:

Classical Conditioning Phenomena 202-208

RING BELL ⟶ CR?

The observer should record whether or not an eyeblink occurred. the training and testing sequences can be continued until the eyeblink response is conditioned. Each group can then decide how to demonstrate stimulus generalization, discrimination and extinction. After the groups have finished these procedures the observer from each group can report their results to the class. After the class discussion, the same groups can be formed to test for spontaneous recovery. Did the eyeblink reappear in the subjects who had undergone extinction? Transparency 6-3 illustrates acquisition, extinction, and spontaneous recovery of a conditioned response. If the research groups collected data, they can match their data records with the curves shown in the transparency to see how closely the "real" data corresponds to "theoretical" curves.

Instrumental Conditioning 208-217

Instrumental Conditioning. Reinforcement is a key concept in instrumental conditioning. Transparencies 6-4 and 6-5 illustrate various aspects of reinforcement. After pointing out that acquisition is faster with 100 percent reinforcement than with partial reinforcement (less than 100%), show 6-4 to illustrate what effect the acquisition reinforcement schedule has on resistance to extinction. Transparency 6-5 contrasts positive and negative reinforcement and punishment and the effects each has on responsivity. With these concepts as background, introduce Garcia's work on taste aversion.

Garcia combined his work in taste aversion with Gustavson's interest in the foraging behaviors of wild animals to attack a problem involving sheep-killing coyotes (Gustavson & Garcia, 1974). They tainted lamb meat with lithium chloride, a drug which causes nausea and vomiting, to condition coyotes to avoid lamb meat. They report that the treatment worked by suppressing coyote attacks, although once the effect wore off (extinction) the attacks resumed.

Expectancies and Learned Helplessness 227-229

Learned helplessness research is another topic that students seem to find interesting (Alloy & Seligman, 1979). Learned helplessness is a cognitive approach in learning and has interesting developmental implications as well. It proposes to apply across species and to be synonymous with such terms as perception, belief, or expectation of control. Such terms have been used in the past to express subjective representations of the degree to which outcomes are dependent upon behavior. The important point is that learned helplessness theory proposes that helplessness interferes with one's ability to learn future response-outcome contingencies.

Controversy 220-221

Biofeedback: Monitoring Physiological Reactions During Stress. Biofeedback has become a familiar term to most students due to the emphasis the media has placed on stress-related disorders and their treatment (see Chapter 12). The equipment used as monitoring devices are now compact enough to be brought into the classroom for a demonstration. If the instructor is not familiar with psychophysiological recording equipment, ask a colleague who is to assist with the demonstration. Usually several students are willing to volunteer. The subject's EMG and HR will be measured and a baseline obtained. Then the subject will be "stressed" (e.g., by counting backward by 7's from 500). This shows the class how bodily changes occur as a result of psychological stress. Stern and Ray (1977) provide basic information about biofeedback that will be useful in answering student questions. They state that "the primary function of biofeedback is to help us tune in to our bodies..." (page 5) and suggest that people need to become "good listeners" and pay attention to the internal signals of their bodies.

AUDIOVISUAL AIDES

Films

Classical and Instrumental Conditioning. Harper & Row, 21 minutes. Describes and compares classical and instrumental conditioning, includes laboratory demonstrations.

Cognition, Creativity, and Behavior. Research Press, 30 minutes, 16 mm, color, includes discussion guide. B. F. Skinner and R. Epstein report their work on "symbolic communication," "self-awareness," and "insight" with pigeons, challenging the validity of such concepts. Skinner and Epstein put their research firmly in the historical work on animal learning.

B. F. Skinner and Behavior Change. Research Press, 45 minutes, 16 mm (also video), color. S. Bijou, J. Cantela, C. B. Ferster, J. Fletcher, F. Keller, G. Patterson and R. Stuart join B. F. Skinner to discuss issues generated by behavioral psychology. On-site intervention programs are shown.

Learning. CRM/McGraw-Hill, 30 minutes, color. Classic experiments in species-specific behaviors and modern conjugate reinforcement techniques are demonstrated.

Observational Learning. Harper & Row Media, 23 minutes, color. Robert Liebert narrates a review of observational learning which includes the work of Albert Bandura and Richard Walters, a demonstration of vicarious emotional conditioning, and concept formation by film modeling. Children's imitation of television receives special treatment.

Business, Behaviorism, and the Bottom Line. CRM/McGraw-Hill, 22 minutes, color. B. F. Skinner defines behaviorism, conditioning, reinforcement and shaping and gives an interpretation of an applied program in an industrial setting.

Audio Cassettes

Toney Buzan. Learning and Memory. Psychology Today Cassettes, Jeffrey Norton Pub., Inc. Buzan gives specific instructions on how to improve both learning and memory by tapping into the brain's unused capacities.

Martin, E. P. Seligman. Learned Helplessness. Psychology Today Cassettes, Jeffrey Norton Pub. Inc. Seligman's research on helplessness in animals provides a new view of the problem of human depression.

Lee R. Steiner. Learning: The Basis of Human Existence. Jeffrey Norton Pub., Inc., 27 minutes. Discussion of our awareness of change through his learning experience, and his fear of changing due to the conformity taught by the educational systems.

Charles W. Simon. Sleep and Learning. Jeffrey Norton Pub., Inc., 17 minutes. Popular and scientific history of attempts to learn during sleep is reviewed. EEG illustrations for use on opaque projector accompany tape.

REFERENCES AND ANNOTATED SOURCES

Alloy, L. B., & Seligman, M. E. P. (1979). On the cognitive component of learned helplessness. In G. H. Bower (Ed.), *The psychology of learning and motivation* (vol. 13). New York: Academic Press.

Fancher, R. E. (1979). *Pioneers of psychology.* New York: W. W. Norton.

Gardner, R. M. (1980). *Exercises for general psychology.* Minneapolis, MN: Burgess Publishing Co.

Gustavson, C. R., & Garcia, J. (1974). Pulling a gag on the wily coyote. *Psychology Today*, Aug.

Miller, N. E. (1978). Biofeedback and visceral learning. In M. R. Rosenzweig & L. W. Porter (Eds.), *Annual review of psychology* (vol. 29) (pp. 373-404). Palo Alto, CA: Annual Review Inc.

Miller, N. E. (1969). Learning of visceral and glandular responses. *Science, 163,* 434-445.

Miller, N. E., & Sworkin, B. R. (1974). Visceral learning: Recent difficulties with curarized rats and significant problems for human research. In P. A. Obrist, A. H. Black, J. Brener, & L. V. Dicara (Eds.), *Cardiovascular psychophysiology.* Chicago: Aldine Publishing Co. The three references cited above will provide a solid overview of Miller's work on conditioning of autonomic responses.

Stern, R. M., & Ray, W. J. (1977). *Biofeedback: Potentials and limits.* Lincoln: University of Nebraska Press.

Tighe, T. J. (1982). *Modern learning theory: Foundations and fundamental issues.* New York: Oxford University Press. Includes many examples of shaping including a baby's first words, a child's first attempts to print letters, and the attempts of a person to remain upright while learning to skate.

Chapter 7

MEMORY

CHAPTER OVERVIEW

The experimental study of memory is one of the oldest continuous themes in psychology and generally dates to the work of Ebbinghaus in the late 19th century. Concepts developed by Ebbinghaus such as trials-to-criterion, relearning, and savings continue in use.

Contemporary psychologists distinguish three parts of the memory storage system --sensory, short-term, and long-term. Discussion of sensory storage focuses on iconic storage (vision) and echoic storage (audition) and covers phenomena such as serial position effects (privacy and recency). The authors next describe short-term storage, often referred to as working memory, and show how it is affected by rehearsal. In the section on long-term memory the authors define memory codes (linguistic, imaginal, motor) which assist storage of information.

Next the authors review two major theories of forgetting, interference and décay. Proactive and retroactive interference are defined and experimental procedures for demonstrating each are illustrated.

From forgetting, the authors move to a discussion of recoding of information. They explain Paivio's dual coding theory, Craik and Luckhart's levels of processing approach to memory, and in *Controversy*, the phenomenon of eidetic imagery or photographic memory.

The fact that memory often involves a recoding of information suggests that constructed memory may not always match initial information. The authors note that Bartlett was one of the first to point out the alterations in memory due to reconstruction. Central themes of stories were recalled rather accurately--Bartlett referred to these as schema--whereas other aspects of a story were not be remembered as well. In *Applying Psychology* the issue of reconstructive memory is examined in the context of eyewitness testimony in court cases.

The chapter then considers the factors influencing retrieval. The Von Restorff effect and "flashbulb memories" illustrate that distinctiveness often aides retrieval. Tulving refers to this phenomena as the *encoding specificity hypothesis.* In the *Focus on Research* section, the authors examine the effects of pharmacologic state on memory and retrieval (state dependent retrieval).

Retrieval from semantic memory is considered from the perspective of association networks. The authors describe phenomenon such as spreading activation, lexical decision tasks, and paradox of interference. The chapter closes with a discussion of mnemonic devices including the link method, the method of loci, and the peg method.

LEARNING OBJECTIVES

07-1. Distinguish the three stages of the memory process: acquisition, storage, and retrieval. Describe an appropriate metaphor for memory.

07-2. Describe the methods and materials Ebbinghaus used to study verbal learning. State the general conclusions that can be drawn from his relearning method and from his forgetting curves.

07-3. Distinguish the three memory storage systems: sensory stores, short-term store, long-term store. Contrast iconic and echoic storage. List and define three different types of codes used to store information in long-term memory.

07-4. Define decay theory and interference theory. Distinguish between retroactive and proactive interference.

07-5. Define recoding. Describe verbal and imaginal recoding processes.

07-6. Summarize the main ideas behind the levels-of-processing approach to memory. Briefly discuss the research which supports remembering as a constructive process.

07-7. Define encoding specificity and relate this concept to the relative effectiveness of different types of retrieval cues.

07-8. Describe research dealing with the memory of unusual events, such as the vonRestorff phenomenon and flashback memories.

07-9. Distinguish between episodic and semantic memory. Cite evidence which either does or does not support that distinction. Why may the distinction not be a valid one?

07-10. Briefly discuss the link method, the method of loci and the peg method as mnemonic devices. Specify the two critical ingredients of all successful methods of remembering.

ATTENTION GETTERS

Recall Memory
235-236

Ebbinghaus studied memory using experimental techniques. He found that he often seemed unable to recall material. But when he relearned the material it did not take as long. Have you noticed this effect in your own life? Under which situations are you likely to get the most "savings"?

Sensory Stores
237-240

It has been suggested that echoic storage should last longer than iconic storage? Why would you expect this to occur? What characteristics about iconic and echoic storage support this view?

Forgetting
243-245

Several theories have been advanced to explain why forgetting occurs. Describe what happens when forgetting occurs due to retroactive interference? What happens when proactive interference occurs? Do you think this interference is occuring because the information is no longer being stored or because of difficulties retrieving the information?

State Dependent Retrieval 258-259

Research on state dependent retrieval shows that a person will recall information better when s/he is in the same pharmacological state as s/he was in when the information was originally learned. What implications does this have for studying and test-taking? Which types of tests would you expect the state dependent effects to be greatest for? In which types of test would you expect fewer state dependent effects to occur?

LECTURE SUGGESTIONS AND CLASS DEMONSTRATIONS

Contemporary study of memory has been influenced greatly by information processing research, which itself is a direct outcome of computer technology. The "little black box" representation of mind has yielded to models that stress encoding, storage, retrieval, and decoding processes. Transparency 7-1 illustrates Atkinson and Shiffrin's model of memory storage and serves as an excellent starter for introducing the student to short-term memory, long-term memory, and control processes. Transparency 7-2 illustrates how events can interfere with memory retroactively and proactively and Transparency 7-3 shows how alterations in level of consciousness induced by drugs can affect memory (state-dependent retrieval). The following two demonstrations can be used to explain additional influences on memory; namely, chunking information into smaller units, and constructing memories from experience. The first demonstration involves the short-term store and the second the long-term store.

Short-Term Store 240-242

Now I said my ABCs... Wingfield (1979) states that the singing rhyme used by children to learn the alphabet "exploits every memory device possible" (p. 335). How does this rhyme bring the 26 letters of the alphabet into a span that can be retained in short-term store?

Wingfield explains that the letters are divided into three chunks:

abcdefg hijklmnop qrstuvwxyz

Each of these chunks has two elements:

(abcd)(efg) (hijk)(lmnop) (qrstuv)(wxyz)

Each of these element has two units, with a unit consisting of one to four letters:

"(ab-cd)(ef-g) (hi-jk)(lmno-p) (qrs-tuv)(w-xyz)

Students can discuss how the rhyme of the song organizes the material and how through chunking the number of items to be remembered is reduced (from: Norman, D. A. (1976). *Memory and attention: An introduction to human information processing* (2nd Ed.). New York: Wiley. (Cited by Wingfield, 1979, p. 335.)

The Long-Term Store 242-243

Remember when... The text explains how we construct memories from our experiences rather than coding information as exact copies of our experiences. This can be demonstrated by showing the class the stimulus figures shown below. The entire class receives pieces of paper with the same four stimulus figures but the verbal labels vary:

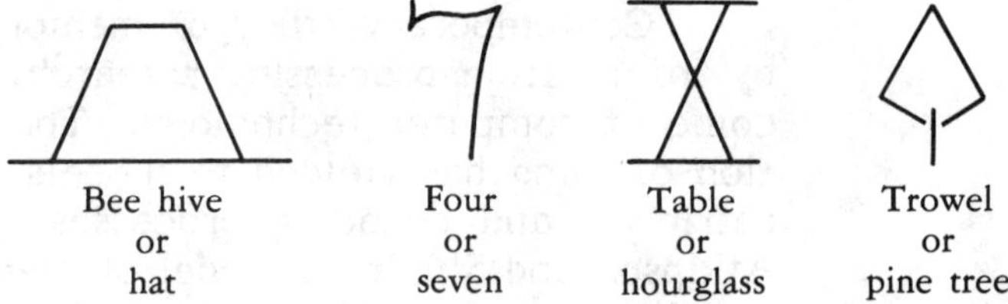

FIGURE 4

Students should study the figures and then write their name on the paper and turn it into the instructor. At the end of class each student should be asked to draw the four figures and turn them in. Students will find that the verbal labels distorted their reconstructions of the figures:

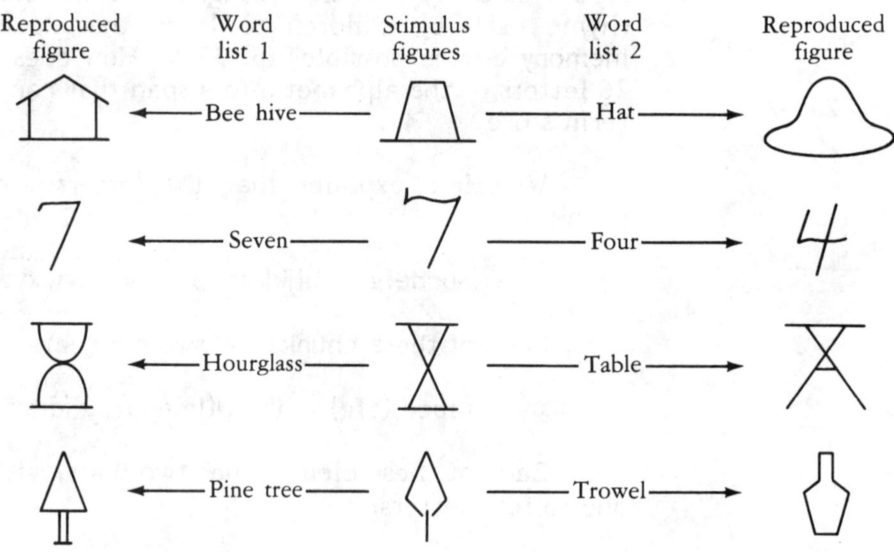

FIGURE 5

Figures 4 and 5: From L. Carmichael, H. P. Hogan, and A. A. Walter. (1932). An experimental study of the effect of language on the reproduction of visually perceived form. *Journal of Experimental Psychology, 15,* 80. (In the public domain.)

Tip of the tongue. The strategies involved in retrieval processes can be investigated by recording the words people produce when a target word is "right on the tip of the tongue." Wingfield (1979, page 287) suggests that a tip-of-the-tongue state can be produced by reading a person a definition for an uncommon object and then asking the person to name the object:

> "Give the name of this object:
>
> 'A navigational instrument used in measuring angular distances, especially the altitude of the sun, moon, and stars at sea.'"

The correct word is "sextant." However, many adults experienced the tip-of-the-tongue phenomenon when trying to name this object: "...normal adult subjects (in a 1966 study by R. W. Brown and D. McNeill) produced words of similar sound (secant, sextet, sexton) and of similar contextual association (astrolobe, compass, dividers, protracter). Further,...they fully realized in most cases that their answers were close to the target, but nevertheless incorrect" (Wingfield, 1979, p. 288). When doing this demonstration ask students not to blurt out the answer immediately. The class can divide into pairs with one member receiving the definition sheet and correct answer. This person can then record the other person's solutions until the target word is retrieved. Those pairs that do report a tip-of-the-tongue experience can share their results with the class.

Do you remember when Katie fell on the ice? The study of memory for discrete real-life events (episodic memory) receives little attention in memory research despite the fact that people engage in such recall efforts daily. The text defines Tulving's (1972) distinction between episodic and semantic memory and points out that many facts that we remember (semantic memory) become divorced from the time and/or place when the events occurred (episodic memory). Transparency 7-4 illustrates a theory of semantic memory which conceptualizes memory as consisting of a network of associations, the strength of which vary, in part, as a function of the individual's experience.

Just how well do we remember the times and events of our past? A detailed explanation of a clever, but time-consuming, study by Marigold Linton (1979) can serve as a good attention-getter for a lecture on retrieval processes while simultaneously orienting students to consider the recall of everyday events. Over a six-year period, Linton recorded on cards two or more events each day, concentrating on events unique to her daily activities such as where she dined and how well she enjoyed the meal. On the back of each card she recorded the date and a rating (1 to 5 scale) of the importance, affective quality, or novelty of the event. Over the six year period she accumulated 5,500 items. Monthly, she selected 150 cards at random and tested her memory for events ranging in time from the previous day to years in the past. After reading the description of the event, she recorded her estimate on when the event occurred, how long it took her to arrive at her estimate, and the reasons she used to date the item. She also re-rated the item using the same scales as before. She then entered the original information and the recalled information into a computer to determine the accuracy of her memory for events. Linton reports that by the end of a calendar year she forgot 1% of the events recorded for that year. Tests for memory of events two years in the past produced an additional 5.1% forgetting, and by the end of the study she had forgotten 31% of the events. Most of the events she remembered were unique, as for example, a traffic accident. In many instances she recalled the general nature of an event but forgot the details. In other words, episodic memory had shifted to semantic memory. Rate of memory loss was relatively even from year to year in contrast to the immediate memory loss Ebbinghaus reported in his classic studies using nonsense syllables.

Students could perform a mini-version of Linton's study by recording two events daily during the first week of class. Later in the term, they could follow Linton's procedure and attempt to recall the day that the event took place. Discussion in class could focus on episodic and semantic memory in relation to eyewitness testimony as highlighted in *Applying Psychology.* (See Linton, M. (1979). I remember it well. *Psychology Today*, 81-86.)

Mnemonic Devices 266-268

Memory aides. Students may be unaware that they have been relying on mnemonics to remember information. Just by asking them, "How many days are in this month?", the instructor can point this out. Many students will find themselves saying, "30 days hath September, April, June, and November..." Another example is to ask them how to spell "receive" or "sleigh". Once again they are likely to come up with a rhyme:

"i before e
except after c
or when sounded like a
as in neighbor or weigh."

AUDIOVISUAL AIDES

Films

Human Memory. Harcourt, Brace, Jovanovich, Inc., 28 minutes. Describes the basic phenomena of human memory and presents studies on aphasia, intermediate and long-term memory and mnemonic devices. STM and LTM experiments discussed by Gordon Bower.

Memory. CRM/McGraw-Hill, 30 minutes, color. This film opens with a description of sensory memory, STM and LTM. A variety of methods of catagorizing and referencing memories is illustrated. The goal is fast, efficient recall.

Information Processing. Psychology Today Films (CRM), 27 min., color. Information processing at a cocktail party. Some unusual guests demonstrate attention, language processing, short- and long-term memory, mnemonics, and problems solving.

Audio Cassettes

McGaugh, James L. Biological bases of memory storage processed: The state of the art. APA Tape 10-13, 1974. Selected aspects of research on neurobiological correlates of training and treatments that modulate memory storage processes is reviewed. To date, no coherent theory of how information is stored in the brain exists. More must be known about electrical and chemical stimulation of the brain on memory, as well as more about memory as an information processing system.

REFERENCES AND ANNOTATED SOURCES

Bransford, J. D. (1979). *Human cognition: Learning, understanding and remembering.* Belmont, CA: Wadsworth Publishing Co. Includes many attention-getting illustrations, all of which can easily be made into transparencies.

Brown, A. L. (1975). The development of memory: Knowing, knowing about knowing, and knowing how to know. In H. W. Reese (Ed.), *Advancements in child development and behavior,* (Vol. 10). New York: Academic Press. Refers to LTM as "memory as knowing." Also distinguishes "memory as knowing how to know," which changes developmentally, and "knowing about knowing," which refers to metacognition.

Hasher, L., & Zacks, R. T. (1979). Autonomatic and effortful processes in memory. *Journal of Experimental Psychology: General, 108,* 356-388. The effects of mood on memory are pointed out by linking depression to suppression of strategy use. Also useful for discussion of automatic and controlled processing.

Luria, A. R. (1968). *The mind of a mnemonist.* New York: Basic Books. This classic study provides many interesting examples for lecture.

Tulving, E. (1972). Episodic and semantic memory. In E. Tulving and W. Donaldson (Eds.), *Organization of memory.* New York: Academic Press.

Wickelgren, W. A. (1979). *Cognitive psychology.* Englewood Cliffs, NJ: Prentice-Hall. Contains a good overview of iconic, echoic, graphic, and phonetic STEM. Includes a detailed discussion of the four types of experiments used to demonstrate echoic memory and to measure its duration (Probe, Modality, Interference, Repetition).

Wingfield, A. (1979). *Human learning and memory: An introduction.* New York: Harper and Row.

Wood, G. (1983). *Cognitive psychology: A skills approach.* Monterey, CA: Brooks/Cole Publishing Co. Argues that use of mnemonics as pegs can be linked to an inability to use schemata for information processing. When schemata are unavailable, more mental effort is required to achieve satisfactory performance.

Chapter 8

DEVELOPMENT

CHAPTER OVERVIEW

Chapter 8 opens with a discussion of the defining features of developmental psychology and a brief historical overview. Five views of development are summarized including the developmental stages proposed by Piaget, Freud, and Erikson. The nature-nurture controversy is noted along with the more contemporary interactionist position. Following this general presentation of the theories, methods, history, and factors of development the authors shift to an age-period format. The section on prenatal development reviews the major events of each of the three periods of prenatal development--zygote, embryo, and fetus--focusing particularly on growth changes and potential complications to the fetus.

Infancy is the next topic. The newborn as helpless and dependent is contrasted with the ways in which the newborn is biologically prepared to make rapid adaptations to events in the environment. Piaget's period of sensorimotor intelligence is introduced with special attention to object permanance, the appearance of early vocalizations, and the organization of social behavior as it emerges from the attachment of caregiver and infant. In *Applying Psychology* the authors highlight research and theory related to the long-term effects of early experience noting especially research on infants reared in institutions.

The section on early childhood reviews Piaget's description of the preoperational child as well as research which suggests that he underestimated the cognitive abilities of the preschool-aged child. Socialization and the origins of self- and gender-identity are reviewed within the context of Erikson's theory and Baumrind's research on family rearing patterns and child behavior. *The Research Process* focuses on development of children's understanding of the intentions of others.

The next section, middle childhood, reviews Piaget's studies of classification and conservation in the elementary age child as well as studies that qualify his theory. In contrast to Piaget's structural approach to cognitive development, information processing approaches emphasize the importance of selective attention and memory strategies, metacognition, and the role of feedback in cognition. Acquisition of cognitive strategies and awareness and self-control of thinking, combine with the child's emergent system of logical operations to make the elementary years truly ones of discovery and adventure. Social development highlights the reciprocity of interaction and the development of moral reasoning as viewed from Kohlberg's six-stage revision of Piaget's theory of moral development.

The section on adolescence begins with the physical and physiological changes that occur during puberty and then examines physical and psychological concomitants of early and late maturing. Adolescent sexuality, identity formation, and consolidation of values provide a context within which the student can consider the conflicts of adolescence. A discussion of Piaget's formal operational thought and abstract reasoning closes the section.

The last section of the chapter opens with Levinson's stages of adulthood and Erikson's final stages of psychosocial development. The text summarizes problems young adults face then views midlife transitions in the context of aging, children separating from the family, changes in cognitive skills, and degrees to which personality is stable. *Controversy* highlights current debate concerning the stability of personality during adulthood. Finally, Kubler-Ross's stages in the resolution of death and dying are highlighted.

LEARNING OBJECTIVES

08-1. State the primary goal of the developmental psychologist. What sets developmental psychology apart from other subfields of psychology?

08-2. List and define six important views of psychological development.

08-3. Describe the process of prenatal development. Name and briefly discuss the three periods of prenatal growth. List three probable causes of complications during prenatal growth.

08-4. State the central feature of infant development. Explain the relationship between infant mental development and learning and memory.

08-5. Describe three characteristics of a child's behavior which indicate that an attachment has occurred. Relate the concept of attachment to separation anxiety and to stranger anxiety.

08-6. Define preoperational thinking. Give examples of perceptually based reasoning and nonlogical thinking. Define socialization. Name and describe the two fundamental processes which help children learn to behave according to social values.

08-7. Name and discuss three major skills included in cognitive development during middle childhood. Include in your discussion the two major accomplishments which accompany Piaget's concrete operations period, and two examples of cognitive strategies children develop during middle childhood.

08-8. Briefly describe the changes in social understanding and behavior which take place during middle childhood.

08-9. Discuss the biological, cultural, and psychological characteristics which help to define adolescence. Your discussion should focus on the physical changes during puberty, adolescent sexuality, and the acquisition of identity and values.

08-10. According to your text, what are the central concerns of young adults, the middle-aged, and the elderly?

ATTENTION GETTERS

Child Studies 278-279

Before 1750 the odds were 3 to 1 against a child's living to age five. Children in earlier historical periods were therefore more familiar with death as they saw siblings and peers die. How do you think today's children conceptualize death? How would the child's level of cognitive development affect their ideas about death? To stimulate class discussion on this issue, the instructor could assign the following article: Kastenbaum, R. The kingdom where nobody dies. In R. Fulton, E. Markisen, G., Owen, and J. L. Scheiber (Eds.). (1978). *Death and dying: Challenge and change.* Reading, MA: Addison-Wesley.

Piaget's Theory 287-311

What are the most important characteristics of the child's thinking at each of the four periods of cognitive development suggested by Piaget? Do you think that there should be a 5th period of thinking that would characterize the cognitive abilities of adults? What would be the important characteristics of the 5th period? How would it differ from formal operational thought?

Research Methods 277-315

A psychologist is interested in determining whether children who stand, crawl, and walk early also reach puberty early. What type of research method should be used to investigate this question: longitudinal or cross-sectional? What are the advantages and disadvantages of longitudinal and cross-sectional designs? What type of questions would be investigated using the cross-sectional method?

Overcoming Disadvantage 291

A social service agency discovers a 4-month-old infant that has had his physical needs met but has been deprived of interactions with people. What behaviors would you expect this child to show? What kind of care would you suggest to reverse these effects, if, in fact, they are reversible?

LECTURE SUGGESTIONS AND CLASS DEMONSTRATIONS

Psychological Studies of Children 278-281

Different approaches to development. Students often have difficulty understanding the different viewpoints found in developmental psychology. Therefore a demonstration that clarifies these views can be quite helpful. The instructor could place the information contained in Table 1 on an overhead projector by using a Xerox process to make a transparency. Once each of the views has been explained, the instructor can give an example of how each view leads to a different interpretation of a specific behavior or activity. In discussing the example, the instructor could first "become" a behaviorist then a cognitive-constructivist, and so on, successively advocating each view. If the instructor is familiar with these views, the class can be asked to give an example of a behavior and then can collectively generate various interpretations. Finally, at universities with large graduate programs, graduate students could be recruited to role play each of

TABLE 1

Basic Components of Four Views of Development

	Behavioristic-Learning	Cognitive-Constructivist	Psychoanalytic	Comparative-Evolutionary
Goals of Theory	explain and control behavior	explain the nature and origins of knowledge	explain personality and treat psycho-pathology	explain adaptive behavior
Primary Units of Data	stimuli, responses, reinforcements	behavioral schemes	free associations, self-reports	fixed action patterns, releasers
What Develops?	stimulus-response associations	schemes, schemas, structures	ego, superego redistribution of instinctual energies, defense mechanisms, fixations	adaptive behavior
Developmental Processes	learning	accommodation, assimilation, equilibration, organization	channeling of instinctual energies	genetic programing, environmental releasers
Determinants of Greatest Interest	environmental contingencies	maturation, experience, social transmission, equilibration	instinctual impulses, innate ego potentialities, id-reality conflicts	natural selection

Adapted by permission of Macmillan Publishing Company from *Research in Developmental Psychology: Concepts, Strategies, Methods* by Thomas M. Achenbach.

the views. Careful preplanning could make this debate a lively supplement to the lecture.

Piaget and Concrete Operations 298-300

Concrete operational thought. Dramatic changes occur during the preschool years. Children begin to talk, sing, count, memorize, expand their social environment, express independence, and encounter the institutions of society. These changes during the transitional period from preschool to the elementary years collectively are called the 5-to-7 shift. The school-age child no longer faces the cognitive limitations of preschool years. Perhaps the most dramatic of the cognitive achievements is that of conservation of the properties of things. Certainly this topic has been the most extensively studied of any aspect of Piaget's theory of cognitive development. If there are ten buttons in a row, and they are rearranged into a circle, there are still ten buttons. Adults certainly know this as do adolescents and older school-age children. But the young school-age child does not seem to understand that properties of objects stay the same (they are conserved) even when transformations change their appearance. The changes that occur during Piaget's period of concrete operational thought are almost always of interest to students (see Ginsburg & Opper, 1979).

Transparencies 8-1 and 8-2 will help students to follow a lecture on Piaget's theory by providing a visual cue to the periods of cognitive development (8-1) and to the tasks used to investigate conservation (8-2), the hallmark of concrete operational thought. Transparency 8-3 shows the pendulum problem, which has been used to study changes in logical thinking that take place as the child moves from concrete operations to formal observations.

Products of Socialization 296-297

Dare to discipline. Students generally respond well to lectures reviewing studies of observational learning and modeling. This topic provides good background for subsequent discussions of aggression as well as certain theories of child abuse. Moreover, it provides a context for discussing parental disciplinary techniques. A review of Baumrind's (1978) research on authoritative, authoritarian, and permissive parental rearing styles is one way to bring the topics of discipline, aggression, and observational learning together in the broad context of socialization of the child.

Dollinger and Brown (1979) devised a simulation of parent-child interaction to illustrate types of discipline and to integrate the student's knowledge of children with research and theory. Moreover, the simulation provides an example of factorial design. Context: Christmas shopping in a department store. Child demands purchase of an expensive toy. Students are arranged in triads with one student each acting as parent, child, and observer. Players are given written instructions describing their role and suggestions for how to play. "Parents" are given suggestions for disciplinary techniques and are instructed to see what works. One-half of the parents are told that they were embarrassed by the child, had a long shopping list, and wanted to avoid a scene. "Children" are given suggestions for persuasion. One half of the children are told to back down when parent gets angry. The other half are told that their sense of being loved is tied to parental purchase of the toy. Observers are to keep notes and to look for four types of discipline: reason-oriented, power-assertion, guilt-inducing, and evasion (ignoring). Role playing begins with a child request for the toy and a parent refusal. Then for 5 to 10 minutes the players are on their own. At the end, the parent and child answer questions and are briefly interviewed by the observer about their feelings. The observers then report to the class on the interactions observed and types of discipline used. Thus students are able to compare two types of discipline and two types of child reaction. For further information see S. J. Dollinger and D. F. Brown. (1979). Simulated parent-child interaction in an undergraduate child psychology course. *Teaching of Psychology, 6*, 180-181.

Home leaving. The changes that occur during adolescence go far beyond those associated with sexual development. The adolescent also is attempting to establish his or her identity; to arrive at some answer to the question "Who am I?" When identity diffusion results, it often shows up in antisocial or psychopathological behavior. Indeed, the rise in adolescent suicide is alarming inasmuch as it now is the third leading cause of death among teenagers. Depression during adolescence often is associated with home leaving and becoming independent. What does it mean to leave home and yet be economically dependent on parents for educational support? Erikson argued that college delayed resolution of identity formation. As a prelude to lecturing on Erikson's theory, or after providing an overview, have the class discuss the general issue of identity versus diffusion in the context of college living and home leaving. Even in today's highly mobile society, this may be the first time that some students have "left home" for any length of time. For those who have returned between semester breaks, have they noticed any changes in their parents' orientation to them? If graduate assistants are to lead these discussions, the activity should be carefully planned and some attention given to group process.

Mid-Life Transitions 313-315

Myths of aging. Paul Panek (1982) uses a quiz developed by McKenzie to test student knowledge about aging. This short test (Table 2) contains ten true-false items constructed according to ten "myths" about older adults. The questions could be written on an overhead projector and students' asked to vote on each question in succession. These questions and results could be an excellent way to open a lecture about aging, or could be used in a general lecture on life-span development. The correct answer to all of the questions is "false." For further information see: Panek, P. E. (1982). Do beginning psychology of aging students believe in 10 common myths of aging? *Teaching of Psychology, 9*, 104-105.

TABLE 2

Quiz Questions to Test Student Knowledge about Aging

1. As older adults grow older, they become more alike. T F
2. If people live long enough, they will become senile. T F
3. Old age is generally a time of serenity. T F
4. Older people tend to show little interest in sex. T F
5. Older adults tend to be inflexible. T F
6. Most older people lack creativity and are unproductive. T F
7. Older people have great difficulty in learning new skills. T F
8. When people grow old, they generally become "cranky." T F
9. Most older people are lonely and isolated. T F
10. As people become older, they are likely to become more religious. T F

(From Panek, P. E. (1982). Do beginning psychology of aging students believe in 10 common myths of aging? *Teaching of Psychology, 9.* Copyright 1982 by the American Psychological Association. Reprinted by permision of the author.)

AUDIOVISUAL AIDES

Films

Development. CRM/McGraw-Hill, 33 minutes, color. Research methods used to study human development are demonstrated. Psychologists working in different areas of study within this field explain their research. Among those featured are Jerome Kagan who discusses infants' perceptual responses and Sylvia Bell who conducts an experiment using Mary Ainsworth's "Strange Situation" procedure. The film provides a good introduction to research in the field of developmental psychology.

When Life Begins. CRM/McGraw-Hill, 14 minutes, color. This film follows the development of the fetus through the three periods of growth discussed in the text: zygote, embryo, and fetus. Live motion picture photography is used to show the various stages of development from fertilization of the ovum to birth. The film ends with a scene of a natural childbirth. After showing the film the instructor may direct the students' attention to the text explaining prenatal development in more detail.

Childhood: The Enchanted Years. Films Incorporated, 52 minutes, color. This film gives an overview of the early years of childhood. It provides a bridge between early lectures on infancy and lectures on childhood. Animated sequences illustrate the egocentrism of the child and the tendency to develop misconceptions. A wide variety of topics is covered including: temperamental differences among children, motor development, peer interaction among toddlers, early concepts of morality, competency.

The Eight Stages of Human Life: Part III: Early Childhood. Human Relations Media. This is the third of a four-part program designed to describe the human life cycle. It deals specifically with children from 2 to 6. Several topics discussed in the chapter are included here. Piaget's preoperational stage of development is discussed. There also is information on the development of gender identity and sex-typed behavior.

Personality: Adolescence. CRM/McGraw-Hill, 21 minutes, color. Short vignettes are used to illustrate the problems and challenges that teenagers face. Adolescent sexuality, the development of self-esteem, conflicts with authority, and the desire for independence are issues that are discussed.

The Eight Stages of Human Life: Adolescence to Old Age. Human Relations Media, color. This four-part program is designed to explore issues in the last four stages of human life: adolescence, young adulthood, the mature adult, and old age. The discussion of young adulthood includes a description of Erikson's theory. Major responsibilities of this stage include marriage, parenthood, and work. The film on the Mature Adult provides information on the mid-life transitions encountered by men and women. Among the topics included are: the empty nest syndrome, the tendency toward career and lifestyle changes, menopause, the mid-life re-evaluation.

Audio Cassettes

Eleanor E. Maccoby. Sex differentiation during early childhood development. APA Tape 11-17, 1975. The text poses the question "What determines gender identity?" This lecture discusses the effects of biological factors such as hormonal levels on sex-differentiated behavior. The interactions between biological factors and socialization patterns are stressed.

John Money. Differentiation of Gender Identity. APA Tape 10-15, 1974. This tape also considers the factors that influence sexual identity. Case studies are presented regarding endocrine malfunction and errors in prenatal sexual development.

John J. Conger. Current issues in adolescence development. APA Tape 11-12, 1975. Several myths about adolescent development are discussed. The following are among the topics covered: Adolescence as a development stage, the extent to which adolescence is a period of turmoil, identity development, social institutions that affect adolescent development.

Filmstrips

Attitude Toward Children. 5 filmstrips, 5 audioscript booklets and discussion guide. Sound available on record or cassette. Parents' Magazine Films, Inc. These filmstrips present an historical look at American attitudes about the basic notions of children and what is best for them. It includes discussion of the child as inherently sinful, as tabula rasa, and as inherently good. The argument is made that clerics and philosophers have been replaced by child care specialists as authorities on childrearing.

Understanding Human Reproduction. Sound is available on cassette or record. A discussion guide also is available. Guidance Associates. This filmstrip explains reproduction, intercourse, conception, and development of the embryo and fetus. It also shows labor and birth.

The Child's Point of View. Sound available on records and cassettes. Parents' Magazine Films, Inc. This filmstrip illustrates the nonlogical thinking discussed in the text. David Elkind explains how fantasies are real to a young child and how all things are assumed to be purposeful.

The Black Child, The Puerto Rican Child, The Chicano Child, The Indian Child. Parents' Magazine Films. Audio script booklets and discussion guides are included. Sound records available. These filmstrips present information about the needs of minority children.

Other Instructional Aides

Human Reproduction. A discussion guide is available. Guidance Associates. This slide package contains 80 full color slides depicting structures and functions of the male and female reproductive systems.

Child Development: The Early Years. 3/4" V-Matic Video Cassette, B/W. Harper & Row Media. This videotape demonstrates developmental changes from 4 weeks of age to 6 years. The development of communication skills, mastery of the physical environment, and attachment to the mother are among the topics covered.

Child Development: The Middle Years. 3/4" V-matic, B/W. Harper & Row Media. Clinical interviews with children from 6 to 11 reveal some of the issues of middle childhood including peer relationships, the need for achievement, and conscience formation.

Child Development: The Adolescent Girl. Child Development: The Adolescent Boy. 3/4" V-Matic Cassettes. B/W. Harper & Row Media. The first videotape shows interviews of 5 girls aged 14 to 20. They discuss emerging sexual feelings, conflicts with mother, relationships with boys, and feelings upon leaving the parental home. The second videotape presents interviews with 3 teenage boys (13-17). They discuss feelings about work, sex, girls, and life goals.

REFERENCES AND ANNOTATED SOURCES

Baumrind, D. (1978). Parental disciplinary patterns and social competence in children. *Youth and Society*, *9*, 239-276. Contains a description of each of three patterns of rearing: authoritative, authoritarian, and permissive.

Ginsburg, H., & Opper, S. (1979). *Piaget's theory of intellectual development.* Englewood Cliffs, NJ: Prentice-Hall. Provides examples of Piagetian cognitive tasks that are easily adapted to lectures on cognitive development.

Kubler-Ross, E. (1969). *On death and dying.* New York: Macmillan Publishing Co.

McKinney, J. P., Fitzgerald, H. E., & Strommen, E. A. (1982). *Developmental Psychology: The adolescent and young adult.* Homewood, IL: The Dorsey Press. An overview of adolescence including chapters on physical development; sexuality; cognitive, social, and emotional development; family relations; peers; values; and adjustment problems.

Osofsky, J. D. (Ed.) (1979). *Handbook of infant development.* New York: John Wiley & Sons. Includes chapters on physical development, socio-emotional development, perception, learning, and intellectual functioning in infancy.

Sherrod, K., Vietze, P., & Friedman, S. (1978). *Infancy.* Monterey, CA: Brooks/Cole. Contains brief overview of prenatal development at a level that is suitable for introductory psychology. Among the topics covered are conception, implantation, physical growth and development of the embryo and fetus.

Shneidman, E. S. (1977). The college student and death. In H. Feifel (Ed.), *New meanings of death.* New York: McGraw-Hill. An interesting chapter written from a perspective counter to Kubler-Ross's sequential stage approach.

Tanner, J. M. (1970). Physical growth. In P. H. Mussen (Ed.), *Carmichael's Manual of Child Psychology.* New York: John Wiley & Sons. Shows how adolescents of the same chronological age may have amazing differences in the degree of physical development around puberty.

Chapter 9

LANGUAGE AND THOUGHT

CHAPTER OVERVIEW

The chapter begins by explaining the functions of language (in social exchanges, learning, and memory) and its structure (phonemes, morphemes, phonological rules, grammatical rules, syntax, and semantics). The authors then review the study of language comprehension pointing out the difference between linguistic performance and linguistic competence. Cited evidence suggests that people remember the deep structure of a sentence but quickly forget the surface structure, that meaningful context aids language comprehension, and that comprehension is a constructive process influenced by a person's expectations, knowledge, and personal interests.

The chapter then shifts to a consideration of human language acquisition beginning with prelinguistic forms of communication: gestures, crying, and facial expression. Following are characteristics of babbling, first words, and the semantic and syntactic rules followed by young children. Evidence is cited suggesting that even preschoolers often adjust their speech to the listener. The authors discuss different explanations for language acquisition and conclude that innate dispositions, cognitive development, and social interactions are all necessary ingredients. *The Research Process* reviews studies showing that children may be unaware of how to ask questions in order to listen more effectively.

Next, the authors consider whether nonhuman animals can be taught to use language. They point out that early difficulties in teaching language to chimpanzees (such as Gua and Viki) may have been due to the use of verbal language which is not well suited to the chimp's anatomy. In *Controversy*, the authors note that initial enthusiasm over recent efforts to teach nonverbal languages to chimpanzees has subsided.

Whorf's hypothesis of linguistic determinism is explained next. The authors note that most people do not accept it; instead, language *reflects* thought rather than *determines* thought. Cross-cultural research suggests that people who speak different languages nonetheless seem to perceive the world in similar ways.

The final section of the chapter explores the relationship between thinking and problem solving. Three steps in problem solving are stated: formulating the problem, generating solutions, and deciding which alternative is best. Obstacles that can occur in this process, such as functional fixedness and mental sets, are discussed.

LEARNING OBJECTIVES

09-1. Describe three functions of language. Provide an example of each function.

09-2. Discuss the structural rules of language as they apply to sounds, words, and sentences.

09-3. Describe the difference between linguistic performance and linguistic competence.

09-4. Three general propositions have been derived from research on language comprehension. State what these are and provide an example of each one.

09-5. Give examples of the biological changes, social interactions, and cognitive advances during infancy which contribute to language acquisition. How do infants communicate their needs before they are able to speak?

09-6. Describe the syntactic and semantic relationships which characterize early speech. Discuss the rules children acquire for increasing sentence complexity. Describe the progression from egocentric speech to socialized speech.

09-7. What are the current views regarding the role of imitation and reinforcement in language development?

09-8. Describe how chimpanzees have been taught symbolic language.

09-9. What is meant by the concept of linguistic determinism? Discuss the evidence which contradicts the Whorfian hypothesis of linguistic determinism for perception and thought.

09-10. Distinguish the three steps in problem-solving: formulating the problem, generating possible solutions, and making decisions. For each step, give an example of an obstacle which might be encountered.

ATTENTION GETTERS

Comprehension 325-330

What evidence can you cite to support the view that language is a *constructive* process?

Language Acquisition 330-338

The text describes the course of linguistic development. Given the fact that this course occurs universally many psychologists have argued that language development must be genetically regulated. Other psychologists emphasize the role of learning. Where do you stand in this debate? How can you support your position?

Animal Communication 338-341

After reading the animal language studies in the text do you feel that the languages learned by the chimpanzees are qualitatively similar to human language? Support your view with evidence cited in the text.

Thinking and Problem Solving 345-350

Functional fixedness occurs when you fail to recognize alternative uses for an object. What situations have you been in when you failed to recognize a possible solution to the problem you were attempting to solve?

LECTURE SUGGESTIONS AND CLASS DEMONSTRATIONS

Language often is viewed as the essential characteristic that separates Homo Sapiens from all other animal species. Indeed, there is little that humans do that is not tied to language. Language plays an obvious role in communication, and it also influences memory, social discourse, and thinking. Transparency 9-1 shows stimuli used in an experiment designed to study recall memory. The relationship between language and cognition can be demonstrated by the project described below.

Comprehending and Using Language 324-328

Linguistic and cognitive development. Gardner (1980) describes an exercise useful for lectures on language development. List a series of sentences that a student can ask a 2-year-old and a 4-year-old to repeat.

1. The ball is blue.
2. Cows can eat hay.
3. The pretty girl is wearing a red dress.
4. Tomorrow will be a very cold day.
5. The jolly fat man walked fast.
6. The boy who we met yesterday talked loud.
7. Where is the ball?
8. Mommy is too tall.
9. The little boy is in the car. (Gardner, 1980)

Write down each child's response exactly as it is stated. Then the instructor can pose a variety of discussion questions--Gardner suggests the following:

1. What aspects of the adult sentences are retained best by each child?
2. What kinds of words or ideas are omitted from the sentences when repeated by the child?
3. What can you infer about the development of language ability in children from a study of these responses? (Gardner, 1980)

Of course, other questions are possible. Ask students to compare differences among different children's responses and to predict (and justify) which children are advanced in language development and which may be showing language delay. Or, show Transparency 9-2 and ask students to select the longest child sentence from their data set and diagram it. Then ask them to identify its surface structure and its deep structure. In addition, show them Transparency 9-3 and have them identify grammatical misconstructions that you would expect to find in a 2- or 4-year-old. Note that to do this part of the demonstration it is important that students record child utterances exactly as they are made.

Applying Psychology 362

Verbal humor. The authors explain how humor is often derived from violations of our expectations. Chukovsky (1963) points out the attraction that nonsense rhymes hold for a young child. He notes that nonsense rhymes would probably not exist in so many cultures if they did not contribute to the child's psychological development and suggests that the child is actually verifying his/her knowledge of the world by violating the relationship that he knows is true. For a class demonstration each student should bring in an example of a nonsense rhyme or an example of verbal humor. The student should be able to explain what level of humor is illustrated in the example (e.g., phonological ambiguity, lexical ambiguity, syntactic ambiguity, semantic ambiguity), what age groups would find this type of humor most appealing and why. Students can be encouraged to find examples from within their own families, and from jokes and books that appealed to them as children (such as Mother Goose). Chukovsky's description of his interaction with his 2-year-old daughter can be read as an example of the type of humor that appeals to a very young child:

> ...one day in the twenty-third month of her existence, my daughter came to me, looking mischievous and embarrassed at the same time--as if she were up to some intrigue. I had never before seen such a complex expression on her little face.
>
> She cried to me even when she was still at some distance from where I sat:
>
> "Daddy, 'oggie--meow!"--that is, she reported to me the sensational and, to her, obviously incorrect news that a doggie, instead of barking, meows. And she burst out into somewhat encouraging, somewhat artificial laughter, inviting me, too, to laugh at this invention.
>
> But I was inclined to realism.
>
> "No," said I, "the doggie bow-wows."
>
> "'oggie--meow!" she repeated, laughing, and at the same time watched my facial expression which, she hoped, would show her how she should regard this erratic innovation which seemed to scare her a little.
>
> I decided to join in her game and said:
>
> "And the rooster meows!"
>
> Thus I sanctioned her intellectual effrontery. Never did even the most ingenious epigram of Piron evoke such appreciative laughter in knowledgeable adults as did this modest joke of mine, based on the interchange of two elementary notions. This was the first joke that my daughter became aware of--in the twenty-third month of her life. She realized that not only was it not dangerous to topsy-turvy the world according to one's whim, but, on the contrary, it was even amusing to do so, provided that together with a false conception about reality there remained the correct one. It was as if she perceived in an instant the basic element in comedy, resulting from giving simultaneously to a series of objects an opposite series of manifestations. Realizing the mechanics of her joke, she wished to enjoy it again and again,

thinking up more and more odd combinations of animals and animal sounds.

...To participate in this game, I immediately composed for her a whole series of similar topsy-turvies:

The piglet meowed--Meow! Meow!
The kittens oinked--Oink! Oink!
The ducklings clucked--Cluck! Cluck! Cluck!
The chickens quacked--Quack! Quack! Quack!
The sparrow came skipping and like a cow mooed--Moo-oo-oo!
The bear came running and started to roar--Kukareku!

(From Kornei Chukovsky, *From Two to Five*, Revised ed., translated and edited by Miriam Morton. This translation copyright 1963 by Miriam Morton. Reprinted by permission of The University of California Press.)

After collecting examples of children's humor, the class can share them and discuss how humor relates to the person's level of cognitive development.

Remembering the Meaning 326-328

Language comprehension: Remembering the meaning. Lachman, Lachman and Butterfield (1979) describe the study done by Sachs in 1967, which makes an interesting demonstration of Chomsky's theory of transformational grammar. (Be sure to perform the demonstration before the students read Chapter 9.) The instructor should read the following story to the class:

> There is an interesting story about the telescope. In Holland a man named Lippershey was an eyeglass maker. One day his children were playing with some lenses. They discovered that things seemed very close if two lenses were held about a foot apart. Lippershey began experimenting and his spyglass attracted much attention. *He sent a letter about it to Galileo, the great Italian scientist.* Galileo at once realized the importance of the discovery and set about to build an instrument of his own. He used an old organ pipe with one lens curved out and the other in. On the first clear night he pointed the glass toward the sky. He was amazed to find the empty dark spaces filled with bright gleaming stars. Night after night Galileo climbed to a high tower, sweeping the sky with his telescope. One night he saw Jupiter, and to his great surprise discovered near it three bright stars, two to the east and one to the west. On the next night, however, all were to the west. A few nights later there were four little stars. (From Sachs, J. S. (1967). Recognition memory for syntactic and semantic aspects of connected discourse. *Perception and Psychophysics, 2*, 438-439).

The italicized sentence should not be emphasized in this reading--this is the test sentence that will be transformed in the demonstration. After the reading the instructor should pass out sheets of paper with the heading, "Is this the same sentence that was in the story I just read to you?" followed by one of the following four sentences:

1. He sent a letter about it to Galileo, the great Italian scientist.
2. Galileo, the great Italian scientist, sent him a letter about it.
3. A letter about it was sent to Galileo, the great Italian scientist.
4. He sent Galileo, the great Italian scientist, a letter about it.

The responses should then be collected and tabulated as indicated in Figure 6 below:

Sentence 1 Identical	Sentence 2 Semantic Change	Sentence 3 Syntactic Change	Sentence 4 Formal Change
Is it the same? Yes No	Is it the same? Yes No	Is it the same? Yes No	Is it the same? Yes No

FIGURE 6

Students should report similar answers when given questions 1, 3, and 4 because the deep structure of these sentences remains consistent with the sentence in the story itself. Students receiving sentence 2 as a test sentence should report that it was not in the story since it involves a semantic change which affects the deep structure. This demonstration illustrates how several sentences may have the same deep structure meaning (see page 328 of text). It also illustrates that people remember the meaning rather than the particular surface structure form when information is presented.

Animal Communication 338-342

Talking to the animals. If the instructor knows sign language he or she can teach the students a few signs as an attention getter. Or, if the instructor does not know signing, perhaps someone can be invited to class to put on the demonstration and explain the difference between finger spelling and signing.

When the Gardners published the results of their attempts to teach a gestural communication system to the chimpanzee Washoe, they sparked intense interest and nearly wild enthusiasm among language researchers, primatologists, and the public as well (Gardner & Gardner, 1969). Nearly every publication designed to communicate science to the lay public carried articles about Washoe and her gestures. Criticisms were sure to follow. Terrace's (1979) attempts to teach Nim the same gestural communication system with less impressive results. Recently, Fouts, Hirsch and Fouts (1982) criticize Terrace's approach. Specifically, they charge that Terrace's efforts to provide tight experimental control of the teaching environment failed to take into account the social behavior of chimpanzees. On the other hand, Fouts et al.'s claim that Washoe "taught" an infant chimpanzee to sign is sure to provoke controversy.

The Premacks' did not try to teach a chimpanzee to gesture. Rather they taught Sarah to attach meaning to individual plastic chips which varied in size, shape, and color. Transparency 9-4 shows two sets of chips and the meaning of each. Training procedures were based on operant conditioning. The Premacks argue that "Sarah" learned to "speak" rather complex sentences by placing chips in sequence.

Thinking and Problem Solving 345-350

Problem solving: Insight. A lecture on problem-solving provides an excellent opportunity to contrast the Gestalt and associationist approaches in psychology. Prepare a few overhead transparencies of jumbled letters and ask students to rearrange the letters to make an English word (e.g., THORMAGLI; algorithm). Most students will have had prior experience with anagrams. After someone arrives at the correct answer, review two approaches to this task: algorithms and heuristics (Newell & Simon, 1972). Survey the class and see if any students used heuristics (short-cut strategies) to arrive at the solution. Discussion of functional fixedness is a natural next topic to consider.

Reviewing the stages of problem solving can serve as an lead-in to a discussion of insight. Problem solving involves: problem identification, hypothesis generation, hypothesis testing, incubation, and illumination or insight. Transparency 9-5 shows the now classic Luchins Water Jar Problem, which in effect is six problems, each requiring the solver to pour water from each of three jars in order to obtain a specified amount. In addition, Sternberg and Davidson (1982) cite a variety of insight problems that can easily be integrated into lecture. For example, ask the students the following question: "How can one plant a total of 10 trees in 5 rows of 4 trees each?" (The answer is to arrange them along the line segments of a star.) Give the students about 5 minutes to try to solve the problem. If none has the correct answer at the end of the time period, draw a single diagonal line on the overhead and see if this hint sparks an "aha" experience. Sternberg and Davidson found a relatively high positive correlation between the ability to solve insight problems and scores on tests of mental ability. They argue that an important aspect of insight problem solving is the ability to distinguish necessary information from unnecessary information. They review evidence suggesting that selective coding, selective combination, and selective comparison are key cognitive processes involved in insight-learning performance. Sternberg (1979) discusses the steps involved in solving analogy problems: encoding, inferring, mapping, applying, justifying.

AUDIOVISUAL AIDES

Films

Silent Speech. Films Incorporated, 50 minutes, color. French biologist Hubert Montaguer studies nonverbal comunication in young children. Leadership and maturity derive from the child's success in using silent signals and that success in turn correlates with the mother's behavior.

Language Development. CRM/McGraw-Hill, Inc., 20 minutes, color. This film notes that children worldwide progress through the same sequence of language stages at about the same rate. Premack's studies with chimpanzees are highlighted.

Development of the Child: Language. Harper and Row Media, 24 minutes, color. Viewing the remarkable, orderly, and exciting process of language development of the first four years, this film begins with a child's initial utterances and examines the development of phonemes, syntax, and semantics.

Discovering Language: How Words Get New Meanings. Coronet, 11 min., color. Shows how we take old words and change their meanings to fit new needs.

Piaget's Developmental Theory: Classification. Davidson Films:Sterling Educational Films, 17 min., color. Piaget's theory of cognitive development with emphasis on tasks that highlight different mental operations.

Piaget's Developmental Theory: Conservation. Davidson Films, 30 min., color. Children in individual interviews given tasks involving conservation of quantity, length, area, and volume. Includes discussion from a physicist and an educator.

Audio Cassettes

Ervin-Tripp, Susan M. Language development. APA Tape 11/14, 1975.

Kagan, J. Cognitive development. APA Tape 11/16, 1975.

Desmond Morris. The Language of Gestures and Communication. Psychology Today Cassettes, Jeffrey Norton Pub., Inc. Morris discusses the meanings of nonverbal messages and culturally determined gestures and body movements.

Ernst Beier and James Gill. Non-Verbal Communication. Psychology Today Cassettes, Jeffrey Norton Pub., Inc. Body language, gestures, facial expressions, and other kinds of non-verbal "speech" form a rich language that we all use.

Film Strips

Thinking Skills: Introduction to Critical Thinking. Human Relations Media, 4 part, 35 mm filmstrips and audio cassette, 13-15 minutes, includes Resource Guide.

REFERENCES AND ANNOTATED SOURCES

Bowerman, M. F. (1978). Semantic and syntactic development. In R. L. Schiefelbusch (Ed.), *Bases of language intervention.* Baltimore: University Park Press. Attempts to strike a compromise between Clark's perceptual feature hypotheses and Nelson's shared function hypothesis of the acquisition of word meaning.

Braine, M. D. S. (1976). Children's first word combinations. *Monographs of the Society for Research in Child Development, 41,* Serial No. 164. Research on early word combinations suggests the hypothesis that children arrive at syntactic knowledge of language by attempting to communicate meaning.

Chukovsky, K. (1963). *From two to five.* (Miriam Morton, Ed. and Trans.) Berkeley: University of California Press.

Fouts, R. S., Hirsch, A. D., & Fouts, D. H. (1982). Cultural transmission of a human language in a chimpanzee mother-infant relationship. In H. E. Fitzgerald, J. A. Mullins, & P. Gage (Eds.), *Child Nurturance 3: Studies of development in nonhuman primates.* New York: Plenum Press.

Gardner, R. A., & Gardner, B. T. (1969). Teaching sign language to a chimpanzee. *Science, 165,* 664-672.

Lachman, R., Lachman, J. L., & Butterfield, E. C. (1979). *Cognitive psychology and information processing.* Hillsdale, NJ: Lawrence Erlbaum Associates.

Newell, A., & Simon, H. A. (1972). *Human problem solving.* Englewood Cliffs, NJ: Prentice-Hall.

Savage-Rumbaugh, S. (1982). A pragmatic approach to chimpanzee language studies. In H. E. Fitzgerald, J. A. Mullins, & P. Gage (Eds.), *Child Nurturance 3: Studies of development in nonhuman primates.* New York: Plenum Press. Questions whether chimpanzees know what they are saying, assuming that they can in fact learn a gestural communication system. She reports research indicating chimpanzees intentional, rule-based use of symbols.

Sternberg, R. J., & Davidson, J. E. (1982). The mind of the puzzler. *Psychology Today,* June.

Sternberg, R. J. (1979). Stalking the IQ quark. *Psychology Today,* September.

Terrace, H. S. (1979). *Nim.* New York: Alfred A. Knopf.

Chapter 10

INTELLIGENCE AND MENTAL ABILITIES

CHAPTER OVERVIEW

The chapter begins with a brief description of Galton's definition of intelligence (sensitivity to physical stimuli) and his methods of measurement. From Galton, the text follows the development of intelligence tests by Binet and Simon and defines Stern's formula for computing an intelligence quotient. The deviation IQ is explained in the context of modern intelligence testing. The authors discuss such characteristics of psychometric tests as standardization sampling, stratified random sampling, and the assumption of normal distribution as well as several types of validity (construct, concurrent, predictive). The authors raise the question, "Is intelligence a stable characteristic?" and follow with a discussion of developmental changes from infancy to old age.

The next section on uses and abuses of intelligence tests emphasizes that tests are not absolute measures of one's capacity to learn. *Applying Psychology* focuses on early abuses of IQ tests, including immigration quotas. Next begins a debate over the relationship between heredity, environment, and IQ scores which analyses research from twin studies and adoption studies. Racial differences in IQ provide a background for an explanation of heritability. The section concludes with a confluence model of intelligence relating family size to IQ scores.

Controversy: IQ Tests on Trial reports two court cases in which black children sued in court charging that they were placed in special education programs for the retarded on the basis of IQ scores.

The authors discuss mental retardation, its classification, and its possible causes such as PKU, Down's Syndrome, anoxia, and environmental factors. *The Research Process* details a study by Brown and Barclay which shows that teaching cognitive strategies to older retarded children can improve their learning methods. The authors then point out that less attention is focused on the other end of the intelligence scale--the intellectually gifted. Terman's classic study refutes the myth that bright children are socially maladjusted and narrowly specialized.

The last section deals with varying ways of conceptualizing intelligence, comparing Spearman's factor analytic method identifying a general (g) factor, Thurstone's seven primary abilities, and Guilford's 120 factor-structure of intellect model. Next the author's present three theories of intelligence involving levels of cognitive process: (1) Cattell's division of intelligence into fluid and crystallized intelligence, (2) Jensen's theory involving associative and conceptual abilities; and (3) Campione and Brown's description of an architectual system and an executive system. Sternberg's distinction between components in problem solving (the steps used to solve the problem) and metacomponents in problem solving (how to solve the problem) leads to a different view of intelligence than that proposed by psychometricians. And finally, the authors describe how Piagetian notions have been combined with information processing concepts to form a framework for investigating intelligent behavior.

LECTURE OBJECTIVES

010-1. Describe briefly the development of modern IQ tests. Name some of the most popular current tests. Describe how these tests are used by psychologists.

010-2. Define standardization, reliability, and validity and specify how these test characteristics affect the interpretation of IQ scores.

010-3. Be able to discuss the factors which determine stability of IQ scores over the life span.

010-4. Give examples of the misuses of IQ tests and explain why misuses occur.

010-5. Be familiar with arguments on both sides of the nature-nurture debate concerning intelligence, including the evidence drawn from twin studies and adoption studies.

010-6. Understand the term *heritability* and how it relates to the debate over causes for racial differences in IQ scores.

010-7. Identify the possible effects of birth order on IQ scores and describe the confluence model of intelligence.

010-8. Distinguish between four types of mental retardation. Give examples of hereditary and environmental causes of retardation. Describe some common treatments.

010-9. Be familiar with Terman's study of gifted children. Be able to discuss the educational opportunities for the gifted.

010-10. Describe briefly Spearman's and Thurstone's models of intelligence. Be familiar with current models and how they divide cognitive skills.

ATTENTION GETTERS

Intelligence Testing 354-359

What were intelligence tests designed to measure? Do the tests measure a person's absolute mental abilities or do they measure the person's relative performance compared to others? Why would it be important for a standardization sample to represent the population that may take the test?

IQ Stability 359-361

Why do you think that intelligence test scores obtained from infants and toddlers do not correlate well with scores obtained in later childhood and adolescence? When would you expect to see more stability in test scores?

IQ and Heredity 363-370

What methods have been used to determine whether heredity or environment plays a greater role in the development of intelligence? What problems have arisen in interpreting data based on these methods? What conclusions did you reach after reading the studies cited in the text?

Creativity and Intelligence 377

Is creativity different from intelligence? If so, how can it be defined? Would it be possible to measure creativity without also measuring intelligence?

LECTURE SUGGESTIONS AND CLASS DEMONSTRATIONS

An interesting way to introduce this topic is to read excepts from Terman' s (1917) account of Francis Galton's childhood. Galton knew both English and Latin alphabets by 18 months of age, could read both languages by 4 years, and designed a flying machine powered by a steam engine by 13 years. A discussion of Galton's intellectual abilities can lead to a brief historical survey of the intelligence testing movement (see Nunnally, 1978, pp 502-508). Galton's definition of intelligence (sensory keenness) can be assessed in terms of its validity (Chapter 1) and contrasted with Piaget's theory of intelligence (Chapter 8). With this material as background students should be prepared to understand the distinctions Cattell and Horn make between fluid and crystallized intelligence.

The Rapid Decline of Intelligence! The text describes the intelligence quotient formula as suggested by Wilhelm Stern:

$$IQ = \frac{MA}{CA} \times 100$$

Modern Intelligence Tests 354-356

It also reports that the method for calculating an IQ has changed so that a deviation IQ is now used. The instructor can demonstrate why this method proves more useful in the calculation of IQ scores.

After the age of 15 or 16 a person's absolute performance on some IQ test items does not increase (e.g., digit span remains at 7 digits from 15 years to 50 years). This means that mental age remains constant while chronological age increases. Transparency 10-1 shows performance items similar to those included in the Wechsler Adult Intelligence Scale. Ask students to predict which items best correspond to what Cattell and Horn refer to as fluid and crystallized intelligence. Which does digit span reflect? Transparency 10-2 illustrates the distribution of intelligence, showing a distribution that is slightly skewed to the right. This suggests that most people score fairly close to the population mean, but that slightly more people are above the mean than are below the mean. Most IQ tests standardize the distribution so the mean is 100 and the standard deviation is 15 or 16, depending on the test. Finally, Transparency 10-3 shows the difference between high and low test-retest reliability. In order to be credible, a test must have high test-retest reliability, although several factors influence reliability independent of the test, such as the amount of time that intervenes between testing. The closer together in time, the higher the test-retest reliability.

Using the intelligence quotient formula stated above a person's IQ might show the following changes:

Age 15 $\quad IQ = \frac{15\,(MA)}{15\,(CA)} \times 100 = 100$

Age 30 $\quad IQ = \frac{15\,(MA)}{30\,(CA)} \times 100 = 50$

Age 60 $\quad IQ = \frac{15\,(MA)}{60\,(CA)} \times 100 = 25$

Using this method a person would become much less intelligent over time! The deviation IQ bases a score on a person's performance when compared to others of the same age; thus, a person is not penalized for growing older! (Example adapted from: Holmes, D. L., & Morrison, F. J. (1979). *The child: An introduction to developmental psychology.* Monterey, CA: Brooks /Cole.)

Cultural Bias in IQ Tests: The Chitling Test. The authors report that many immigrants to the United States were labeled "feebleminded" because of their poor performance on intelligence tests. Often the reason was due to language differences--English speaking individuals scored higher than non-English speaking immigrants. The following examples show that subtle biases still exist. Sattler (1974) illustrates this point in both the Stanford-Binet and the WISC-R. In the Stanford-Binet children are asked, "What's the thing for you to do if another boy hits you without meaning to do it?" To respond correctly children should say that they would walk away. Children who respond that they would hit back do not receive any points. Sattler suggests that in some neighborhoods to walk away would be fatal and that hitting back has survival value.

Uses and Abuses 361-363

Adrian Dove, a black sociologist, constructed a test to point out how culture affects a child's score on IQ tests. In this "Chitlings" test, the items are constructed using the language of inner city blacks rather than of the white middle class. For example, the child must be able to recognize that the word "gray" does not belong in the same category as the words "splib," "blood," "spook," and "black." As part of a class demonstration give this test to your class (it can be found in the July 15, 1968 edition of *Newsweek.*) This experience will stimulate discussion of the problems of cultural bias. Ask the class to try to devise some items that would be culture fair. Point out the need for items that do not require constant revisions. For example, one of the questions in the "Chitling" test requires that the child estimate the wages earned by a person picking cotton for the entire day. In 1968 the correct answer was $5.00, but by 1983 this answer would be incorrect.

Racial Differences 367-369

Transparency 10-4 shows several items used in a "culture-free" test of fluid intelligence. Culture-free tests purport to measure aspects of intelligence that show little cultural variation, the assumption being that these aspects of intelligence are characteristic of the species and are relatively uninfluenced by education or other cultural influences.

Intellectually Gifted Children 376-379

Gifted revisited. Lewis Terman began his now famous longitudinal study of gifted children in 1921. All of the children enrolled in the study scored above 135 on the Stanford-Binet IQ test, putting them in the top 1 percent of the population. In 1921, as today, popular stereotypes of gifted children ascribed personal and social difficulties to them far in excess of what one would expect for children in general. Today, Robert and Pauline Sears (Goleman, 1980) are continuing the study of individuals in Terman's original sample with some surprising results. For example, although many individuals in Terman's study had quite successful careers, few achieved distinction in the creative arts. Men and women differed in a variety of ways related to life satisfaction. In other words, many findings fail to support common stereotypes about gifted individuals. The following activity serves as an attention getter for consideration of giftedness but also brings in the topic of stereotyping. Prepare a handout which contains two sets of identical questions, one set for males and one for females. The students' task is to respond to each item as they think subjects in Sears' study responded. Use the following format:

TABLE 3

Life Satisfactions Ratings

How do you think males (females) responded?

	Not Important				Extremely Important
Occupation	1	2	3	4	5
Family Life	1	2	3	4	5
Friendship	1	2	3	4	5
Richness of Cultural Life	1	2	3	4	5
Service to Society	1	2	3	4	5
Overall Joy in Living	1	2	3	4	5

(Repeat the items, but now have students rate how they perceive female responses.)

(Composed from textual material in Goleman, D. (1980). 1,528 little geniuses and how they grew. *Psychology Today*, Feb.)

> Rate each of the following categories in answer to the question: How important was this for obtaining the satisfactions you had hoped for in life? (Remember that the subjects in the Sears' study are in their 60's.) You are to rate the categories as if you were one of the individuals who was in Terman's original study of giftedness; that is, you are now 65 years old.

The Sears study found three major differences between men and women: Work is more satisfying for men than for women; friendships and cultural activities are more satisfying for women than for men. Men and working women are more similar than are men and women in general.

Collect the anonymous questionnaires, summarize the results and compare the class responses with those reported by the Sears. Ask the students to explain any discrepancies in their responses with the responses of individuals from Terman's original sample?

Creativity and Intelligence 377

Measuring creativity. The text discusses problems distinguishing creativity from intelligence. Transparency 10-5 illustrates items used to assess creativity in children. How do these items differ from those in a culture-free test of fluid intelligence? Or, do they? The following example highlights this issue (see Barron, F. (1969). *Creative person and creative process.* New York: Holt, Rinehart and Winston). The formation of anagrams is used to study creativity. Write the work "generation" on the board or overhead projector. Instruct the students to form as many anagrams as possible from this word. Point out that anagrams will be judged for originality and correctness (they must be in the dictionary). Allow 5 minutes to complete the task. Then record all of their responses on the board. As each response is given, ask for a show of hands to indicate how many people thought of that word. The class can discuss what should constitute an original response (in the study cited by Barron, the criterion was one instance in 100). Unusual possibilities include: onager (a wild ass), argentine (silver), or ergot (a fungal disease of cereal grasses). Students can determine their creativity score as follows:

1 point: a word generated by 1 person per every 100 people.

0 points: common words generated by more than 1 person per every 100 people (examples: nation, rate, gene).

0 points: "made up" words that are not found in the dictionary (examples: tanion, etar, nege).

The instructor should bring a dictionary to class to settle disputes over the legitimacy of a word.

After generating these scores the class can discuss whether this was a good way to measure creativity. The distinction between convergent and divergent thinking can be mentioned at this point. In what ways does the formation of anagrams involve convergent thinking?

AUDIOVISUAL AIDES

Films

Intelligence: A Complex Concept. CRM/McGraw-Hill, Inc., 28 minutes, color. What is intelligence? When the average layperson was asked this question, answers revealed considerable confusion between intelligence as tested and intelligence as it is viewed in everyday life. The film explores definitions of Jean Piaget and J. P. Guilford among others.

Three Cognitive Skills: Middle Childhood. CRM/McGraw-Hill, Inc., 21 minutes, color. Reading memory and creativity provide the foundation of the child's ability to assimilate into society and the world as a whole. The film shows that a variety of factors, including individual intelligence and school and home environment can affect the development of all three skills.

A Cross-Cultural Approach to Cognition. Harper & Row Media, 22 minutes, color. Japan, Guatemala, and Kenya and sequences of milestones in psychological development. Task-oriented experiments are demonstrated. Play, cognition, perception, and memory development, reflectivity, and concrete operational thinking are illustrated.

Cognitive Development. CRM/McGraw-Hill, 20 min., color. Piaget's theory set to animation! Interviews with Siegfried Engelmann contrast Piaget's approach with that of behaviorism.

Thursday's Children. KETC TV Channel 9, 34 min., B & W. Film for parents and professional designed to stimulate early recognition of learning disabilities.

Audiocassettes

David Campbell. Psychological Testing. Psychology Today Cassettes, Jeffrey Norton Pub., Inc. Campbell discusses what can be tested, test differences between men and women, cultural preferences of women, characteristics of business executives, and testing in industry.

Gertrude H. Hildreth. Understanding the Gifted. Psychology Today Cassettes, Jeffrey Norton Pub., Inc., 24 minutes. Identification and education of the gifted is of interest in relation to promoting full development of human resources and leadership.

J. McV. Hunt. The Stimulation of Early Cognitive Learning. Jeffrey Norton Pub., Inc., 45 minutes. The epigenesis of intrinsic motivation and cognitive learning.

Bernard Rimland. Idiots Savants: The Gifted Retarded. Psychology Today Cassettes, Jeffrey Norton Pub., Inc. A few severely retarded individuals perform feats beyond abilities of non-retarded persons. Rimland describes their abilities.

REFERENCES AND ANNOTATED SOURCES

Dove, A. (1968). Taking the Chitling test. *Newsweek*, July 15.

Goleman, D. (1980). 1,528 little geniuses and how they grew. *Psychology Today*, Feb.

Hallahan, D. P., & Kauffman, J. M. (1982). *Exceptional children: Introduction to special education*, (2nd ed.). Englewood Cliffs, N.J.: Prentice-Hall, Inc. Discussion of mental retardation at a level appropriate for an introductory class. Among the topics covered are: definitions and classifications of mental retardation, causes of retardation, methods of measurement, and educational considerations.

Plomin, R., DeFries, J. C., & McClearn, G. E. (1980). *Behavioral genetics: A primer.* San Francisco: W. H. Freeman, Co. Contains a clear and detailed explanation of heritability and links this concept to path analysis and multivariate techniques.

Sattler, J. M. (1982). *Assessment of children's intelligence and special abilities.* Boston, MA: Allyn and Bacon, Inc. Reviews the historical development of the IQ test, including a discussion of the deviation method for calculating IQ. Many examples of modern assessment standards are in ample appendices.

Suran, B. G., & Rizzo, J. V. (1979). *Special children: An integrative approach.* Glenview, IL: Scott, Foresman & Co. Discusses prevention and ethical issues in mental retardation and points out that it is easier to understand the special needs of retarded children than those of gifted children. They report the characteristics of gifted children and educational interventions designed to meet their special needs.

Terman, L. M. (1917). The intelligence quotient of Francis Galton in childhood. *American Journal of Psychology, 28*, 204-215.

Chapter 11

MOTIVATION

CHAPTER OVERVIEW

The chapter begins with a description of three biologically based motives: hunger, thirst, and sex. The concept of homeostasis introduces the topic of food intake. Included in this section are discussions of glucostatic, lipostatic, aminostatic theories; the importance of the liver, and the role of the brain. The text then considers explanations for human obesity showing the many factors involved in weight regulation. *Applying Psychology* reports the increase in the incidence of anorexia nervosa and offers possible explanations for this disorder. Though not causally connected, drinking often occurs in the same context as eating. The text describes volumetric and osometric thirst as well as adipsia, which is caused by lesion of the lateral hypothalamic region of the brain.

The authors point out several differences between sexual motivation and other biological motives (such as hunger and thirst): sex is not necessary for a person's survival, sex reduces energy rather than restoring it, deprivation has little effect on sexual activity. Human sexual behavior shows rather broad cultural differences in preferred circumstances, positions, and erotic aspects of the body. The text then examines organizational and activational characteristics of androgens and estrogens, the continuing debate between biological and social learning theories of gender identity, and the development of homosexual behavior. *Controversy* examines sex differences in response to erotic stimulation.

After considering biologically based motives the text shifts to a discussion of learned motives, highlighting McClelland's work on achievement motivation and Atkinson's theory which emphasizes conflict between hope for success and fear of failure. Maslow's theory suggests that motives may be organized hierarchically with biologically based motives demanding satisfaction before learned motives can achieve full expression. *The Research Process* reviews research contrasting the relative importance of intrinsic and extrinsic motivation.

The final topic in the chapter addresses theories of motivation, beginning with drive theory. Problems with the drive reduction analysis of behavior leads to a discussion of incentive theory and arousal theory as alternative explanations. The text contrasts incentive--a "pull" theory--with drive--a "push" theory--highlighting expectancy and value as key aspects of incentive motivation. Arousal theory emphasizes multiple determinants of general organismic activation that influence performance, particularly as predicted by the inverted U-shaped curve. The text concludes with a review of opponent-process theory.

LEARNING OBJECTIVES

011-1. Define motivation and homeostasis. Give examples of how these two concepts are related.

011-2. Be familiar with three theories of food regulation: glucostatic, lipostatic, and aminostatic. Summarize the experimental evidence showing the importance of the liver and hypothalamus in food regulation.

011-3. Identify the following factors in obesity: responsiveness to external cues, set point, stress, endorphins, metabolism, social situations, and learning. Describe the condition known as anorexia nervosa.

011-4. Distinguish volumetric and osmometric thirst. Summarize the role of the hypothalamus and septum in water regulation.

011-5. Be familiar with the major surveys and cross-cultural comparisons concerning sexual behavior.

011-6. Identify the major sex hormones and distinguish between their organizational and activational effects on humans and animals. Give examples of situational and external factors in sexual motivation.

011-7. Be able to discuss evidence of the effects of upbringing on gender identity. Distinguish between types of homosexuality.

011-8. Define need for achievement and be familiar with research procedures used to measure this motive.

011-9. Understand Maslow's hierarchy of needs and the concept of reciprocal inhibition. Distinguish extrinsic and intrinsic rewards.

011-10. Outline the main features of drive theory, incentive theory, opponent-process theory, and arousal theory. Be able to distinguish the theories from one another.

ATTENTION GETTERS

Regulation of Water Intake 400-401

What is the difference between volumetric thirst and osmometric thirst? Why would they be expected to generally occur together? What role does ADH (antidiuretic hormone) released by the pituitary play in the regulation of water in the body?

Human Sexuality 401-406

Many studies of human sexual behavior have relied on questionnaires and interviews to obtain data. What problems may occur in this type of data collection? What do cross-cultural studies reveal about human sexual behavior?

Gender Identity 406-409

What impact does the social context have on gender identity? What evidence supports your view? Is there evidence that is contrary to your view?

Reciprocal Inhibition of Motives 414-415

What is meant by the term "reciprocal inhibition." Give an example of how one motive may dominant other motives. Could a motive that is low in a hierarchy of motives ever dominate over higher motives? What practical implications does this have in terms of motivating people?

LECTURE SUGGESTIONS AND CLASS DEMONSTRATIONS

Regulation of Food Intake 392-398

Lose 10 pounds in less than one week! Considering the effort and money spent by business to promote slimness and the fact that much of this effort is aimed at the older teen and young adult, it usually is a topic that college students find interesting. Beck's (1978) set point theory for the regulation of body weight can serve as a starting point, after first exposing the students to a variety of advertisements about weight control. Making transparancies of the advertisements and choosing blatent examples of "false" claims can be a good attention getter. According to Beck's theory, the number of fat cells that an individual has is determined in infancy. If one has more fat cells, he or she will have a higher set point than an individual who has fewer fat cells. Nisbett's (1972) explanation for obesity is based on the set point theory of fat cells. Nisbett claims that, "Simply put, this view suggests that some individuals have no choice but to be fat....They are biologically programmed to be fat" (1972, p. 433). As students react to Beck's theory, opportunities will arise to weave sociobiological, behavioral, and psychoanalytic views of weight control into the discussion. In addition, the instructor can show Transparency 11-1 which summarizes research suggesting that the liver plays a key role in regulating food intake, perhaps a more important role than the brain.

The instructor can ask how many students have been on a diet in the past year. The students who raise their hands can then consider their motivations for dieting in terms of the questions suggested by the authors.

(1) Why did they initiate this behavior; that is, why did they begin a diet?
(2) What determined the direction that their behavior took; that is, why did they adopt a particular diet?
(3) How vigorous is the behavior; that is, how hard did they try to lose weight? Did they reach the goals that they had set?

Share the answers to these questions with the class to demonstrate basic issues in motivation. Then ask the students to design a weight-loss plan based on the principles explained in chapter 11. This can be done as a class or in small groups.

Transparency 11-2 illustrates items from an eating restraint scale. Individuals who score high on the scale are dieters, those who score low are not. As indicated in the text, priming restrained eaters prior to an ice cream tasting caused them to eat more ice cream than restrained eaters who were not primed (by a milkshake).

Applying Psychology 399

At the other end of the weight scale, anorexia nervosa is a problem involving the same age group to which advertisers aim weight loss programs and gimmicks. Moreover, media interest in anorexia has brought the problem to the attention of the public so most students will probably be somewhat familiar with the topic. Anorexia should particularly be of interest to female students since it usually occurs in adolescence and affects women more than it does men. Bemis (1978) describes the criteria used to diagnose anorexia: it begins before age 25 and involves a weight loss of at least 25 percent below original weight; it involves a distorted attitude toward eating that overrides hunger; the weight loss cannot be explained by any obvious physical or psychiatric illness; and it involves at least two of the following: amenorrhea (abnormal cessation of the menses), lanugo (fine, soft hair on forehead, ears), bradycardia (slowness of heartbeat), overactivity, bulimia (morbidly increased appetite), and vomiting. Bemis also reviews research on premorbid characteristics of anorexic patients, precipitating factors, and family environments. At this point it might be interesting to introduce Maslow's notion that there is a hierarchy of needs with physiological needs posed as most fundamental. Transparency 11-4 shows Maslow's hierarchy. Ask students to contrast Maslow's needs hierarchy with the phenomena of anorexia, which could be interpreted as engaging in self-destructive behavior. With good preparation, this topic is almost a sure winner for maintaining student interest.

Sexual Motivation 401-409

Sexual misinformation. Human sexual behavior, broadly defined, also is a hot topic and a sure bet for student interest. Collins (1980) offers an interesting perspective to the topic of socialization and sex role differentiation. She argues that organized religion is a source of social learning that is resistent to change and discusses Judaic, Catholic, and Protestant views of human sexuality and gender role. As an attention getter, present the results of the survey on sexual misinformation, for regardless of the factors that shape our views of human sexuality, it is clear that many young adults continue to be misinformed about much of human sexual behavior. Students can fill out the survey on sexual information (see Table 4) several class meetings prior to the lecture to give the instructor ample time to score and summarize the results.

Need for Achievement 410-412

Women and achievement: Is there a fear of success? One of the limitations of the Atkinson-McClelland model of achievement motivation is the fact that it describes male behavior more accurately than female behavior. Matina Horner suggests that women have a stronger fear of success than do men. To demonstrate this to the class, hand out papers giving the sentences used in her study (Horner, 1969): "After first term finals, Anne (John) finds herself (himself) at the top of her (his) medical school class." Ask the students to complete the story. Compare the results of the class to her finding that two-thirds of the women in her study avoided success. Class discussion can focus on whether any

TABLE 4

Sexual Information Survey

Purpose: This survey is designed to help you locate areas in which you may have misinformation about human sexuality. It is also intended to serve as a starting point for class discussion. It will *not* ask you to reveal your values, morals, or practices. Your participation is requested, but it is not required. If, for any reason, you do not wish to complete this survey, just leave it blank. In any case, *do not put your name on this sheet.*

Instructions: Mark each item true (T) or false (F).

1. (F) The incidence of sex crimes such as rape and child molestation is correlated with the availability of pornographic material.
2. (T) Masturbation occurs more frequently among highly educated males than it does among males with very little formal education.
3. (T) Most married couples have violated the law in their private sexual practices.
4. (T) Impotence in men and frigidity in women are usually learned responses (rather than responses with a biological cause).
5. (F) Most studies find that homosexuals are usually people who have had unsatisfactory sexual experiences in childhood or in the early teenage years.
6. (F) Excessive masturbation can cause serious physical and emotional consequences.
7. (F) The hymen is a very tough membrane that is intact in the virgin female.
8. (F) Prostitutes are the most common source of V.D.
9. (T) Some form of incest taboo is found in all societies.
10. (T) Sexual arousal can occur without stimulation of the erogenous zones.
11. (F) The major function of the small tooth-like projections (vagina dentata) just inside the vaginal opening is probably to increase friction and to give increased pleasure to the male during intercourse.
12. (F) After a vasectomy sexual desire may diminish slightly because the male hormones are no longer generated by the testes.
13. (T) A hysterectomy produces no loss in sexual drive or ability to respond to sexual stimulation.
14. (T) The sole function of the clitoris is apparently sexual: it is a main focus of sexual arousal in women.
15. (T) Nearly all men have experienced several hundred orgasms by the time they get married.
16. (T) In the space of a few minutes a woman may have a series of orgasms, while a man is only capable of having one orgasm in that short time period.
17. (T) Women--as well as men--have dreams that produce orgasm.
18. (T) To become pregnant, the best time for sexual intercourse is during the middle of the menstrual cycle.

(Adapted from: Johnson, R. L. 1980. *Instructor's manual to accompany Understanding Human Behavior* (p. 95), (3rd Ed.). (New York: Holt, Rinehart and Winston). Copyright 1980 Holt, Rinehart and Winston. Reprinted with permission.)

differences found may be due to changing roles of men and women in our society. (For further information see: Horner, M. S. (1971). Femininity and successful achievement: A basic inconsistency. In M. H. Garskof (Ed.), *Roles women play: Readings toward women's liberation.* Belmont, CA: Brooks/Cole Publishing Co.)

AUDIOVISUAL AIDES

Films

The Psychology of Eating. Harcourt, Brace, Jovanovich, Inc., 29 minutes, color. Elliot S. Valenstein poses questions with respect to food-seeking. Valenstein introduces the work of Lewis Lipsitt (infant taste preferences), John Garcia (taste aversions), Terry Powley (regulation of food consumption), Judith Rodin (insulin reactions) and Albert Stunkard (obesity). A key point made is the relation between psychology and physiology and clinical practice with respect to eating behavior.

A New Look at Motivation. CRM/McGraw-Hill, Inc., 32 minutes, color. This film contrasts affiliation, power, and achievement motives. Individuals with these types of personality are shown to have motivation levels that are very clearly linked to social and environmental factors in the workplace.

Pain: Where Does It Hurt Most? Films, Inc., 51 min., color. Research at three institutions covers psychological, behavioral, and physiological ways to control or alleviate pain.

Psychling. CRM/McGraw-Hill, 25 min., color. Explores reasons why individuals set seemingly impossible goals by focusing on an example involving an athlete who supposedly would never again be able to participate in sports.

Audio Cassettes

A Dialogue on Education and the Control of Human Behavior: Rogers vs. Skinner. Jeffrey Norton Pub., Inc. A 6-tape summary of a famous 2-day debate between these two noted psychologists. Each cassette has accompanying materials.

Film Strips

Why We Do What We Do: Human Motivation. 3 filmstrips, audiocassettes, instructor's guide. Human Relation Media. A 3-part filmstrip program that introduces students to the basic concepts of the drives, needs and motivations that make each individual unique. One part each is devoted to physiological, psychological, and learned drives.

REFERENCES AND ANNOTATED SOURCES

Atkinson, J. W., & Raynor, J. O. (1974). *Motivation and achievement.* Washington, D.C.: V. H. Winston and Sons. Provides a detailed overview of the research and theory underlying present conceptualizations of achievement motivation.

Beck, R. C. (1978). *Motivation: Theories and principles.* Englewood Cliffs, NJ: Prentice-Hall.

Bemis, K. M. (1978). Current approaches to the etiology and treatment of anorexia nervosa. *Psychological Bulletin, 85*, 593-617.

Collins, S. (1980). Religion and the sexual learning of children. In E. J. Roberts (Ed.), *Childhood sexual learning.* Cambridge, MA: Ballinger Publishing Co.

Luria, Z., & Mitchel, R. D. (1979). *Psychology of human sexuality.* New York: John Wiley & Sons. An extensive overview of the psychology of sexuality appropriate for an introductory lecture. Among the topics covered are cultural differences in sexual behavior, hormonal influences on sexual behavior, and variations in sexual behavior.

Maccoby, E. E., & Jacklin, C. N. (1974). *The psychology of sex differences.* Stanford, CA: Stanford University Press. An extensive review and analyses of research aimed at documenting evidence for (and against) the existence of sex differences.

Nisbett, R. E. (1972). Hunger, obesity and the ventromedial hypothalamus. *Psychological Review, 79*, 433-453. This article re-examines the manner in which the ventromedial hypothalamic syndrome and hunger have been viewed and suggests an alternative view. The behaviors of hungry organisms are compared to the behaviors of obese humans. The author notes the striking similarities in these behaviors.

Weiner, B. (1972). *Theories of motivation: From mechanism to cognition.* Chicago: Markham Publishing Co.

Weiner, B. (1980). *Human motivation.* New York: Holt, Rinehart & Winston. The two books by Weiner provide an extensive review of four theories of motivation: drive, field, achievement, and attribution. A review of current research in the field highlights the more recent volume.

Chapter 12

EMOTION AND STRESS

CHAPTER OVERVIEW

The authors begin by showing how important it is to understand emotion when explaining behavior. They note that there is a genetic basis to the physiological reactions and facial expressions of emotion, whereas descriptions of emotions and emotional behaviors are learned. Three types of evidence support genetic interpretations for the facial expression of emotion: cross-cultural interpretations of facial expressions, similarity between blind children's and normal children's facial expressions, and similarity between animal and human facial expressions. The authors briefly review basic concepts about the autonomic nervous system (these concepts are introduced in chapter 2). They then show how the sympathetic nervous system becomes active during strong emotion and consider the roles of the cerebral cortex and the hypothalamus in emotion. *Controversy* cites research suggesting that men show more emotional reactivity by physiological measures whereas women appear more emotional by facial expression and verbal report.

The authors then discuss several theories of emotion. They carefully define the James-Lange theory of emotion and then review Cannon's criticisms to this theory as well as more recent data including the work of Stanley Schachter. The next section focuses on frustration which the authors employ as an example of how a person learns to respond to an emotion.

The remainder of the chapter covers the topic of stress. The authors describe several common sources of stress: prolonged emotional reactions, changes in life that require adaptation, the minor hassles and annoyances of daily life, chronic exposure to environmental noises or occupational tensions, and unresolved conflicts (approach-approach, approach-avoidance, avoidance-avoidance). *Applying Psychology* discusses the link between divorce and physical or emotional disorders.

The discussion of the effects of stress begins with a description of the stress reaction and the three stages of the general adaptation syndrome (alarm reaction, resistance stage, stage of exhaustion). Outlining the relationship between stress and specific diseases such as high blood pressure, heart disease and ulcers, the authors describe Type A and Type B personalities.

Several factors affect the ability to cope with stress: being able to predict when a stressful event will occur, being in control of the stressful situation, and having a sympathetic confidant. Also, the amount of stress depends on the person's cognitive evaluation of the situation. *The Research Process*, dealing with control and stress, closes the chapter.

LEARNING OBJECTIVES

012-1. Define emotion and be able to list four ways in which psychologists measure emotion.

012-2. Be familiar with evidence showing that facial expression of emotion is innate.

012-3. Understand the role of the sympathetic and parasympathetic nervous system in emotional reactions.

012-4. Summarize the James-Lange theory of emotion and outline the four criticisms of the theory made by Cannon. How do contemporary psychologists view the relation between physiological arousal and emotional reaction?

012-5. Define frustration and be able to identify four responses to frustration which appear to be learned.

012-6. List and give examples of the most common sources of stress: life changes, minor annoyances, chronic discomfort, and conflict. Give examples of approach-approach, avoidance-avoidance, and approach-avoidance conflicts, and how they can be resolved.

012-7. Identify the three stages in the general adaptation syndrome to stress and describe the physiological changes in each stage.

012-8. Summarize current research into the relation between stress and disease.

012-9. Understand the effects of predictability, control, sympathetic support, and cognitive appraisal on stress. Review the experimental evidence showing the relation of control to stress.

ATTENTION GETTERS

Facial Expression 424-427

List three reasons why the expression of emotion through facial expressions seems to be innate. Are there particular emotional expressions that seem more likely to be inborn? Which facial expressions would be harder to substantiate as innate?

Physiological Reaction 427-429

What role does the autonomic nervous system play in the body's reaction to emotion? Is the sympathetic or parasympathetic nervous system dominant during times of emotional arousal? What brain structures are involved in emotion?

Sources of Stress 437-442

The Homes and Rahe Social Readjustment Rating Scale (Table 12.1) shows various life changes that may produce stress. Among the items on the list are marriage, marital reconciliation, outstanding personal achievement and vacation. Why would these types of changes which are generally considered to be positive changes also tend to lead to stress? What factors might determine whether or not these changes have a negative impact on the person?

Conflict 440-442

The authors point out that conflicts that have not yet been resolved are often a major source of stress to a person. What are three different types of conflict that may occur? Which would be the easiest to resolve? In what ways could these conflicts be resolved? Explain your answers through the use of examples.

LECTURE SUGGESTIONS AND CLASS DEMONSTRATIONS

Expression of Emotion 424-428

One way to open the lecture is to quote sentences or passages from Darwin's *Expression of the Emotions in Man and Animals* (1872). Darwin suggested that the baring of the fangs of a wolf can be related to the sneer of the human adult. He argued that emotional expressions have two major characteristics: survival value and communication value. Sylvan Tomkins' (1970) views about the development of emotions are clearly within the evolutionary framework. Tomkins suggests that there are eight innately patterned emotions which are expressed through facial expressions: interest, surprise, joy, disgust, rage, anguish, fear, and shame.

Facial Expression 424-427

Facial expression of emotion. Figure 12-1 of the text shows the high level of agreement found in naming particular emotions to match facial expressions. In a class demonstration, student volunteers can be asked to demonstrate various emotions (happiness, disgust, fear, anger, sadness, surprise, interest, anguish, contempt, shame). The class can decide which emotions are being portrayed. For which emotions is there a high level of agreement? Are certain emotions more difficult to distinguish than others? An alternative demonstration would be to show the class pictures of various emotions (such as those presented in Izard, 1977, Figures 4-5 to 4-13) and ask them to label the emotions shown.

Physiological Reactions 427-429

Lie detection: Measuring emotional reactions. The autonomic nervous system mediates emotional reactivity, with the sympathetic branch (SNS) most active during intense emotional experiences and the parasympathetic branch (PNS) active during low levels of arousal. Transparency 12-1 illustrates the organization of the autonomic system and shows examples of the functions of its components. In fact, the SNS activating--PNS inhibition dichotomy has so many exceptions that it is probably better to distinguish the two by the major neurotransmitters related to each: SNS--norepinephrine; PNS--acetylcholine. The autonomic nervous system is that which mediates behaviors polygraphers use in lie detection. After reviewing the material in Transparency 12-1, the following class activity will likely provoke active discussion about the "science" of lie detection.

The use of polygraphs to detect lying has generated much debate both among psychophysiologists and among lawyers. Recently, F. Lee Bailey's television show has brought lie detection to public attention. Assign students to watch the show one week in advance of a planned lecture on lie detection. Prior to presenting the lecture, show some polygrams of heartrate, GSR, and EMG. Perhaps a colleague can provide an example if one is not available personally. After showing what these physiological records look like, the instructor can ask for responses to the show. Point out that the Federal Government recently announced that individuals suspected of being security risks will have to undergo lie detector tests. Ask students to comment on this procedure. Businesses also use lie detection, especially those that employ many teenagers and young adults. Would students in the class submit to a lie detector test as part of the employment interview?

Effects of Stress 442-446

The General Adaptation Syndrome. Stress is a topic that has received a great deal of public attention during the past 10 years. A lecture based on Seyle's (1976) general adaptation syndrome is almost a must. After reviewing Seyle's three stages of stress reaction--alarm, resistance, exhaustion--one can have the class take a short-form version of the Social Readjustment Scale (Holmes & Holmes, 1970). This stress scale consists of a listing of life events which can be ranked in terms of perceived stress. For example, adults rank death of spouse, divorce, and marital separation highest in stress; whereas, vacation, Christmas and minor violations of the law are lowest in rank. Despite all sorts of controversy in this area, few would disagree that psychological stress now is recognized as a major contributor to physical as well as mental illnesses. Students can be asked to compare this example to the discussion of the General Adaptation Syndrome. Transparency 12-3 illustrates Seyle's three stages of the stress reaction and will serve as a helpful visual guide during lecture.

Students sometimes have difficulty understanding the fact that the General Adaptation Syndrome is a nonspecific reaction to all stressors that results in a specific syndrome. Selye's analogy illustrates this:

> "Suppose that all possible accesses to a bank building are connected with a police station by an elaborate burglar-alarm system. When a burglar enters the bank, no matter what his personal characteristics are--whether he is small or tall, lean or stout--and no matter which door or window he opens to enter, he will set off the same alarm. This primary change is therefore nonspecifically induced from anywhere by anyone. The pattern of the resulting secondary change, on the other hand, is highly specific. It is always in a certain police station that the burglar alarm will ring, and the policemen will rush to the bank along a specified route according to a predetermined plan to prevent robbery" (Selye, 1976, p. 58).

Stress situations interact with other variables, such as personality characteristics. Students nearly always find discussion of Type A and Type B personalities interesting. Goldband (1980) and Friedman & Rosenman (1974) link Type A personality to cardiovascular dysfunction. In fact, Type A personalities can be as much at risk for cardiovascular problems as are individuals who smoke, have high blood pressure, or high cholesterol levels. Type A personality refers to an individual who is competitive, achievement oriented, in a hurry, impatient and angry when confronted by perceived incompetence, and has difficulty relaxing.

Presenting material on Type A personality can be a good lead into a general discussion of biofeedback and relaxation training techniques.

Coping strategies for dealing with stress. Table 12-1 shows various life events that are stress producing for most individuals. Many students may assume that these events create stress and that the person experiencing these events must simply put up with it. It is important to point out that a person's reactions to an event influence whether it could be considered stressful. Shaffer (1982) illustrates this point:

> "It is late afternoon on the last Friday of the month. At the bank, the lines of customers waiting to deposit their paychecks or to withdraw money for the weekend have stretched practically to the front doors. At one window, a customer finishes and the next person, a merchant, steps up. He opens a cloth bag and produces a stack of checks, cash, and deposit slips almost two inches thick. The teller's eyes widen. This will be at least ten minutes' work, maybe fifteen. What about those other customers waiting in line? How will they react?
>
> Interestingly enough, the reactions of the customers waiting in line behind the merchant vary considerably. Gary Johnson, for instance, is furious. He grinds his cigarette under his heel and mutters about inconsiderate jerks who wait until the last minute to deposit their week's receipts. Gary shifts back and forth from foot to foot, the swaying of his body telegraphing his frustration. He probes his pockets to see whether any of his antacid mints are left. Finding none, he curses under his breath and lights another cigarette.
>
> Several places behind Gary, Mike Harlow is waiting in a different way. Mike has a dinner date at six, and he felt his anger rise when the merchant at the head of the line began his lengthy transaction. Unlike Gary, however, Mike is working hard to cope with his irritation. He takes several deep breaths, reminds himself that there is nothing he can do to speed up the line, and then gazes out the windows--focusing his attention upon the beautiful trees that line the street.
>
> Directly behind Mike, Ginny Caldwell is dealing with the situation in yet another way. Before she came into the bank, Ginny knew that she might be in for a long and frustrating wait, what with it being Friday afternoon and payday as well. So she made sure she had plenty of time to spend, and she brought along an Agatha Christie novel to occupy her time. Ginny vaguely noticed when the merchant stepped up to the window to deposit his time-consuming pile

of work, but she thought little or nothing about it. She simply adjusted her stance to feel more comfortable and continued reading Chapter Six. Would Miss Marple, she wondered, really be able to figure out who had murdered the Duchess?

Gary, Mike and Ginny have all been subjected to a typically stressful situation, not unlike the stresses each of us encounters every day. What is significant, however, is that each of them has reacted to that stress in a dramatically *different* way." From Shaffer, M. (1982). *Life after stress.* (New York: Plenum Press), (pp. xi-xii). Copyright 1982 by M. Shaffer. Reprinted with permission of Plenum Press.

This example can be used to illustrate the different methods of coping with stress as discussed in the text. For example, the authors report that unpredictable events are more stressful than predictable events. Certainly, a Friday afternoon could be predicted to be a busy time at a bank! Ginny's strategy of predicting the occurrence of a stressful event and then preparing for it by bringing a book is an effective means of coping. Students can discuss what events in their lives are stressful and which of the methods discussed in the text might be effective in forming coping strategies.

AUDIOVISUAL AIDES

Films

Learning to Live with Stress: Programming the Body for Health. Document Associates, Inc., 19 minutes, color. Hans Selye and Herbert Benson discuss stress as a causal factor in cardiovascular dysfunctions and other threats to health. Air traffic controllers are highlighted as individuals in high stress occupations.

Emotional Development: Aggression. CRM/McGraw-Hill, 18 min., color. Takes a social learning approach to aggression. Interviews with Gerald Patterson and Stephen Johnson.

Managing Stress. CRM/McGraw-Hill, 33 min., color. Examines the types of stress that arise from within the individual and that are generated by an organization. Animation and interviews are used to show how stress management can have positive effects.

Love and Film. Zagreb-Film, Yugoslavia; BFA, 9 min., color. A satire on the ways that love is presented in motion pictures cross-culturally. Animation.

Resolving Conflicts. CRM/McGraw-Hill, 22 min., color. Two basic approaches to conflict resolution are illustrated. More common approaches such as avoidance, "passing the buck" and pseudointervention are shown to be ineffective ways to resolve conflicts.

Audio Cassettes

Herbert S. Strean. Adolescence: The Stormy Years. Psychology Today Cassettes, Jeffrey Norton Pub., Inc. Strean discusses the emotional turmoil experienced by many young people entering adulthood and suggests ways to ease stress.

Film Strips

Masks: How We Hide Our Emotion. Human Relations Media, 2-part filmstrip, color/audio cassette.

Psychological Defenses. Human Relations Media, 3-part.

Managing Stress, Anxiety and Frustration. Human Relations Media, 4-part.

REFERENCES AND ANNOTATED SOURCES

Ekman, P., & Oster, H. (1979). Facial expressions of emotions. In M. R. Rosenzweig & L. W. Porter (Eds.), *Annual Review of Psychology, 30*, 316-354. An up-to-date review of research on the facial expressions of emotions, including cross-cultural and developmental studies, measurement issues, and neural control factors.

Goldband, S. (1980). Stimulus specificity of physiological response to stress and the Type A coronary-prone behavior pattern. *Journal of Personality and Social Psychology, 39*, 670-679.

Gurin, J. (1979). Chemical feelings. *Science 80*, Nov/Dec. A popular review of brain peptides containing good material for a lecture including a summary chart of the "peptide hit parade."

Holmes, T. S., & Holmes, T. H. (1970). Short-term intrusions into life-style routines. *Journal of Psychosomatic Research, 14*, 121-132.

Izard, C. E. (1977). *Human emotions.* New York: Plenum Press.

Miller, N. E. (1983). Behavioral medicine. Symbiosis between laboratory and clinic. In M. R. Rosenzweig & L. W. Porter (Eds.), *Annual Review of Psychology, 34*, 1-31.

Plutchik, R. (1975). Emotions. In C. N. Cofer & H. E. Fitzgerald (Eds.), *Psychology: A programmed modular approach* (pp. 461-510). Homewood, IL: Learning Systems Company. An easily digested overview of three major traditions in the study of emotions: Darwin, James and Cannon, and Freud.

Seyle, H. (1976). *Stress in health and disease.* Woburn, MA: Butterworth.

Shaffer, M. (1982). Life after stress. New York: Plenum Press. A presentation of stress as an adaptation response. Effective and ineffective ways of coping with stress are described.

Tomkins, S. S. (1970). Affect as the primary motivational system. In M. Arnold (Ed.), *Feelings and emotions: the Loyola symposium.* New York: Academic Press.

Chapter 13

PERSONALITY

CHAPTER OVERVIEW

This chapter introduces five major approaches to personality: trait, psychoanalytic, sociobiological, behavioral-social learning, and phenomenological. The section on the trait approach emphasizes its contributions in the measurement of personality and the prediction of behavior. The authors explain the work of trait theorists R. B. Cattell and H. Eysenck and note such tests as The Sixteen Personality Factor Questionnaire, the Eysenck Personality Questionnaire, the Minnesota Multiphasic Personality Inventory (MMPI), the California Personality Inventory (CPIO) and the Personality Research Form (PRF). Using the scores obtained from the inventories and the ratings, trait theories predict performance on various tasks related to each trait. For example, the authors cite a study by Harry A. Murray and his associates in which student ratings of their professors predicted which professors would be good teachers or good researchers! *Controversy* addresses the issue of consistency in personality versus situational specificity.

The chapter then takes up the psychoanalytic approach to personality. Beginning with a brief description of Freud's early life and career the text outlines the psychoanalytic model of personality (id, ego, superego) as well as its development.

The text then reviews psychoanalytic assessment including dream analysis, free associations and projective personality tests, and completes the survey of psychoanalytic concepts by summarizing the neoFreudian work of Jung, Adler, Fromm, Horney and Erikson.

For the sociobiological approach, the chapter first explains Sheldon's theory of body types and then explores the genetic components in personality formation shown by studies of monozygotic and dyzygotic twins. These studies suggest that personality may be more of a matter of heredity than has been realized. *The Research Process* examines studies of the heritability of personality.

The behavioral-social learning approach to personality emphasizes the objective study of a person's behaviors. The authors point out how this approach differs from those mentioned above in that one can alter a person's personality just as one can change other learned behaviors. Several concepts first introduced in Chapter 6 are reexamined in the context of personality development. Among these are: classical conditioning, instrumental learning, reinforcement, observational learning, vicarious conditioning, vicarious reinforcement, generalization, and discrimination learning. In order to assess personality these theorists measure specific behaviors under specific conditions. An example of a behavioral assessment method used in spy selection is shown in the section on *Applying Psychology.*

The final approach covered is the phenomenological view of personality. Carl Roger's Self-Theory is presented to show that how individuals view themselves is a central issue to phenomenological approaches. The development of the self-concept is discussed in terms of an actualizing tendency and a desire for social approval. Maslow's study of 49 self-actualized people is reported and his hierarchy of needs is examined.

The chapter concludes with an attempt to integrate the various approaches to the study of personality and emphasizes the need for including the person, behavior, and situation in the analysis of personality.

LEARNING OBJECTIVES

013-1. Define the study of personality.

013-2. Define the trait approach to personality. Identify major assessment techniques for measuring traits, including the work of Cattell and Eysenck.

013-4. Describe Freud's conceptualization of personality and Freud's view of the stages of personality development.

013-5. Outline the dynamics of personality in psychoanalytic theory and identify the assessment techniques used by psychoanalysts.

013-6. Distinguish between the neo-Freudian approaches to personality of Carl Jung, Alfred Adler, Erich Fromm, Karen Horney, and Erik Erikson.

013-7. Define the sociobiological approach to personality and be able to discuss evidence showing the heritability of personality.

013-8. Compare and contrast radical behaviorism and social learning approaches to personality. Present examples of how classical conditioning, instrumental learning, and observational learning can influence personality.

013-9. Distinguish the phenomenological approach to personality from the trait, psychoanalytic, sociobiological, and social learning approaches. Define Roger's theory of self-actualization.

013-10. Define interactionism and indicate how the five approaches to personality can be integrated in such a system.

ATTENTION GETTERS

Controversy 466-467

In *Controversy* the authors present evidence that was collected in order to determine whether there is stability in personality traits over situations or whether behavior is specific to a particular situation. In what ways can the evidence be supportive of arguments for consistency? In what ways can the evidence be supportive of arguments for specificity?

Psychoanalytic Theory 469-477

Why does anxiety originate according to psychoanalytic theory? What are the three basic types of anxiety? What defense mechanisms might people use to deal with anxiety?

Heritability of Personality 480-482

Twins studies have been carried out to determine whether or not a genetic component is important in determining personality. What evidence on the heritability of personality has been gathered through these studies? What criticisms have been made of the twin studies?

Self Theory 489-490

According to Carl Rogers, childhood is a critical period for the formation of personality. How might conflicts arise between choices leading to self-actualization and choices leading to social approval? What should parents do to promote growth?

LECTURE SUGGESTIONS AND CLASS DEMONSTRATIONS

Sigmund Freud's theory of personality certainly stands as one of the most influential theories in the history of psychology. Transparencies 13-2, 13-3, and 13-4 provide excellent classroom aides for reviewing Freud's theory and for setting the stage for discussion of personality assessment and other theories of personality. Transparency 13-2 illustrates Freud's structure of mind into the conscious, preconscious, and unconscious. 13-3 follows with a depiction of the three structures of personality; id, ego, and superego. 13-4 provides a systems view of the Oedipal complex, the resolution of which leads to superego and appropriate sex role identification in the male. Freud's description of the structure and dynamics of personality certainly stimulated development of other theoretical views, and no doubt played a role in attempts to develop instruments to assess personality.

The Trait Approach 458-469

Personality assessment. A lecture on methods of assessing personality provides an opportunity to review the importance of validity, reliability, and standardization in test evaluation. Students can be asked to apply concepts learned in Chapter 10 to the material in this chapter. Projective tests, objective tests, interviews, and observations can be compared as to their use in personality assessment. Transparency 13-1 provides illustrations of items similar to those that are in the Minnesota Multiphasic Personality Inventory; a widely used objective personality test, and Transparency 13-5 illustrates an inkblot from the Rorschach Ink Blot Test, a widely used projective technique for assessing personality. The following two demonstrations can serve as attention-getters.

Personality tests attempt to assess personality quantitatively and are among the most misunderstood types of assessment instruments. Personality tests, like all psychological tests, must be reliable and valid. Four types of validity traditionally are differentiated: face, predictive, concurrent, and construct. The following demonstration illustrates the problem of using personal agreement as a validation method.

First the instructor must prepare an adjective checklist personality test. Select any 12 adjectives or use the ones listed in Table 5. Next, administer the "test" during the class immediately preceding the day in which you will lecture on personality assessment. Collect the tests and tell students that they each will receive a confidential personality sketch based on the test results. Next, prepare an "official" personality sketch for distribution to students or use the one in Table 5. Note that each student is to receive the same sketch! Before discussing the sketches, ask students to rate them on a scale from 0 (poor) to 5 (perfect) as to how effectively the personality test revealed their personality. Finally, have students rate each statement in their sketch as either true or false about their personality. Reveal the deception involved in your demonstration and use student reactions to lead to discussion of validity and reliability issues in all types of personality assessment.

TABLE 5

12-Factor Personality Inventory

Student's Name

Instructions: Check the adjectives that apply to you as you feel you actually are, not as how you'd like to be. Work quickly, giving your first impressions.

____nervous	____humorous
____likeable	____insecure
____cold	____shy
____musical	____critical
____intelligent	____fearful
____generous	____warm

Sample Personality Sketch

You have a great need for other people to like you.
You have a tendency to be critical of yourself.
You have a great deal of unused potential.
You are generally able to compensate for your personality weaknesses.
Your heterosexual relationships present problems for you.
Your appear well-controlled on the outside but are worrisome and insecure on the inside.
You often have serious doubts about the decisions you make.
Your prefer change and variety and dislike being limited by restrictions.
You take pride in being an independent thinker.
You are very careful in what you reveal to others about yourself.

(Adapted by permission from Activity 71, "Personality Tests" by N. F. Russo in L. T. Benjamin, Jr. and K. D. Lowman, eds., *Activity Handbook for the Teaching of Psychology.* Copyright 1981 by the American Psychological Association. All rights reserved.)

Personality Assessment 474-475

Doodling. Gardner (1980) suggests a class demonstration to determine how doodling can be used as a method of assessing personality. Each student should be given a paper with the designs shown below in Figure 7:

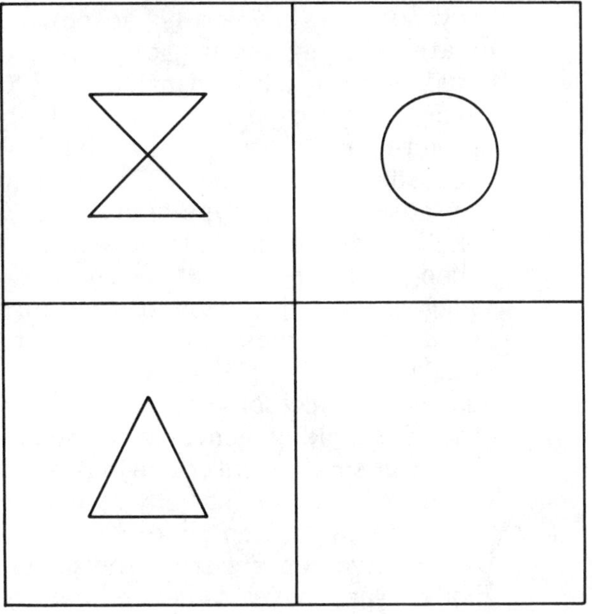

FIGURE 7

After filling in each of the four squares, the doodles can be evaluated according to the following criteria:

Square objects--masculine
Round objects--feminine
Sharp protrusions--aggression
Shaded areas--obsessive personality
Houses--security
Common domestic animals--well adjusted
Bugs, spiders--phobias

(Adapted from Rick M. Gardner, *Exercises for General Psychology.* Copyright 1980 by Burgess Publishing Company. By permission of Burgess Publishing Company, Minneapolis, Minnesota.)

Students should ask themselves if the descriptions of the personality characteristics fit their own perceptions of their personality? Would they consider this an accurate method of assessing personality? Which of the five approaches discussed in the text would be more likely to accept this method?

Sociobiological Approach 478-483

Body types. Although the layperson often has been said to use body type as a quick method of personality assessment (fat=jolly; slender with glasses=scholarly; muscular=adventurous) this is a theory that has not gained wide acceptance in American psychology. In fact, American psychologists have resisted theories emphasizing a strong link between personality and genetic factors. Nevertheless, considerable evidence is accumulating from studies of twins to suggest that the genetic influence in behavior may be greater than psychologists generally acknowledge. Transparency 13-6 illustrates the heritability of a variety of disorders as suggested by studies comparing identical and fraternal twins. Sociobiological approaches to personality challenge traditionalism, and indirectly prompt new interest in Sheldon's classification of personality according to body type. Students may assume that a person is able to change body type and hence change personality. However, Sheldon suggests that body type remains constant. Nutritional changes do not lead to changes in the somatotype. "Sheldon suggests that just as a starved mastiff does not become a poodle, so a starved mesomorph does not become an ectomorph" (Hall & Lindzey, 1970, p. 356). Indeed, if changes in body type did lead to changes in personality, it would provide strong evidence against theories linking genes to personality. Why then is there such a boom in surgical interventions, diets, and other techniques designed to alter body type or body appearance?

For attention-getters, select a variety of advertisements or descriptive reports from the popular press that link personality to body type; have someone who recently experienced significant weight loss appear before the class to describe personality changes that occurred as a result of the weight loss; or, if possible, have someone who has recently started to use a prosthetic device or who received significant cosmetic surgery describe their "before-after reactions. Such anecdotal accounts provide good starting points for contrasting sociobiological and social learning explanations for correlations between body type and personality characteristics.

The Phenomenological Approach 488-493

Self-monitoring: Will the real you stand up! Phenomenological approaches to personality emphasize analyses of conscious experience; that is, all of the factors that enter into the individual's perceptions and valuations of his or her life experiences. Carl Rogers refers to these perceptions as the self-concept and distinguishes between the actual-self and the ideal-self. Snyder (1980) argues that the individual's concept of self is, in part, defined by how others perceive us and that individuals vary with respect to their ability to control the impressions others form about them. The following abridged version of Snyder's Self-Monitoring Scale (Table 6) can serve as an attention-getter to introduce the topic of self-theory. Distribute the questionnaire as students enter the classroom, instructing them to complete it as soon as they sit down. Open the lecture by having students score their own responses and then use Snyder's hypothesis to lead into class discussion or a formal lecture or self-theory in personality.

TABLE 6

Snyder's Abbreviated Self-Monitoring Scale

These statements concern personal reactions to a number of different situations. No two statements are exactly alike, so consider each statement carefully before answering. If a statement is true, or mostly true, as applied to you, circle the T. If a statement is false, or not usually true, as applied to you, circle the F.

1. I find it hard to imitate the behavior of other people. T F
2. I guess I put on a show to impress or entertain people. T F
3. I would probably make a good actor. T F
4. I sometimes appear to others to be experiencing deeper emotions than I actually am. T F
5. In a group of people I am rarely the center of attention. T F
6. In different situations and with different people, I often act like very different persons. T F
7. I can only argue for ideas I already believe. T F
8. In order to get along and be liked, I tend to be what people expect me to be rather than anything else. T F
9. I may deceive people by being friendly when I really dislike them. T F
10. I'm not always the person I appear to be. T F

Instruct the students to score their answers as follows: Give yourself one point for each of questions 1, 5, and 7 that you answered F. Give yourself one point for each of the remaining questions that you answered T. Add up your points. If you are a good judge of yourself and scored 7 or above, you are probably a high self-monitoring individual; 3 or below, you are probably a low self-monitoring individual. (Reprinted from: M. Snyder. The many me's of the self monitor. *Psychology Today* magazine. Copyright 1980 American Psychological Association. Used by permission.

Snyder suggests that obese people, politicians, lawyers, recent immigrants and black freshment in a predominately white university, are likely to score high because they will tend to be sensitive to how others react to them. Low self-monitoring individuals tend to accept behavior of others at face value, whereas high self-monitoring individuals are sensitive to deception and attempts by others to manage impression formation.

AUDIOVISUAL MATERIALS

Films

Transitions: Letting Go and Taking Hold. CRM/McGraw-Hill, 29 minutes, color. Changes involving personal, internal and emotional adjustments are life transitions. Shows changes occurring in an organization.

Personality: Adolescence. CRM/McGraw-Hill, Inc., 21 minutes, color. Short vignettes are used to illustrate sexual maturation, self-esteem, independence, self-concept, conflicts with authority, and peer interactions during adolescence.

Happy to be Me. Arthur Mokin Productions, Inc., 25 minutes, color. Perceptions of masculinity and femininity are important aspects of social phenomena. This film provides a view of young people's attitudes toward gender, and male and female roles.

Ego Development: The Core of a Healthy Personality. Davidson Films; Sterling Educational Films, 19 min., color. Bettye Caldwell analyzes the first three levels of personality development as designated by Erik Erikson. Emphasizes that early development is essential to healthy emotional life.

Growth Failure and Maternal Deprivation. Counterpoint Films, McGraw-Hill, 26 min., B & W. Two case studies of young children living in poor conditions and suffering from growth failure. Shows positive results of intervention. Can serve as excellent attention getter to consider the effects of early experience in personality development.

Psychotherapy. CRM/McGraw-Hill, 26 min., color. Provides an introduction to the process of psychotherapy and cites several examples of encounters between patient and therapist.

Audio Cassettes

Garmazy, N. Vulnerable and invulnerable children: theory, research, and intervention. APA Tape 11/15, 1975.

Leonard Berkowitz. Understanding and Controlling Human Aggression. Psychology Today Cassettes, Jeffrey Norton Pub., Inc. Answers are given to questions relating to the understanding, control, and containment of aggression in children and adults.

Philip Zimbardo. Overcoming Shyness. Psychology Today Cassettes, Jeffrey Norton Pub., Inc. A social psychologist discusses the nature, causes, and consequences of shyness, and explains how it can be overcome.

Film Strips

Perspectives on Death. 2 filmstrips, audiocassettes, and instructor's guide. An examination of complex issues associated with death such as legal definition and euthanasia. Various attitudes toward death are considered.

Personality Disorders: Failures of Adjustment. Human Relations Media, 3-part program each 13-15 minutes with resource guide.

Evaluating Personality. Human Relations Media, 3-part series, 13-15 minutes each.

Your Personality: The You Others Know. Guidance Associates, 2 filmstrips, 2 cassettes, discussion guide.

REFERENCES AND ANNOTATED SOURCES

Corsini, R. J. (Ed.) (1977). *Current personality theories.* Itasca, IL: F. E. Peacock Publishing, Inc. This volume includes chapters on ten major theoretical approaches to personality, a chapter on Soviet personality theory and one on Asian theory, and ends with a chapter in which Corsini reviews twelve specific theories.

Ewen, R. B. (1970). *An introduction to theories of personality* (2nd ed.). New York: John Wiley & Sons. Provides summaries of the major terms in psychoanalytic theory, of the defense mechanisms, psychosexual stages and of the structures of personality. The summary charts are excellent for lecture preparation.

Hall, C. S., & Lindzey, G. (1970). *Theories of personality* (2nd Ed.). New York: John Wiley & Sons.

Mischel, W. (1981). *Introduction to personality.* New York: Holt, Rinehart and Winston. Discusses Skinner's radical behavioral theory and then explains how its concepts changed into social learning theory. Includes a review of the implications of social learning theory for personality change.

Pervin, L. A. (1978). *Current controversies and issues in personality.* New York: John Wiley and Sons. Explores the question, "Am I me or am I the situation?" and advances the argument that neither consistency nor specificity adequately accounts for research results and suggests an interactionist approach.

Chapter 14

ABNORMAL PSYCHOLOGY

CHAPTER OVERVIEW

The chapter opens with a discussion of various criteria used to distinguish between normality and abnormality: the statistical criterion, cultural criterion, and personal distress criterion. The concept of a normal-abnormal behavior continuum is introduced as is the legal criterion for abnormality.

The historical overview of different conceptualizations of abnormality includes the superstitious approach, the medical approach, the psychoanalytic approach, and the behavioral approach. *Controversy* addresses the issue of whether mental illness is, in fact, a myth. Szasz's definition of abnormality as "problems in living" is presented in this context.

The authors point out that a good system for classifying abnormal behaviors allows one to make a prognosis, develop appropriate treatments for different disorders, and to study the causes of specific disorders. DSM-III is introduced, and relying on DSM-III, the remainder of the chapter describes various disorders but fits each disorder within the traditional tripartite scheme: neuroses, psychoses, and character disorders.

In a discussion of the neuroses the authors describe anxiety disorders, (phobias, generalized anxiety disorders, panic attacks, obsessive-compulsive disorders), somatoform disorders (conversion disorders), and dissociative disorders (amnesia, fugue, multiple personality disorders). In *Applying Psychology* the authors discuss acquittal on criminal charges due to insanity.

Among the character disorders described are substance use disorders, psychosexual disorders (divided into 3 categories: gender identity disorders, sexual deviations, and sexual dysfunctions) and impulse control disorders (gambling, kleptomania and pyromania). *The Research Process* demonstrates how the social learning theory concepts of observational learning and reinforcement can explain adolescents' use (and abuse) of alcohol and marijuana.

The final section details the psychoses. The authors describe delirium and dementia as examples of organic brain syndrome and then review the essential characteristics of schizophrenic behavior (thought disorders, delusions, hallucinations) as well as the major types of schizophrenia (disorganized, paranoid, catatonic, and undifferentiated). Next the text describes the major characteristics of paranoid disorders and the extremes of affective disorders, mania, and depression. In considering the causes of depression the authors review psychoanalytic, biomedical, and learning theory formulations. The chapter concludes with an emphasis on the various explanations for abnormal behavior.

LEARNING OBJECTIVES

014-1. Understand and distinguish the four criteria used to define abnormality: statistical, cultural, personal, and legal.

014-2. Distinguish the four approaches to explaining abnormality: superstitious, medical, psychoanalytic, and behavioral.

014-3. Be familiar with the DSM III classification of abnormal behavior and its uses.

014-4. Identify neuroses and be familiar with categories and subcategories of anxiety disorders, somatoform disorders, and dissociative disorders.

014-5. Identify character disorders and be familiar with categories and subcategories of substance use disorders, psychosexual disorders, and impulse disorders. Be able to discuss evidence showing the relative importance of biological and learning factors in character disorders.

014-6. Be familiar with categories and subcategories of organic disorders and schizophrenic disorders.

014-7. Identify the biomedical, psychoanalytic, and learning models for explaining the causes of schizophrenia.

014-8. Be familiar with categories and subcategories of paranoid and affective disorders.

014-9. Identify the psychoanalytic, biomedical, and learning models for explaining the causes of depression.

ATTENTION GETTERS

Concepts of Abnormality 500-503

Do you think that mental illness is comparable to physical diseases or do you think that abnormal behaviors are problems in living? What evidence can you cite to support your view?

Phobias 507-508

It is suggested that phobias may have an evolutionary basis because people tend to develop phobias toward objects that might affect (or have affected in the past) survival. What types of phobias are more common? Do you think there is a tendency for people to be "prepared" to develop fears of some objects more than others?

Substance Use/Abuse 512-514

What is the most abused drug in the United States? Why do the effects of alcohol seem paradoxical? Why do some people have difficulty understanding that alcohol is a depressant?

Psychosexual Disorders 514-516

What is the difference between transsexualism, transvestism, and gender identity or role disorder? How do psychoanalysts view these disorders? How do learning theorists view these disorders?

LECTURE SUGGESTIONS AND CLASS DEMONSTRATIONS

What is Abnormal Behavior 498-503

Defining abnormality. Reference to Transparencies 14-1 and 14-2 at the beginning of lecture will alert the student to DSM III and to the major categories of mental disorders. After reviewing the material in these transparencies, students can be asked to consider what, in fact, constitutes abnormal behavior. The following demonstration is a useful method of introducing students to the topic of abnormality. In order to obtain student perceptions of abnormality have them perform the task before reading Chapter 14. Ask students to define what constitutes normal behavior and what constitutes abnormal behavior. Responses can be charted on the board.

TABLE 7

Sample for Charting

What Constitutes Normal or Abnormal Behavior

Abnormal	Normal	Problems with this Definition
That which deviates from a society's conventions.	Behavior accepted by the majority of a society.	It doesn't allow for an entire society to behave abnormally, e.g., Nazi Germany.
Behaviors indicating severe depression.	Behaviors indicating little anxiety or depression.	In some cases, such as the death of a loved one, the lack of depression or sorrow, rather than their presence, would be abnormal.

The instructor can encourage students to form as many definitions as possible. Once the list has been generated, the instructor can compare these definitions with those discussed in the text. Transparencies 14-3 and 14-4 provide a context to consider the heritability of criminal behavior or of schizophrenia. If these types of "abnormal" behavior do have a base in the genotype, what are the implications for environmental influences? How would knowledge of genetic origins influence students' definitions of abnormality?

Controversy 502-503

Myths about mental illness. Coleman and Broen (1972) cite several popular misconceptions about mental disorders. These can be presented to the students in the form of a quiz:

1. Abnormal behaviors are always bizarre. (False--Coleman and Broen point out that this view may be perpetuated by the media since the extremes of behavior are being reported.)

2. A clear distinction can be drawn between "normal" and "abnormal" behaviors. (False--Coleman and Broen explain that there are not two groups of people, the "normal" and the "mad." Instead abnormality is a matter of degree.)
3. Geniuses are particularly prone to insanity. (False--Terman's study of high IQ children, discussed in Chapter 10, showed that these people actually may be more well adjusted than the population in general.)
4. Most mental disorders are incurable. (False--According to Coleman and Broen, between 70% and 80% of those hospitalized as mental patients eventually recover.)

Classifying Abnormal Behavior 504

Normal or abnormal: Classifying behaviors. After the students have read Chapter 14, the following demonstration aids in developing an understanding of the classification of various disorders. Student volunteers should be asked to portray various disorders to the class. These can be decided upon by the students after reading the chapter or assigned by the instructor. The instructor should ask some of the volunteers to enact behaviors that would be considered "normal" rather than deviant. The following situations might be expanded for use as examples of normal behavior:

"When the end of the school term approaches and I begin to study for final examinations, I find myself getting anxious."

"I get very uncomfortable at the sight of blood and so I try to avoid movies, etc. that are likely to contain bloody scenes."

Students can see how problems of reliability can occur when the same example is given different diagnoses by various students.

The Neuroses 506-511

Robert Meister's (1980) study of hypochondriasis also provides a good example for discussion of the classification of normal and abnormal behavior. He describes the case of a women who, quite routinely, five times daily, would give her body a thorough 30-minute tactile and visual examination. She used a magnifying glass to examine her skin and a mirror arrangement to observe every part of her body. Meister notes that, "Her rapport with her body was absolute and awesome to behold." Yet, this woman was quite satisfied with her life and career, not concerned about her preoccupation with her body, nor did she run to physicians to obtain cures for supposed illnesses. Or, take the case of the middle-aged male businessman whose confidante was his secretary.

> It was only during such (business) trips that he talked about his complaints, usually after dinner. She (his secretary) initiated these confessionals with the question, "How have you been feeling?" and the answer was often half an hour long. He believed that he had colitis and talked at great length about his stool. For weeks at a time, he "lived on" caster oil, which was "like champagne" to him. He medicated himself extensively with nonprescription drugs, and had absolute confidence in them. On his trips he carried a special

> attaché case filled with medications....Although he never married, he seemed to like women and bragged about his affairs. To all outward appearances, he was an energetic, fastidious, cheerful man, with a wide variety of interests (Meister, 1980, p. 34).

Meister differentiates such "closet hypochondriacs" from true or "abnormal" hypochondriasis, which involves the use of illness to express a deficit of self-esteem. For example, Meister notes that individuals with true hypochondriasis tend to maintain a slavishly submissive and dependent relationship with a parent or a parent substitute. He advances several conclusions which both characterize hypochondriacs and distinguishes them from closet hypochondriacs:

> -Hypochondria can occur at any age in both sexes.
> -Hypochondria can occur either as a separate, independent disorder, or it can coexist with any number of mental and/or physical disorders....
> -For hypochondria to occur, there is likely to have been exposure in early life to numerous, persistent complaints and evidence of illnesses, invalidism, life-threatening experiences of various sorts, or death of close family members....or a pronounced dependency relationship with a parent or parent substitute....
> -The suffering of hypochondriacs is genuine....
> -The case material dispels the widely held fallacy that hypochondria is fear of illness....
> -The attitude of the medical profession toward hypochondria is decidedly an aloof one (Meister, 1980, p. 34).

Class discussion can focus on the following question: Are behavior patterns that do not interfere with everyday performance or do not interfere with others, justifiably labeled "abnormal?" Apparently Meister does not believe so, at least with respect to closet hypochondriasis.

Causes of Depression 527-529

Dare to be perfect. Setting unrealistic and unattainable goals may contribute to affective disorders such as depression. Perfectionists are individuals who set personal standards so high that they cannot attain them (Burns, 1980). Perfectionism is related to poor self-control, low self-esteem, poor health, and to a variety of mood disorders such as depression and loneliness. David Burns identifies three types of mental distortions common among perfectionists: all or none thinking, overgeneralization, and use of "should" statements. Thus, when perfectionists fail they do not engage in constructive self-evaluation, but rather engage in nonproductive self deprecation. Burns links the inefficiency and defeatism of perfectionism to learned helplessness, and suggests that children learn to fear failure and to overvalue success as a result of their interactions with perfectionist parents. These are parents who dichotomize positive and negative emotional consequences of the child's successes and failures.

A lecture on perfectionism enables the instructor to link depression and other affective disorders to self-concept, child-rearing, values, need for achievement, and fear of failure. The combined impact of these topics should have immediate relevance to college students who routinely are in situations that challenge their immediate course goals as well as their long-range vocational and life goals. As an attention getter, ask students to complete Burns' Perfectionism Scale (Table 8), which can be distributed to students as they enter the classroom.

TABLE 8

The Perfectionism Scale

Decide how much you agree with each statement using the following scale: +2 = I agree very much; +1 = I agree somewhat; 0 = I feel neutral about this; -1 = I disagree slightly; -2 = I disagree strongly. Fill in the blank preceding each statement with the number that best describes how you think most of the time. Be sure to choose only one answer for each attitude. There are no "right" or "wrong" answers, so try to respond according to the way you usually feel and behave.

____ 1. If I don't set the highest standards for myself, I am likely to end up a second-rate person.
____ 2. People will probably think less of me if I make a mistake.
____ 3. If I cannot do something really well, there is little point in doing it at all.
____ 4. I should be upset if I make a mistake.
____ 5. If I try hard enough, I should be able to excel at anything I attempt.
____ 6. It is shameful for me to display weaknesses or foolish behavior.
____ 7. I shouldn't have to repeat the same mistake many times.
____ 8. An average performance is bound to be unsatisfying to me.
____ 9. Failing at something important means I'm less of a person.
____ 10. If I scold myself for failing to live up to my expectations, it will help me to do better in the future.

Scoring: Add up your scores on all items, noting that plus numbers and minus numbers cancel each other out. A score of +20 = high perfectionism; a score of -20 = nonperfectionism....About half the population scores between +2 and +16, indicating varying degrees of perfectionism. Reprinted from: Burns, D. D. The perfectionist's script for self-defeat. *Psychology Today* Magazine. Copyright 1980 American Psychological Association. Used by permission.

AUDIOVISUAL AIDES

Films

Depression: A Study in Abnormal Behavior. CRM/McGraw-Hill, 27 minutes, color. A young housewife-teacher is followed through the course of a depressive episode. Upon resolution of her treatment she is released from hospital care but has need of follow-up therapy.

Abnormal Behavior: A Mental Hospital. CRM/McGraw-Hill, 28 minutes, color. A documentary involving Gateways Mental Hospital in California. Shows patient-therapist sessions during which the two discuss symptomotology, diagnosis, treatment, and prognosis.

Neurotic Behavior: A Psychodynamic View. CRM/McGraw-Hill, 20 minutes, color. Illustrates neurotic behaviors and defense mechanisms in a male college student. Relates current neurotic behavior to maternal induced trauma early in his development.

Madness and Medicine. CRM/McGraw-Hill, 49 minutes, color. A two-part film presentation exploring aspects of a mental institution and its patients (Part 1) and the use of electroshock and psychosurgery (Part 2). Patients discuss their difficulties adjusting to society after leaving the hospital setting.

Audio Cassettes

Stein, L. Biochemical substrates of schizophrenia. APA Tape 10-11, 1974. Stein reviews various theories of schizophrenia in relation to the biochamistry of catecholamines--dopamine and norepinephrine. He argues that to date no firm relationship has linked dopamine to thought disorders or to affective disorders, both of which are symptoms of schizophrenia. Norepinephrine, however, is linked to cognitive and affective function.

Film Strips

Who's OK, Who's Not OK. Human Relation Media, 3-part filmstrip, 13-15 minutes each, audiocassettes and guides. Presents guidelines for distinguishing among normal, neurotic, and psychotic behavior. Topics include: phobias, depression, obsessive-compulsive behavior, schizophrenia, paranoia, manic-depression, hypochondria, and melancholia.

Origins of Mental Illness. Human Relation Media, 2-part filmstrip, 13-15 minutes each, audiocassettes and guide. Points out the prevalence of mental illness and discusses its causes. Four etiological aspects are reviewed: genetic defects, faulty personality development, environmental stress, and socio-cultural influences.

Psychosomatic Disorders. Human Relation Media, 3-part filmstrip, 13-15 minutes each, audiocassettes and guides. Discusses a variety of physical disorders whose origins are linked to mental and emotional factors. Included are: migraine headaches, asthma, insomnia, hypertension, obesity, anorexia nervosa, ulcers, and eczema.

REFERENCES AND ANNOTATED SOURCES

Burns, D. (1980). The perfectionist's script for self-defeat. *Psychology Today, 44,* 34-52.

Coleman, J. C., & Broen, W. E., Jr. (1972). *Abnormal psychology and modern life.* Glenview, IL: Scott, Foresman and Co.

Cytryn, L., & McKnew, D. H., Jr. (1972). Proposed classification of childhood depression. *American Journal of Psychiatry, 129,* 149-155. Three distinct categories of childhood depression are proposed: masked depression, active depression, and chronic depression. Some controversy exists with respect to masked depression.

Draguns, J. G. (1980). Psychological disorders of clinical severity. In H. C. Triadis, J. G. Draguns (Eds.), *Handbook of cross-cultural psychology, Vol. 6: Psychopathology.* Boston: Allyn and Bacon. Key aspects of abnormal behavior across cultures are reduced to four dimensions: affective disorder, schizophrenia, neurosis, and personality disorders. Although no disorder is completely free of cultural influence, neither is any disorder entirely the result of cultural influence. Draguns argues that psychoses are less influenced by culture than are non-psychotic disorders.

Katchadourian, H. A., & Lunde, D. T. (1972). *Fundamentals of human sexuality.* New York: Holt, Rinehart & Winston. A comprehensive overview of human sexuality, including anatomy and physiology of reproduction, contraception, sexual behavior and development, intercourse, deviations, and such cultural aspects as human sexuality as occur in art, literature, law, and film. This book is loaded with information, well written, and contains much information on historical and cultural aspects of human sexual behavior.

Meister, R. (1980). Closet hypochondriacs. *Psychology Today,* 28-37.

Mineka, S. (1982). Depression and helplessness in primates. In H. E. Fitzgerald, J. A. Mullins & P. Gage (Eds.), *Child Nurturance 3: Studies of development in nonhuman primates.* New York: Plenum Press. Argues persuasively for the usefulness of primate models of depression with respect to their significance for advancing understanding of the phenomenon and for understanding human depression. Even if one is constrained in generalizing from nonhuman primates to human beings, studying depression in primates allows us to understand them better.

Seligman, M. E. P. (1975). *Helplessness: On depression, development, and death.* San Francisco: Freeman.

Chapter 15

THERAPIES

CHAPTER OVERVIEW

The authors begin the chapter by showing methods that have been used throughout history to "treat" abnormal behavior. A series of figures illustrates the conditions in various institutions and the devices used to restrain patients. The authors introduce the psychoanalytic, humanistic, behavioral, and community approaches to therapy pointing out that each defines abnormality in a different way. They review differences in the training of psychiatrists, clinical psychologists, counseling psychologists, psychiatric social workers, and psychiatric nurses.

First the authors consider psychoanalysis as a therapeutic method and include information on free association, resistance, transference, and catharsis. They discuss NeoFreudian variations of psychoanalytic theory as well as modern changes in psychoanalytic techniques. Approaches to encourage release of repressed tensions include transactional analysis, psychodrama, and primal scream.

Next the text discusses humanistic therapies focusing on Rogers' person-centered approach, Gestalt therapy, Ellis' rational-emotive therapy, and humanistic forms of group therapy.

The authors then show how behavioral approaches, such as systematic desensitization therapy and aversion therapy, are based on a classical conditioning procedure called counterconditioning. The authors also explain how self-management approaches emphasize principles of operant conditioning, as do biofeedback techniques that often are applied to stress management. Observational learning is shown to be effective in the treatment of phobias. *Applying Psychology* highlights the work of Masters and Johnson and various techniques used in sex therapy. Next the text discusses residential therapeutic communities and institutionalization. Token economies and social milieu therapies are efforts to restructure the institution to reinforce appropriate rather than undesirable behaviors. After highlighting problems involved in community half-way houses the authors summarize the three types of services that community mental health centers provide.

Controversy, reviews research assessing whether psychotherapy is effective and whether some methods lead to more improvement. A basic problem in this controversy focuses on the definition of "cure."

The final section deals with biological approaches. Although rare today, psychosurgery was common in the 1940s and 1950s. It has been replaced by use of electroconvulsive therapy (severe depression) and a variety of drugs (anxiety and psychoses). *The Research Process* evaluates the effectiveness of several biological therapies.

LEARNING OBJECTIVES

015-1. Be familiar with major historical advances in the treatment of abnormal behavior and name three modern approaches to treatment. Classify psychotherapy practitioners.

015-2. Describe the methods and goals of Freudian, or classical, psychoanalysis.

015-3. Compare and contrast the different versions of neo-Freudian psychoanalysis with classical psychoanalysis and describe the three modern psychoanalytic therapies: transactional analysis, psychodrama, and primal scream.

015-4. Describe four humanistic or phenomonological approaches to psychotherapy, person-centered therapy, gestalt therapy, rational-emotive therapy, and group therapy.

015-5. Identify two types of classical conditioning used by behavior therapists and indicate when their use is appropriate. In what situations have operant conditioning procedures such as positive reinforcement and punishment been used by such therapists?

015-6. Describe three areas in which modeling therapy has been successfully employed. What are the two goals of cognitive behavior modification?

015-7. Identify three categories of community therapy, and state the rationale for treating patients in the community.

015-8. Be familiar with the arguments for and against the effectiveness of psychotherapy.

015-9. Describe three types of biological therapies. Indicate when such procedures might be used and if these procedures have been shown to be effective.

ATTENTION GETTERS

Historical Aspects 534-537

What methods have been used historically to correct abnormal behavior? What treatments might be expected in institutions of the 19th century?

Therapists 536-537

What five groups practice psychotherapy? What training does one receive as a psychiatrist, clinical psychologist, counseling psychologist, psychiatric social worker, or psychiatric nurse?

Psychoanalytic Approaches 537-540

Freud's psychoanalytic theory has inspired many variations in both theory and technique. Describe these variations from classical psychoanalysis. What do all of the psychoanalytic approaches have in common?

Community Mental Health 555-556

Describe the three types of services provided by Community Mental Health centers. Give examples of each. What community services are available in your community? Are primary services being provided?

LECTURE SUGGESTIONS AND CLASS DEMONSTRATIONS

Over the centuries many changes have occurred in our concept and treatment of the mentally ill. Transparency 15-1 reviews these changes and illustrates four "revolutions" in mental health that have slowly, yet still not completely, suppressed the view that (d)evil is somehow the causal mechanism in mental illness. The principal theories of causation and typical methods for treatment of the mentally ill are listed for each revolution.

Transparency 15-2 contrasts five professions involved with psychotherapeutic treatment of the mentally ill, and Transparency 15-3 shows that deinstitutionalization has greatly reduced the number of individuals in hospitals. Deinstitutionalization in large part became possible because of the last revolution in treatment of the mentally ill; namely, drugs (see Transparency 15-5). Moreover, it will likely require even more psychotherapists since drug intervention often provides the means whereby individuals can now benefit from psychotherapy.

Psychoanalytic Approach 537-540

Rope jumping, rhyming, and psychoanalysis. The text reviews a variety of psychoanalytic approaches to therapy and notes that they share the assumption that causes and cures of dysfunction lie in the unconscious. Psychoanalysis, in particular, strives to bring unconscious material to the conscious awareness of the patient through such classic techniques as free association. However, psychoanalysts use many other sources of information to develop insight into dysfunctional behavior. For example, Herbert Goldings (1974) finds the analysis of jump-rope rhymes useful in explacating the development of girls during the latency period. Goldings suggests that some jump rope rhymes are psychodynamically meaningless:

> Icka-bicka soda cracker
> Icka-bicka boo
> Icka-bicka soda cracker
> Out goes you (p. 440)

whereas, others express such themes as sibling rivalry, anality, hostility, envy, and hatred for boys. Consider, for example,

> Standing on the corner
> Chewing bubble gum
> Along came a boy
> And asked for some
> No you little boy
> No you dirty bum
> You can't have any
> Of my bubble gum (p. 440).

Goldings' description of the case of a 7½-year-old girl serves as an interesting introduction to psychoanalysis and to concepts such as transference. This particular girl began therapy at age 5½ in order to alleviate sleep problems (nightmares, restlessness, fear). When 4½ she had been hospitalized for observation of a potential abnormality of the genitourinary tract. Six months prior to that her brother had a life-threatening attack of idiopathic thrombocytopenic purpura (a bleeding disorder of childhood), which required a long period of aftercare. Goldings notes that the girl's resolution of her resentment of her brother was associated with increased physical activity, including rope jumping. Goldings reports three "Cinderella" jump-rope rhymes which helped him to understand her problem and which helped her negotiate transference.

Cinderella
Dressed in yella
Went upstairs
To kiss her fella.
How many kisses did she give him?
One-two-three-four-etc. (p. 445).

After reciting this rhyme the girl launched into a discussion of kissing, became quite excited, and recited a second rhyme:

Cinderella
Dressed in yella
Went upstairs
To kiss her fella.
By mistake
She kissed a snake
How many doctors
Did it take?
One-two-three-four-etc. (p. 446).

She then made a pair of lips out of clay which Goldings suggested resembled a particular sexual motion she made in a previous session. The girl denied this and gave the third version of the rhyme:

Cinderella
Dressed in yella
Went downtown
To get some mustard.
By mistake
Her girdle busted.
How many people
Got disgusted?
One-two-three-four-etc. (p. 446).

According to Goldings, the analytic and jump-rope rhymes, "....demonstrates the easy movement in (X) from the oedipal and latency material to the oral, sexual, and death elements (including the transference danger of erotic interest in and penetration by the doctor), and, finally, to the anogenital excitement bound by the reaction formation of disgust." Recounting this example from psychoanalytic treatment of a child can serve as an attention-getter for discussion of psychoanalytic therapy and especially for the significance of transference in the analytic work. (For additional information and more examples of jump-rope rhymes see: Goldings, H. J. Jump-rope rhymes and the rhythm of latency development in girls. In R. S. Eissler, A. Freud, M. Kris, and A. J. Solnit (Eds.), (1974). *The psychoanalytic study of the child, 29,* 431-450).

Operant Conditioning 546-548

Dolorology: Behavioral management of chronic pain. Constance Holden (1977) notes that chronic pain associated with amputation, arthritis, degenerative diseases, cancer, lower back disorders, and headache carries an annual price tag estimated to be 50 billion dollars. Standard medical treatment has not been effective in providing relief from such pain. Dolorologists, or pain therapists, attempt to treat chronic pain using a variety of nonmedical techniques such as biofeedback and hypnosis. Their goal is to help chronic pain sufferers become active agents rather than passive patients in the management of their pain. Inasmuch as pain is viewed as learned behavior, pain therapists attempt to help patients change their atitudes toware pain and if necessary, to learn to live with it.

The therapeutic approach developed by William Fordyce at the University of Washington is used in many pain clinics. A thorough description of the Fordyce approach allows the instructor to integrate many concepts and procedures discussed in previous chapters. For example, the Fordyce approach begins by classifying pain as respondent or operant (Holden, 1977). Respondent pain is a conditioned response to the physical source of the pain. Operant pain, on the other hand, is learned as a result of reinforcement for pain behaviors. According to Fordyce, pain reinforcers include attention from others, medications designed to relieve pain, avoidance from activities as a result of pain, disability compensation, and guilt and need for self-punishment. Consistent with the principles of operant conditioning, Fordyce's program aims to reinforce non-pain behaviors and to extinguish pain behaviors. As Holden notes, the $5,000 that patients pay for "dolorology" is often more than 10 times less than the medical bills that they accumulate, with no relief from pain to show for the expense. A major component of the Fordyce program is the removal of the contingent relationship between treatment and pain. In order to eliminate reinforcement for the pain, medications are administered on a fixed schedule, non-contingent on pain. In addition, medication intake is reduced gradually over the course of the several months of therapeutic treatment. All significant individuals who interact with the patient become involved in the treatment program, including nurses and family members. The Fordyce approach, and variations thereof, has been very successful in relieving the misery of chronic pain. Holden describes the Fordyce program in detail as well as other noninvasive approaches, including the use of hypnosis. In addition, she integrates the therapeutic approaches to pain with gate control theory of sensation and reviews evidence suggesting that the central nervous system plays a more important role in pain perception than previously thought.

Reducing fear of the dentist. The following demonstation helps students integrate material from earlier discussions on observational learning with the discussion of therapy in Chapter 15. Students should divide into small groups and be given the following information:

Modeling Therapy 549-551

> A 3-year-old girl, Penny, has visited the dentist several times with her parents for their dental appointments. The unusual appearance of the dental equipment and her recognition of her parents' fears ("I sure hope they don't drill today!") has led her to become worried about her first dental examination. What approach would you recommend to reduce her fear and help her cope with this experience in a positive manner?

Students can discuss which of the approaches discussed in the text (psychoanalytic, humanistic, behavioral, community, biological) best explains this particular case. Once the group choses a particular approach, they can decide on a course of treatment. For example, if the group decides to adopt a behavioral approach, they may wish to use a systematic desensitization, a treatment based on positive reinforcement, a treatment based on observational learning, or some combination of methods. After each group selects a treatment plan they can report their results to the class. The instructor can then read the following example based on a case from a 1970 study by Richard Adelson and Marvin Goldfried (cited by Schaefer and Millman, 1977):

> "Amy (4 years) and Penny (three-and-a-half-years) were scheduled for office visits. Amy was outgoing and had had a prior pleasant dental experience. Penny was shy, withdrawn, and worried about her first dental examination. She was invited to sit in the back of the room and watch Amy's examination (mouth mirror and explorer, visual examination, radiographs, and soft tissue examination). As expected, Amy was cheerful and cooperative throughout. Since she had been so cooperative, she was allowed to select a special prize from a small treasure chest. Amy stood on the chair and jumped loudly to the floor with both feet.
>
> After Amy left, Penny was examined. Although reticent, she willingly cooperated. Before receiving her reward, she jumped to the floor exactly as her "model" had. Six months later, Penny very cooperatively received polishing and fluoride treatments, and got down from the chair in the

same manner. The authors interpret that Penny was aroused (worried and apprehensive), the model had high status (somewhat older, gregarious, and sociable), and the model's behavior resulted in positive consequences (a reward)" (Schaefer & Millman, 1977, pp. 110-111).

Rational-Emotive Therapy 542-543

Irrational behavior and RET. The text explains that, according to Rational-Emotive Therapy (RET), people operate under fallacies that lead them to behave irrationally The following demonstration illustrates this theory and the methods suggested by Ellis (1973) to reduce irrational beliefs. RET clients often are taught to complete homework reports to help deal with their problems. Students can be asked to complete a report about their own behavior using the RET homework approach (Ellis, 1973, page 195). The following information should be included:

1) The event that led you to be upset
2) A rational belief based on the event
3) An irrational belief based on the event
4) What were the consequences of the irrational beliefs concerning this event.

These sample answers will help students in this exercise:

1) I sent in applications for graduate school.
2) It would be very disappointing if I didn't get accepted.
3) If I don't get accepted I'm a total failure.
4) I became very anxious and got a headache.

During the next class those students who would like to share their experiences can do so. The instructor can explain how an RET therapist would challenge the irrational beliefs of the client in order to help the client develop appropriate reactions to life events.

AUDIOVISUAL AIDES

Films

Rational Emotive Therapy. Research Press, 30 minutes, 16 mm or videocassette, color. Rational emotive therapy as explained by its developer, Albert Ellis. The film shows Ellis and his colleagues using RET with clients and students and involves such problems as guilt, social anxiety, and jealousy.

Harry: Behavioral Treatment of Self-Abuse. Research Press, 38 minutes, 16 mm, color (with some b/w), leader's guide. An extraordinary view of therapy in action. Life filming of a behavior modification treatment program applied by Richard Foxx to Harry, a 24-year-old , mildly retarded, self-abusive individual.

Peer-Conducted Behavior Modification. Research Press, 16 mm or videocasettes, 24 minutes, color. Paul Clement discusses the role of peers in shaping deviant behavior as well as the value of peers as positive modifiers in a therapy program.

Primal Therapy: On Search of the Real You. Document Associates Inc., 19 minutes, color. Discussion with Arthur Janov and an examination of his claim that primal therapy is the first therapy to deal with the neurotic patient as a whole.

Psychotherapy. CRM/McGraw-Hill, Inc., 26 minutes, color. An overview of the process of psychotherapy and aspects common to all therapies are reviewed. Three case vignettes illustrate how stages of the therapeutic process are dealt with in therapeutic encounters.

Audio Cassettes (APA Master Lectures)

Miller, Neal E. Fact and fancy about biofeedback and its clinical implications. APA Tape 10-14, 1974. A pioneer in the field of biofeedback research reviews his research as well as that of others which deals with monitoring of visceral activity and provides individuals with information about these functions. Miller considers the possibility that people can learn to control visceral functions by using information provided through biofeedback.

Jacobson, E., & McGuigan, F. J. Principles and practice of progressive relaxation: A teaching primer. Tape 1: Progressive relaxation: Origins and critical concepts. 1 of 4 tapes. BMA Audio Cassettes.

Hoffman, Lynn. Therapeutic Paradox: "Restraint from Change". Techniques in family therapy. 1 cassette (51 min.). BMA Audio Cassettes.

Emery, Gary. Controlling depression through cognitive therapy: Self-management guide and clinical procedure. 3 cassettes (139 min.) and workbooks. BMA Audio Cassettes.

REFERENCES AND ANNOTATED SOURCES

Ellis, A. (1973). *Humanistic psychotherapy: The rational-emotive approach.* New York: Julian Press.

Ellis, A. (1973). Rational-Emotive Therapy. In R. Corsini (Ed.), *Current psychotherapies.* Itasca, IL: F. E. Peacock Publishers.

Eysenck, H. J. (1952). The effects of psychotherapy: An evaluation. *Journal of Consulting Psychology, 16,* 319-324. Concludes that psychology has not provided evidence to support the conclusion that psychotherapy works!

Gomes-Schwartz, B., Hadley, S. W., & Strupp, H. H. (1978). Individual psychotherapy and behavior therapy. In M. R. Rosenzweig & L. W. Porter (Eds.), *Annual Review of Psychology* (Vol. 29). Palo Alto, CA: Annual Reviews, Inc. These authors conclude that psychotherapy does work and they examine the variety of factors that may influence psychotherapeutic outcome.

Holden, C. (1977, April). *Psychology: A Quarterly Journal of Human Behavior.*

Kazdin, A. E. (1975). *Behavior modification.* Homewood, IL: Learning Systems Company. Reviews behavior modification techniques including contingency contracting, extinction, punishment, systematic desensitization, aversion therapy, covert conditioning, self-control, and ethical issues related to behaivoral control.

Rogers, C. (1951). *Client-centered therapy.* Boston: Houghton. Contains lots of examples of therapist-client interaction for use in class.

Schaefer, C. E., & Millman, H. L. (1977). *Therapies for children: A handbook of effective treatments for problem behaviors.* San Francisco: Jossey-Bass.

Smith, M. L., Glass, G. V., & Miller, R. L. (1980). *The benefits of psychotherapy.* Baltimore, MD: Johns Hopkins University Press. Argue that psychotherapy works as indicated by a meta-analysis of published studies.

Strauss, J. S. (1979). Social and cultural influences on psychopathology. In M. R. Rosenzweig & L. W. Porter (Eds.), *Annual review of psychology* (Vol. 30). Palo Alto, CA: Annual Reviews Inc. Reviews social and cultural influences on psychopathology including research on the effects of social class, labeling, family events, and life events.

Chapter 16

SOCIAL PSYCHOLOGY

CHAPTER OVERVIEW

The authors use cultism as an opening ploy to pose questions about the effect that others have on the behavior of the individual. The first section of the chapter reviews the topic of person perception. Impressions we form about others influence cultural stereotypes, which under can become self-fulfilling. Asch's famous study on impression formation illustrates his change-of-meaning hypothesis, which attempts to account for the effects of order of presented information on impression formation.

Attribution theory concerns our perceptions of why others behave as they do. Kelly's recent elaboration of Heider's "naive psychology," which emphasizes the consensus, distinctiveness, and consistency of information in attributing causality to behavior. Category-based expectancies and target-based expectancies also influence our judgments of others. Such factors as object salience and overemphasizing the actor's role while underemphasizing the environmental causes often result in the "fundamental attribution error."

Social psychologists devote much time to the study of interpersonal attraction. The authors review this research first by examining variables that influence liking (physical attractiveness, similarity, gain and loss of self-esteem), and then exploring the dynamics underlying romantic love.

Then the text deals with persuasion and attitude change, highlighting three aspects of persuasion: source of a message, characteristics of a message, and characteristics of the person to whom a message is directed. Festinger's theory of cognitive dissonance provides an analysis of an example of cultism. *The Research Process* explicates field research in the context of cognitive dissonance theory. Self-attribution theory is an alternative to cognitive dissonance theory. Cognitive dissonance argues that attitudes change behavior, whereas self-attribution theory argues that behavior changes attitudes. The authors consider evidence for each theory.

The next section of the chapter examines the topic of social influence, including conformity behavior, compliance, and obediance. Milgram's famous studies of obedience serve as background for considering the ethics of research. *Controversy* further highlights the issue of deception in psychological research.

The chapter closes with the topic of social loafing, which refers to the fact that people work less hard in groups than when alone. *Applying Psychology* reviews research about social loafing and suggests that social loafing can be "cured" by monitoring the work of each individual member of the group.

LEARNING OBJECTIVES

016-1. Define social psychology.

016-2. Describe the influence of stereotypes, physical features, verbal descriptions, and order of information on impression formation. Distinguish between the change-of-meaning hypotheses and the weighted-averaging model.

016-3. Define attribution theory and distinguish between dispositional and situational causes. Identify three basic biases in the attribution process.

016-4. Identify three factors that help determine interpersonal attraction. Describe how romantic love is measured. Describe the Walster-Berscheid theory of love.

016-5. Show how persuasion or attitude change is affected by the source of the persuasive message, the characteristics of the message, and the characteristics of the audience.

016-6. Define cognitive dissonance theory and describe the Festinger and Carlsmith experiment.

016-7. Define self-perception theory and describe how it can account for Festinger and Carlsmith's results. Identify the relationship between attitudes and behavior, and between self-knowledge and behavior.

016-8. Distinguish between conformity and compliance. Describe research which demonstrates these types of social influence.

016-9. Define obedience. Describe the procedure and results of Milgram's experiments.

016-10. Define social loafing and describe attempts to minimize its effects.

ATTENTION GETTERS

Impression Formation 573-577

What role do cultural stereotypes play in impression formation. How could a stereotype become self-fulfilling. Give an example of how a stereotype can lead people to label identical behaviors in a different manner.

Interpersonal Attraction 581-587

Explain the gain/loss theory of interpersonal attraction. Why would someone who gradually comes to like us, be liked more than someone who has consistently liked us?

Persuasion 587-590

What characteristics of the source influence whether or not one is persuaded by an advertising message? What characteristics of the communication itself affect persuasion? How would the audience for the message play a role in attitude change?

Compliance 599-600

A friend asks you for advice in getting people to allow him to put up political signs in their yards. How can you use the research on compliance to help him devise a strategy that will lead to cooperation?

LECTURE SUGGESTIONS AND CLASS DEMONSTRATIONS

Person Perception and Attribution 573-580

Attribution theory. Amabile and Hastorf (1976) provide an account of the Patricia Hearst kidnapping that can be an interesting attention getter to introduce attribution theory. Their account illustrates the tendency to determine the cause of behavior even when little information is known. Among the reasons given for the kidnapping were the following: (1) actually Patricia had been murdered and was being impersonated; (2) She had joined the Symbionese Liberation Army before her abduction; (3) She was pretending to be an SLA member until she had a chance to escape; (4) She had been brainwashed and now was a willing participant in all SLA activities. This example can be used to explain the concepts presented in the text. Which explanations reflect dispositional causes? Which reflect situational causes? How does the discounting principle apply to this example? Which explanation illustrates the fundamental attributional error? If students are having problems answering the questions, a review of Kelly's attribution theory of causality will be helpful. Transparency 16-1 contains a summary of 16-1 in the text and shows attributions made to actor, entity, circumstance, and distinctiveness. After explaining Kelly's analysis ask students to once again examine the Amabile and Hastorf account of the Patricia Hearst case.

Romantic Love 584-587

Love and/or Marriage? The topic of romantic love is one of considerable interest to most college students. The following demonstration involves the effects of parental interference on a couple's relationship. Students should divide into small groups of 4 or 5 members. Each group must form an hypothesis concerning the relationship between parental interference and romantic love. They should be encouraged to base their hypothesis on previous readings from the text, personal experiences, etc. Each group should describe the source used in reaching their hypothesis. Sample hypotheses might be:

> H_1: If the parents interfere, then a couple's feelings of romantic love grow stronger.
>
> Source: In Shakespeare's play *Romeo and Juliet,* the feuding between the Capulet's and the Montague's led Romeo and Juliet to become even closer to one another. Other sources in literature also show this type of relationship. Based on this cultural folklore our group decided that this hypothesis may be accurate.
>
> H_2: If the parents interfere then the couple's feelings of romantic love will grow weaker.
>
> Source: In Chapter 6 of the textbook, the authors discussed the effects of conditioning and learning on behavior. Since the couples's relationship is not being reinforced by the parents and in fact, may be punished (e.g., loss of positive

interactions with the parents, constant lecturing about negative aspects of the relationship), it is likely that the feelings of love may be extinguished.

H_3: Parental interference is not related to a couple's feelings of romantic love.

Source: In Chapter 8, Levinson's stages of the life course lists early adulthood as occurring from ages 17 to 45. During this time the children will probably be separating from their family of origin and focusing on the tasks of adulthood: finding a mate, finding a job, etc. Therefore the attitudes of the parents may not affect the adult children to any great extent. Instead, the peer group may have more impact.

After each group reports to the class their hypotheses and reasoning, the instructor can describe a study designed to test these hypotheses. Driscoll, Davis, and Lipetz (1972) assessed the perceived parental interference and the romantic and conjugal love in the relationships of 49 unmarried and 91 married couples. They found a positive correlation between romantic love and parental opposition to the relationship in a cross-sectional analysis. In a follow-up assessment it was found that changes in parental interference were related to changes in romantic love for the dating couples. They named this phenomenon "The Romeo and Juliet Effect."

The researchers also make a distinction between conjugal love and romantic love. Parental interference did not lead to an increase in characteristics one might expect to be a part of conjugal love. In fact, couples reporting greater parental interference also report less trust, more criticalness, and more negative interpersonal behaviors when describing the partner. Driscoll et al. conclude that "The association between parental interference and lowered conjugal relationship factors suggests that, if such interference continues without resolution, it is likely to undermine the overall quality of the relationship" (page 9).

Persuasive Messages 587-590

Sir Eccles vs. Mr. Olsen: How credible is the source? In describing how certain characteristics of persuasive messages influence attitude change the authors discuss source credibility. This can be illustrated by demonstrating an abbreviated version of Bochner and Insko's (1966) experiment. In their study, students read an essay arguing that people should actually sleep less than most people believe. The source of the essay was either highly credible ("Sir John Eccles, Nobel Prize winning physiologist") or moderately credible ("Mr. Harry J. Olsen, director of the Fort Worth YMCA"). A shortened version of the essay can be adapted from the experimental booklets (ask for document #9049) which are available from:

American Documentation Institute
Auxiliary Publications Project
Photoduplication Service
Library of Congress
Washington, D.C. 20540

At the beginning of class the instructor can announce that the science department asked if psychology classes could serve as a normative population in the development of information packs for non-science majors. All those willing to evaluate the material would then be given an essay advocating either 6, 4, 2, or 0 hours of sleep per night with evaluation questions at the end of the essay assessing the ease of reading, reactions of the author, and the number of hours of sleep per night advocated by the student. Collect the student responses and tabulate a mean source for the various hours of sleep. During the next session compare the results to those found in the actual experiment (a linear curve was found for belief change in the high-credibility condition and a curvilinear relationship for the moderate-credibility condition). Ask students to consider what implications these results have for various speakers. If a speaker recognizes that she or he is a highly credible source, the speaker may be able to use an extreme message to produce the greatest amount of attitude change. A less credible source would have to temper his or her message to remain effective.

Even if the source was highly credible, would a message be obeyed if it ran contrary to the individual's usual ethical standard? Two studies suggest that the answer to this question may depend on context effects. Transparency 16-4 illustrates results of Asch's experiment which demonstrated that group size, situation ambiguity, and uniformity of group opinion influenced conformity behavior. Transparency 16-5 shows results of Milgram's classic study of obedience. Only when the situation included a confederate who defied the experimenter's order to continue an experiment which involved electric shock, did subjects show a marked increase in noncompliant behavior.

How might conformity and obedience have played a role in the Patricia Hearst case?

Cognitive Dissonance 590-593

Cognitive dissonance: Breaking a norm. Aronson (1980) reviews the role that Festinger's dissonance theory has played in social psychology. He notes that the work on persuasion conducted in the early 1950's focused on the external rewards that produce attitude change. One problem with research based on reinforcement theory was the fact that many of the effects were short-lived. Aronson explains how Festinger and Carlsmith's classic experiment led to a new approach to the study of persuasion. In the approach, longer lasting change is expected when the individual's self esteem is involved in the attitude change. Aronson also notes that dissonance research was instrumental in shifting many social psychologists to a cognitive approach. Cognitive dissonance theory asserts that people strive for consistency between their attitudes and their behavior. Transparency 16-3 illustrates this theory and provides a visual model for students as they consider the following class exercise.

Slawski (1981) suggests the following exercise in order to familiarize students with cognitive dissonance theory. Each student should break a norm (The instructor should emphasize that the students should be breaking an everyday norm, and not a law! Slawski recommends the types of behaviors as seen on "Candid Camera.") The student should analyze what ideas were dissonant during this incident and whether any changes in either behavior or ideas occurred as a result of the experience. If no changes occurred students should decide why they think no change occurred. Each student should decide whether they think future behaviors involving this norm will be influenced by the norm-breaking behavior. Students should be asked to write a brief report describing the norm that they violated, the reactions of those who witnessed the norm breaking behavior, and the answers to the questions mentioned above. During the next class session the instructor can use these reports to illustrate how cognitive dissonance theory applies to everyday situations. For example, the instructor can see if any reports reflect the findings discussed by the authors on page 16-38. Did more changes take place among the students who felt there was very little reward (e.g., "It was only a class assignment and not a major course requirement but I still did it.") than among those who felt there was more reward (e.g., "It was a class assignment and I thought this report might bring up my grade")? Did those whose norm violation was a public one report more change than those who broke a norm but did not have an audience? The class can discuss when cognitive dissonance theory provided a good explanation for their behaviors and attitudes.

AUDIOVISUAL AIDES

Films

When Will People Help? Harcourt Brace Jovanovich, Inc., 25 minutes, color. Daryl Bem uses bystander intervention as an example of the kind of problem with which social psychologists deal. Re-enactments of several important experiments illustrate how social psychologists test the hypotheses in both laboratory and field studies.

Invitation to Social Psychology. Harper and Row, 25 minutes, 16 mm, color. Introduction to social psychology by examining its subject matter, methods of investigation, and its findings. Topics include affiliation, attribution theory, cognitive dissonance, conformity, aggression, bystander intervention.

Social Psychology. CRM/McGraw-Hill, 33 minutes, color. Documentary footage of the first bussing of black children to previously all-white schools in the middle-class suburb of Westport, Connecticut. Basic social psychological concepts are introduced with discussion of the possible applications to the social problems presented in the documentary portion of the film.

Productivity and the Self-Fulfilling Prophecy: The Pygmalion Effect. CRM/McGraw-Hill, 28 min., color. The Pygmalion Effect is dramatized in an industry setting. A janitor is trained to be a computer operator.

Prejudice: Causes, consequences, Cures. CRM/McGraw-Hill, 24 min., color. Reviews research dealing with prejudice against women, national, and ethnic groups. Illustrates how stereotyping can be sustained by media, social distancing, and socialization.

Audio Cassettes

Robert Rosenthal. The Pygmalion Effect: What You Expect is What You Get. Psychology Today Cassettes, Jeffrey Norton Pub., Inc. How Teacher expectations affect student performance; new research in the role of nonverbal cues.

Stanley Milgram. Obedience to Authority. Psychology Today Cassette, Jeffrey Norton Pub., Inc. Milgram discusses his classic experiments on obedience to authority and uses his findings to explain why persons comply with orders that are against their own consciences.

Film Strips

Values in a Democracy Series. Guidance Associates, 5 sound filmstrips, each segment 2 filmstrips, cassettes, guide and ditto masters. Consultants Edwin Fenton and Lawrence Kohlberg helped organize five sound filmstrips that review Kohlberg's stages of moral reasoning and present dilemmas which can be used to facilitate class discussion.

Masculinity and Femininity. Guidance Associates, 2 filmstrips/cassettes, discussion guide. Designed to guide students in discussions of physical, social, and emotional aspects of sex role stereotypes.

Dare to be Different. Guidance Associates, 2 filmstrips/cassettes, discussion guide. Examines conformity pressures as well as types of nonconformity. Criteria for distinguishing between positive and negative reactions to group norms and social convention.

REFERENCES AND ANNOTATED SOURCES

Amabile, T., & Hastorf, A. H. (1976). Person perception. In B. Seidenberg and A. Snodowsky (Eds.), *Social psychology: An introduction.* New York: Free Press.

Aronson, E. (1980). *The social animal* (3rd Ed.) San Francisco: W. H. Freeman and Co.

Bem, D. J. (1970). *Beliefs, attitudes and human affairs.* Belmont, CA: Brooks/Cole. Contrasts prevailing view that attitudes cause behavior with his suggestion that behavior causes attitudes. His discussion of how an interrogator can induce belief in false confessions can be quite interesting to students.

Berscheid, E., & Walster, E. H. (1969). *Interpersonal attraction.* Reading, MA: Addison-Wesley Publishing Co. A thorough review of attributions about physical attractiveness including the classic study with college students and the "dating" party.

Bochner, S., & Insko, C. A. (1966). Communicator discrepancy, source credibility, and opinion change. *Journal of Personality and Social Psychology, 4,* 614-621.

Driscoll, R., Davis, K. E., & Lipetz, M. E. (1972). Parental interference and romantic love: The Romeo and Juliet effect. *Journal of Personality and Social Psychology, 24,* 1-10.

Slawski, C. J. (1981). *Social psychological theories: A comparative handbook for students.* Glenview, IL: Scott, Foresman & Co.

Chapter 17

SOCIAL PROBLEMS

CHAPTER OVERVIEW

The text first addresses three biological theories of aggression: Freud's psychoanalytic theory, Lorenz's innate drive theory, and Dollard and Miller's frustration aggression hypothesis. The authors point out that social learning influences the types of aggression acceptable to a society as well as the appropriate recipients of aggressive acts. Instrumental conditioning and observational learning play a role in prosocial behavior. Comparing the biological and learning theories of aggression, leads to the conclusion that the theories are complementary rather than oppositional.

Controversy poses the question, "What can society do to decrease aggression?" After describing catharsis and social learning attempts to answer the question, the authors suggest that there is little evidence to support the catharsis hypothesis.

The text switches to a discussion of prejudice, and stereotyping. Conditioning, observational learning, and personality dynamics influence the development of prejudice. Social learning theory offers several ways to reduce prejudice. An historical sketch of the presumed inferiority of women introduces the topic of sexism, which, despite dramatic changes in men's and women's roles, continue to exist. The text discusses research suggesting that psychological androgyny may be a more effective sex role standard than are traditional masculine and feminine roles.

The text then discusses a more positive aspect of human behavior--altruism. Examples of altruistic behavior include acts of heroism and everyday acts performed by young children. Sociobiology and social learning theory provide contrastive explanation for the origins of altruism. *The Research Process* demonstrates the study of altruism in the context of the family unit.

The mass media is one source for observational learning of social norms, particularly with respect to the portrayal of antisocial behavior. Information obtained from four techniques (case studies, experimental laboratory studies, experimental field studies, correlational studies) illustrates how viewing antisocial activities leads to aggressive behavior. On the other hand, research shows how television can also have a positive effect on children through the portrayal of prosocial behavior. The authors examine how television depicts different occupations and ethnic groups. *Applying Psychology* reviews research which suggests that television can be an effective tool in reducing prejudice.

The final topic is environmental psychology, with emphasis on overcrowding and density. The relationship between density and altruism indicates less altruistic behavior as density increases. The authors present hypotheses to explain this finding. One hypothesis suggests that urban life has high levels of noise which acts as a stressor thereby reducing altruism.

LEARNING OBJECTIVES

017-1. Be familiar with three biological models of aggression: the Freudian, the innate-drive, and the frustration-aggression.

017-2. Describe the acquisition of aggressive behavior through instrumental conditioning and observational learning. Be familiar with Bandura's model for integrating biological and social learning factors in aggression.

017-3. Define prejudice and describe ways in which prejudices can be acquired.

017-4. Describe ways in which prejudices can be reduced. In particular, how might sexism be reduced?

017-5. Cite some everyday examples of altruism and briefly describe the sociobiological model for explaining altruism. Be familiar with evidence showing the effects of observational learning on altruism.

017-6. Be familiar with research into the effects of television on antisocial behavior.

017-7. Relate the concept of vicarious catharsis to television's influence.

017-8. Summarize research into the effects of television on prosocial behavior and prejudices.

017-9. Define environmental psychology. Summarize correlational research into the effects of crowding and density on behavior.

017-10. Outline current research into the effects of noise on behavior.

ATTENTION GETTERS

Aggression 612-620

Do you think it is better to get aggression "out of your system" by engaging in aggression activities or do you think that ventilating aggressive feelings only leads to more aggression? What evidence can you cite to support your position?

Prejudice 620-624

As a social learning theorist you have been asked to try to reduce the prejudice in a local grade school. What changes would you recommend to the school board in order to facilitate positive social interactions?

Sexism 623-624

What is meant by the term "psychological androgyny"? How has androgyny been measured? Do you feel that parents in the United States are encouraging androgyny in their children?

Media Influences 230-235

The authors point out that a 5-year-old child has spent more time watching television than a college student has spent in a classroom after four years at a university. How do you think television affects children? What evidence suggests that television violence leads to more aggressive behavior on the part of the viewer?

LECTURE SUGGESTIONS AND CLASS DEMONSTRATIONS

Aggression 612-620

Television and aggression. Transparency 17-1 integrates two major theories of aggression--biological and social learning. Using this transparency to open the lecture and reviewing evidence in support of each theory will provide a natural context for considering the relationship between televised violence and children's aggression. In a discussion of observational learning the authors show how a child may learn aggressive responses simply by watching others. Students may be particularly interested in investigating the aggressive content of television programs because this has received so much attention in the popular press. Students should divide into groups of four and each group should choose a children's show and an adult show to watch. Each member of the group should then watch these programs and record the number of aggressive acts, the type of aggression, characteristics of the aggressor, and characteristics of the target. When the class meets again the members of each group can compare their results. Did they agree on which acts were aggressive? On which points was there disagreement? Could they summarize the characteristics of the aggressor and the target of aggression? What differences occur in the manner in which aggression is portrayed on a children's show when compared to aggressive acts on an adult program? Each group can then report their findings to the class. The differences between groups can be used to stimulate a class discussion on the definition of aggression itself. An alternative demonstration would be to have students evaluate different video games in terms of aggressive content rather than television programs.

Sexism 623-624

"Equalitarian" relationships or subtle sexism? After many years in which the social conscience has been raised about the effects of prejudice and stereotyping, it is reasonable to ask if changes in attitudes have occurred. Transparency 17-2 presents evidence suggesting that significant change in racial prejudice occurred between 1940 and the early 70s. Since then, much less change has occurred. Transparency 17-3 shows the results of a survey in which men from nine countries were asked if it was reasonable for men to assume responsibility for dishwashing. The wide cultural variation in opinion suggests that sex role stereotyping means different things in different cultures.

Each of the following two class demonstrations can be used to stimulate discussion of sexism and ethnic stereotyping.

In their discussion of sexism the authors note that although there have been dramatic changes in men's and women's roles in our society, discrimination still persists. Many students may be involved in (or plan to be involved in!) "equalitarian" relationships. The following demonstration shows how subtle sexism can be and how it can exist even in "equalitarian" relationships. The instructor should read the following story:

> Both my wife and I earned Ph.D. degrees in our respective disciplines. I turned down a superior academic post in Oregon and accepted a slightly less desirable position in New York where my wife could obtain a part-time teaching job and do research at one of the several other colleges in the area. Although I would have preferred to live in a suburb, we purchased a home near my wife's college so that she could have an office at home where she would be when the children returned from school. Because my wife earns a good salary, she can easily afford to pay a maid to do her major household chores. My wife and I share all other tasks around the house equally. For example, she cooks the meals, but I do the laundry for her and help her with many of her other household tasks (Bem & Bem, 1970).

The class can then discuss this relationship in terms of whether the spouses hold equal positions or whether the traditional roles for men and women remain. Bem and Bem point out that if the relationship is an equal one the tone of the story should remain constant when the roles of the spouses are reversed:

> Both my husband and I earned Ph.D. degrees in our respective disciplines. I turned down a superior academic post in Oregon and accepted a slightly less desirable position in New York where my husband could obtain a part-time teaching job and do research at one of the several other colleges in the area. Although I would have preferred to live in a suburb, we purchased a home near my husband's college so that he could have an office at home where he would be when the children returned from school. Because my husband earns a good salary, he can easily afford to pay a maid to do his major household chores. My husband and I share all other tasks around the house equally. For example, he cooks the meals, but I do the laundry for him and help him with many of his other household tasks. (From: S. L. Bem and D. J. Bem, 1970. Case study of a nonconscious ideology: Training the woman to know her place. In D. J. Bem, *Beliefs, attitudes, and human affairs,* (pp. 97-98). Belmont, CA: Brooks/Cole Publishing Company. Copyright 1970 by Wadsworth Publishing Company, Inc. Reprinted by permission from Brooks/Cole Publishing Company.)

After hearing this version the students will probably be able to pick out the underlying assumption about women's roles that were present (but perhaps unrecognized) in the first story.

Prejudice
620-624

Stereotype and prejudice. The following activity serves as an attention getter for a lecture on stereotyping and prejudice. Give each student in the class a sheet of paper containing the following lists:

RANK	GROUPS	RESPONSES	CHARACTERISTICS
____	Americans	__________	artistic
			cruel
____	Chinese	__________	extremely nationalistic
			ignorant
____	English	__________	imitative
			impulsive
____	Germans	__________	industrious
			intelligent
____	Irish	__________	lazy
			loyal to family
____	Italians	__________	materialistic
			mercenary
____	Japanese	__________	musical
			pleasure-loving
____	Jews	__________	pugnacious
			quick-tempered
____	Negroes	__________	reserved
			scientifically-minded
____	Russians	__________	shrewd
			sly
____	Turks	__________	sportsman-like
			superstitious
			tradition-loving
			very religious

Ask students to rank the groups in order of preference. Next they are to match the characteristics with the groups by writing characteristics on the lines immediately following each group. More than one adjective can be used for a group and adjectives can be used more than once.

After students have finished, have them compare their own sheets with results from a study conducted in 1933 and one in 1951. (Note that Russians have been added to the current list.)

KATZ AND BRALY (1933)

Americans	industrious 48%, intelligent 47%
Chinese	superstitious 34%, sly 29%
English	sportsman-like 53%, intelligent 46%
Germans	scientifically-minded 48%, industrious 65%
Irish	pugnacious 45%, quick-tempered 39%
Italians	artistic 53%, impulsive 44%
Japanese	intelligent 45%, industrious 43%
Jews	shrewd 79%, mercenary 49%
Negroes	superstitious 84%, lazy 75%
Turks	cruel 47%, religious 26%

GILBERT (1951)

Americans	materialistic 37%, intelligent 32%
Chinese	loyal to family 35%, tradition-loving 26%
English	tradition-loving 42%, reserved 39%
Germans	scientifically-minded 62%, industrious 50%, nationalistic 50%
Irish	quick-tempered 35%, religious 30%
Italians	religious 33%, artistic 28%, pleasure-loving 28%
Japanese	imitative 24%, sly 21%
Jews	shrewd 47%, intelligent 37%
Negroes	superstitious 41%, musical 33%
Turks	cruel 12%, ignorant 7%, sly 7%

(Adapted by permission from Activity 59, "Stereotyping," from L. T. Benjamin, Jr. and K. D. Lowman, eds., *Activities Handbook for the Teaching of Psychology.* Copyright 1981 by the American Psychological Association. All rights reserved.)

After the demonstration, begin the lecture on stereotyping and prejudice. Be sure to examine current American society with respect to changes that are or are not occurring in stereotypes and prejudicial attitudes.

Environmental Psychology 635-640

Helpful behaviors and urban density. In order to demonstrate the relationship between urban density and helpful behaviors the students can replicate Latane and Darley's study. Each student should approach four strangers individually asking one of the following questions of each stranger:

(1) "Excuse me, I wonder if you could tell me what time it is?" (Time)
(2) "Excuse me, I wonder if you could tell me how to get to the nearest post office?" (Directions)
(3) "Excuse me, I wonder if you could give me change for a quarter?" (Change)
(4) "Excuse me, I wonder if you could tell me what your name is?" (Name)

When class meets the instructor can record the following on the board: separately for Time, Directions, Change and Name, record the number of people who helped the number of people who didn't help, and the total sample size.

After each student reports his/her findings and the table is completed the instructor can determine the percentage of people who helped. These can then be compared to the appropriate column in Table 17-4 in the text. Are the results similar to those found by Latane and Darley in 1970 and to those reported by Rushton in 1978? If not, the class can consider why. Could there be confounding due to the fact that class members may have asked the questions in different locations (e.g., some asked strangers in their small home town whereas others asked in a city.)? (For more information see: Latane, B., & Darley, M. J. (1970). *The unresponsive bystander: Why doesn't he help?* New York: Appleton-Century-Crofts; and Rushton, J. P. (1978). Urban density and sharing: Helping strangers in a Canadian city, suburb, and small town. *Psychological Reports, 43*, 987-990.)

AUDIOVISUAL AIDES

Films

The People of People's Temple. Film Incorporated, 24 minutes, color. A documentary which examines the attraction and abuses of Jim Jones' People's Temple.

Pleasure Drugs: The Great American High. Films Incorporated, 52 minutes, color. Cocaine, marijuana, barbituates, and alcohol as means to escape from boredom and stress. Edwin Neuman reports on the impact of the drug business on individuals, families, industry and the military. An NBC White Paper.

The Bronswik Affair. CRM/McGraw-Hill, 24 minutes, color. This film examines the power of advertising in a fantasy drawn about a television set with the hyprobic ability to incite people to buy whatever products are advertised.

Battered Spouses. Harper and Row Media, 28 minutes, color. The problem of battered wives has surfaced as a major social concern. This film presents the plight of the victim and the alternatives available to battered wives today. Battered Spouses stresses throughout, the need for more sensitive responses to these individuals.

We Were Just Too Young. MTI Teleprograms, Inc., 30 minutes, color. A documentary that questions the role of parenting in teenagers. The reality of two teens' life situation is contrasted with their expectations. Adolescent sexuality is considered in its broader context as well.

Kids for Sale: A Look at Commercial Television. Mass Media Ministries, 22 min., color. Comments by parents and children intermixed with exerpts from televisions shows and commercials are used to focus attention on problems in children's television.

Human Aggression. Harper and Row Media, 22 minutes, color. Does frustration lead to aggression? The spontaneous occurrences of aggression in real life are depicted and related to scientific principles and findings. Included is aggression as seen through the activities of an actual youth gang.

Audio Cassettes

Roger McIntire. Licensing Parents To Have Children. Psychology Today Cassettes, Jeffrey Norton Pub., Inc. McIntire argues that children should be insured competent parents. To qualify, prospective parents must pass a test.

Film Strips

Suicide: Causes and Prevention. Harper and Row Media, 2 filmstrips, audiocassettes and guide. Suicide is one of the leading causes of death among college students. Part 1 emphasizes causal factors and Part 2 focuses on prevention. Typical warning signs are noted.

Gramp: A man ages and dies. Harper and Row Media, filmstrip, audiocassette, and instructor's guide. Gramp's family cared for him at home through senility and his decision to hasten death by not eating or drinking. An emotionally stirring presentation.

Daddy Doesn't Live Here Anymore. Human Relations Media, 4-part program. Part I. The changing family. Part II. When parents divorce. Part III. One day at a time. Part IV. The step-parent family. Dramatizations based on actual case histories demonstrate the frustrations and satisfactions of learning to manage a family without the presence of a spouse.

Violence in the Family. Human Relations Media, 4-part program. A four-part sound filmstrip package that examines the causes, characteristics, and possible solutions to violence in the family. Separate programs on: Dynamics of Family Violence, Child Abuse and Neglect, Battered Wives, and Adolescent Abuse.

REFERENCES AND ANNOTATED SOURCES

Conway, F., & Siegelman, J. (1978). *Snapping: America's epidemic of sudden personality change.* New York: Harper & Row, Inc. Provides an affirmative answer to the possibility that religious cults use brainwashing to induce conversions in young adults (see Robbins & Anthony).

Freedman, S. L. (1975). *Crowding and behavior.* New York: Viking Press. Reviews human population concentrations since primitive times. Cited research suggests that crowding per se is less important than situational factors such as involuntary crowding and length of time in a crowded condition in influencing behavior.

Gilbert, G. M. (1951). Stereotype persistence and change among college students. *Journal of Abnormal and Social Psychology, 46,* 245-254.

Katz, D., & Braly, K. (1933). Racial stereotypes of one-hundred college students. *Journal of Abnormal and Social Psychology, 28,* 280-290.

Lesser, G. S. (1974). *Children and television.* New York: Random House. Reviews the history and effects of "Sesame Street" on children's behavior and contains much useful information for lecture development.

Nalley, R. (Ed.) (July, 1982). Sociobiology: A new view of human nature. *Science Digest.* A collection of ten brief essays written by individuals sympathetic to the sociobiology position.

Quadagno, J. S. (1979). Paradigms in evolutionary theory: The sociobiological model of natural selection. *American Sociological Review, 44,* 100-109. Offers a harsh critique of sociobiology and charges that it failed to remain consistent with Darwin's ideas of continual organismic change and adaptation in the context of an unpredictable environment.

Robbins, T., & Anthony, D. (May/June, 1978). New religions, families and brainwashing. *Society.* Argues against the possibility of brainwashing in cultism, referring instead to authoritarian control which they suggest characterizes groups ranging from the Boy Scouts to the Moonies (see Conway & Siegelman).

Appendix

AN INTRODUCTION TO STATISTICS

APPENDIX OVERVIEW

The problem of bystander intervention serves as an exemplar for illustration of a variety of statistical concepts and techniques. The text first discusses descriptive statistics including measures of central tendency (mean, median, mode), measures of dispersion (range, standard deviation) frequency distributions, and the normal curve. Next the text discusses correlation and prediction, emphasizing the meaning of the correlation coefficient, and the relationship between correlation and causation.

Inferential statistics is the next topic reviewed. The authors explain the difference between population and sample, pointing out how one structures an experiment to compare two or more sample means. Differences that are reliable are said to be statistically significant. The text explains the meaning of statistical testing, focusing on testing for rejection of the null hypothesis.

Then the text moves to a discussion of the use of statistics to create impressions and relates the misuse of statistics to sampling, graphic displaying of data, and use of statistics in advertising. The appendix closes with a brief discussion of probability theory.

LEARNING OBJECTIVES

1. Distinguish between descriptive and inferential statistics.

2. List and define three measures of central tendency. Tell which measures are preferred and why.

3. List and define two measures of dispersion and state which is preferred.

4. Describe the shape and important features of the normal curve.

5. Defend the statement that "Correlation does not imply causation," and give an example to illustrate the point.

6. Distinguish between a population of scores and a sample of scores.

7. Outline the logic of testing to see whether or not a difference between two samples of scores indicates that they come from different populations. Distinguish between the null hypothesis and the alternative hypothesis.

8. Describe cases in which statistics can be misused by using (a) small samples, (b) exaggerated graphs, and (c) inappropriate comparisons.

9. Outline the reasoning behind the gambler's fallacy and tell how the reasoning is faulty.

LECTURE SUGGESTIONS AND CLASS DEMONSTRATIONS

Of all topics in psychology, statistics is probably the one most likely to be excluded from the introductory course. Most introductory texts reflect the lack of enthusiasm that instructors have for teaching statistics and the lack of endearment with which students approach the topic. Yet, most introductory texts go to great pains to point out that psychology is a science with historical roots in physics, physiology, and biology. We believe that statistics can be presented in a positive and enjoyable way for students and instructors alike. It seems to make sense to have the lecture quite early in the course so that students are well prepared to understand the research findings summarized in subsequent chapters. Moreover, if students are taking only one course in psychology, a lecture on statistics can help to prepare them for interpreting the mass of information that appears daily in newspapers and popular magazines. So, why not give it a try. We think that the materials described in this section will give you new hope that statistics can be included in the lecture repertoire.

A number of computer software programs now are available for assisting in the instruction of statistics and we refer you to the section on computer-assisted-instruction for references to some of these. But whether one chooses to teach statistics with or without reference to issues of design, or whether or not one enlists the aide of a computer, we are convinced that with the help of Huff, Moore, and Isaac (see below) the lecture on statistics can be fun for student and instructor alike.

Statisticulating about the average. Huff's (1954) little book, *How to lie with statistics*, is full of amusing, instructive examples of the misuse of statistics. Especially good examples for a lecture on statistics can be found in the chapters, "The sample with the built in bias," "The well-chosen average," "Post hoc rides again," and "How to statisticulate." In the well chosen average, Huff shows how the mean, median, and mode can give three quite different impressions of the same data. The illustration on page 33 makes a nice overhead transparency for use as an attention-getter. Transparency A-1 can be used to show students how to calculate the mean, median, and standard deviation of two distributions. Even though both distributions have identical means and medians, their standard deviations differ considerably. Transparency A-2, which depicts a normal curve, can be shown to indicate that the distribution of scores within a normal distribution will be about the same regardless of the values for the means or standard deviations. An equally good example, and one often reported in the newspaper, concerns the average income of American families (pp. 104-105). Of course, you may want to update the figures a bit but it really isn't necessary to do so in order to make the point. Huff captures much of the nonsense involved with the use (misuse) of statistics, and we especially like the last two sentences of the book which are part of a longer quote from Mark Twain's *Life on the Mississippi:* "....There is something fascinating about science. One gets such wholesale returns of conjecture out of such a trifling investment of fact."

Using newspapers and/or other media sources, have students collect five articles in which some measure of central tendency is used to describe the "average." At least two of the articles should use the arithmetic mean and two the median. Have students discuss what the data in the article might have revealed if a different measure of central tendency had been used. To what extent do the articles seem to be statisticulating; that is, using statistics to present the strongest support possible for the author's point of view, or attempting to mask a problem by hiding it behind statistics. Transparency A-4 provides an example in which the same data are graphed in different ways. One graph suggests small increase while the other suggests considerably greater increases. How one chooses to scale one's data certainly will affect how others will tend to react to the data.

Sampling and source credibility. A modern day version of Huff can be found in Moore's (1979) paperback on statistics. This book begins with a discussion of sampling and population. Students most likely have heard of sampling via the Harris Poll, Gallup Poll, TV rating systems, and the like. However, they may not be aware that sampling is used in many ways other than rating television programs or to solicit opinions about political candidates.

Population and Sample 658-660

> For example, a radio station that plays a song owes the song's composer a royalty. The organization of composers (called ASCAP) collects these royalties for all its members by charging stations a license fee for the right to play members' songs. But how should this income be distributed among the 20,000 members of ASCAP? By sampling: ASCAP tapes about 60,000 hours of local radio programs across the country each year. The tapes are shipped to New York, where ASCAP employs monitors...to record how often each song was played. This sample count is used to split royalty income among composers, depending on how often their music was played. Sampling is a pervasive, though usually hidden, aspect of modern life (Moore, 1979, p. 5).

Students often place blind faith in data because after all, the data are reported by an individual who is a qualified researcher or teacher. How often students will see the phrase, "According to....," when reading their texts or when listening to lectures. Indeed, knowing the source of the data aides its credibility. But is it enough to know the source of the data. Moore shares the following anecdote which suggests that we should be cautious about data even when the source is known!

> A government energy expert of my acquaintance tells of a booklet on U.S. energy supply written in 1975 for a Federal agency by another energy expert. The booklet contains a graph showing U.S. oil production (which has been declining since 1970) increasing for the rest of the century. The author of the book, my acquaintance says, refers to it in conversation as "the funny book." But he wrote it, because his bosses wanted it that way. Reaching a clear conclusion in an area where extrapolation is necessary and political and economic special interests are strong is extraordinarily difficult. Unfortunately, crucial issues such as future energy supply fall in this category! (Moore, 1979, p. 114).

Each chapter of Moore's book is sprinkled liberally with illustrations and each ends with many exercises that can be adapted for use in class either as part of lecture material or as organizers for class discussion. Chapters 4 (tables, graphs, and distributions), 5 (descriptive statistics), and 6 (the consumer price index) seem especially appropriate for the introductory course and for amplifying topics covered in the appendix.

Research design and sources of error. Isaac (1971) prepared a handbook to meet the needs of individuals who want an overview or listing of the strengths and weaknesses of research design and statistics, and, in our opinion, he has succeeded well. He sampled a wide range of technical books and chapters and compressed information into detailed, step-by-step outlines covering nearly every conceivable aspect of research design and use of statistics. The section on "Common errors made by graduate students" is worth the price of the book alone and certainly has applications beyond the beleaguered graduate student. We have found the book to be an exceptional aide for teaching the undergraduate and for refreshing our own knowledge in matters of research. The handbook contains good illustrations of simple and grouped frequency distributions and the bar graph, frequency polygon, and cumulative frequency curve. Examples of percentile equivalents can be easily adapted for class use as can examples for computing means and standard deviations for ungrouped or grouped data. A summary table on hypothesis testing and statistical significance, definitions of Type I and Type II errors, and other outlines provide for easy assimilation of this material into the formal lecture. In addition, there are superb summaries of descriptive research, developmental research, case and field study, causal-comparative research, and true- and quasi-experimental designs.

If you are inclined to include research design and methodology in your lectures on statistics, Isaac's summary of sources of error in research should be especially relevant. Nine sources of error are listed and defined and we include them here in much abridged form.

Halo effect: tendency for an irrelevant feature of a unit of study to influence the relevant feature in a positive or negative direction.

Rating errors: rating individuals in general, too favorably, too negatively, or too much in the middle.

Hawthorne effect: increasing worker productivity by changing working conditions regardless of the quality of changes (within limits).

Experimenter bias: the subtle, subjective influence that the experimenter has on all facets of his research.

Placebo effect: when a neutral stimulus or stimulus event used in experimental conditions does not occur in control conditions, thereby compromising the effects attributable to the treatment variable.

Post-hoc error: attributing cause merely because one event follows another event when a causal relationship does not really exist.

Error of misplaced precision: carefully collecting data in a study that is poorly designed from the outset.

"Typical" case studies: usually biased and representative examples selected to fit the "experimenters" bias, rather than a truly randomly selected case.

Law of the instrument: Over-extending the use of an instrument or procedure to problems for which other procedures should have been developed.

(For additional information see Isaac, 1977, pp. 58-59.)

REFERENCES AND ANNOTATED SOURCES

Huff, D. (1954). *How to lie with statistics.* New York: W. W. Norton.

Isaac, S. (1971). *Handbook in research and evaluation.* San Diego, CA: Edits Publishers.

Moore, D. S. (1979). *Statistics: Concepts and controversies.* San Francisco: W. H. Freeman.

COMPUTER ASSISTED INSTRUCTION

Technological innovations rarely have universal appeal when they first appear on the market. However, over time, the innovative often becomes the commonplace and the expected. It would be unusual today for instructors to plan an introductory course without including the use of films, slides, or overhead transparancies to supplement their lecture material. On the other hand, few instructors today make liberal use of such instructional aides as audio-visual modules, optical videodisc systems, or computers (King, 1982). Of all technological innovations in education, perhaps none to date has generated as much debate as that involving micro-computers. Although one can find computers in research laboratories, offices, and homes, they have not yet been used extensively in classroom instruction. However, what now seems innovative may be commonplace by the end of the 1980's. As computer prices fall they become more of a cost-effective tool for classroom use. Moreover, more and more elementary and high school students are learning to use the computer and will enter college with a degree of sophistication unknown to past generations. As computer prices fall there is additional impetus for the development of software.

In this section we provide a listing of software programs currently on the market. We have tried to include as comprehensive a listing as possible, but surely we have missed many programs that are not yet widely advertised. Moreover, we are certain that our listing will be obsolete the moment it is published because the field is changing that fast. When making a decision as to whether you will use computer-assisted instruction in your course you may wish to consider Seltzer's (1971) instruction-related criteria for assessing whether or not to bring your course into the computer age.

- If the computer poses a unique solution to an important problem in the instructional process, then it should be used regardless of the cost involved.
- If the computer is more efficient or effective and the cost of its use to instruct is minimal, then it should be used.
- If the cost of development and use of the computer in instruction is relatively high with the relative efficiency or effectiveness only marginal, then the computer should not be used in the instructional process. (Seltzer, 1971, p. 375).

SOFTWARE PROGRAMS

Experiments in Human Physiology (Robert F. Tinker). Human Relations Media. Requires 48K RAM with DOS 3.3. Ten experiments: heartrate measurement, reaction-time measurement, calibration, temperature measurement, homeostasis, reaction-time investigations, physiology of exercise, physiology of stress, physiology of sleep, applications to psychology. Students record physical reactions in real time. Printed documentation.

The Neuro-psych System (Alan Friedlund and Dean Delis). Life Science Associates. Computer battery of neuropsychological tests and procedures. A combination of customized hardward and software. Neuropsychological tests include: test of verbal learning, map orientation test, map-memory test, Benton Visual Retention Test, Rey-Osterriech Complex Figure Test, letter cancellation test, visual tracking task, continuous performance test, Halstead-Reitan Finger-tapping Test, Halstead-Reitan Trail Making Test, Wisconsin Card-Sorting Test, speech structure analyzer, speech prosody analyzer, vocabulary, similarities, proverbs and arithmetic. Custom hardware. Software and documentation.

Computer Programs for Experimental Psychology (Thomas B. Perera). Life Science Associates. All programs supplied with cassette, instructions, and listing. Programs include: Reaction Time, Quantification of the Muller-Lyer Figure, Quantification of the Horizontal-Vertical Illusion, Quantification of the Poggendorf Illusion, Quantification of Size of Line Length Judgments, Concept Formation, Verbal Learning, Multiple Field Tachistoscope, Visual Illusion Demonstrations, Psychophysical Scaling of Line Length using Category Scaling or Magnitude Scaling, Visual Acuity, Operant Conditioning, Latency Analyzer and Histogram Plotter, Interresponse Time Analyzer and Plotter, Event Recorder, Cumulative Recorder, Human Maze Learning, Signal Detection, Pursuit Rotor, Mirror Tracing.

Classical Conditioning Simulation (James O. Benedict). Life Science Associates. Simulates development of fear to an auditory stimulus.

Computer Simulations in Biology (Christopher Kennett). Life Science Associates. Simulation of mitosis, meiosis, Chi square analysis of fruit fly data, respiration.

Hemispheric Information Processing (Joseph G. Dlhopolsky). Life Science Associates. A variety of programs for presentation of stimuli randomly to left and right visual fields. Recall or recognition as dependent variables; stimulus exposure and response latency are timed with millisecond accuracy.

Extra-sensory Perception (Joseph G. Dlhopolsky). Life Science Associates. Experiments in precognition, clairvoyance, or telepathy. Raw data tables, descriptive statistics, and single-subject tests of significance.

Learning Set and Generate (Jesse E. Purdy & Harold Eidson). Life Science Associates. Two programs. Simulations of Harlow's learning set phenomenon. Two-choice discrimination problems.

Laboratory in Cognition and Perception (C. Michael Levy, Ira S. Fischler, Richard A. Griggs). CONDUIT. Experiments emphasizing human information processing. Experiments include: Method of Constant Stimuli, Signal Detection, Span of Apprehension, Iconic Memory, Feature Detection, Pattern Interpretation, Retrieval from STM, Short-Term Forgetting, Comparing Visual and Semantic Information, Concept Learning, Reasoning from Prose.

Laboratory in Memory and Cognition (Janice M. Keenan, Robert A. Keller). CONDUIT. Instructor manual, student manual, and ten programs grouped into five topic areas. Topic areas are: Levels of processing, Encoding specificity, Semantic memory, Sentence-picture verification, and Constructive processes in prose comprehension. A good complement to the Laboratory in Cognition and Perception.

Cognitive Psychology (William Bewley, COMPress, Inc., Wentworth, NH). CONDUIT. Programs for use in courses emphasizing cognitive processes. Topics include: cognitive processes, pattern recognition, concept learning, memory. Student manual, instructor manual, BASIC.

Imprinting (D. W. Rajeck, CONDUIT). Designed to allow students to test theories of imprinting and research techniques used to study imprinting primarily in precocial birds. Student and instructor's guides. FORTRAN.

Schizophrenia (David Malin, CONDUIT). Provides students with opportunity to test theories of schizophrenia through application of research designs. Correlational statistics, Pearson chi-square, and log linear models. FORTRAN.

Changing Attitudes Toward Integration (G. R. Boynton) CONDUIT. A data set composed of variables from national opinion surveys of 1946, 1966, 1972. In addition to described applications, could be used to discuss cohort effects in developmental research. Software for use with SPSS and other statistical packages.

Programs for Instruction in Statistics (Michael Levy, William J. Froming, Marcia Belcher). Tutorials presenting instructions in statistical concepts. Computational programs and exploratory problems. Uses an approach comparable to VisiCalc. Student workbook.

A-Stat (Rosen Grandon Associates). Basic introductory level statistics (mean, median, standard deviation, variance, etc.), tables, correlation, multiple regression, ANOVA, Chronbach's Alpha, report writing, and many other features. Manual available.

ELF: Econometric Linear Forecasting (The Winchedon Group). ANOVA, correlation, discriminate analysis, factor analysis, probabilities of $\underline{t}$, F, chi square, descriptive statistics, stepwise multiple regression, data transformations using BASIC statements. Excellent user's guide.

Statistical Programs for the Apple II Microcomputer (Joseph E. Steinmetz). A variety of ANOVA programs, Pearson R, rho, t-test, Mann-Whitney U, analysis of covariance, descriptive statistics.

Cognitive Experimental Design and Testing System (Instructional Software). Set of over 60 interactive programs. Students can design, run, and analyze experiments with original designs. User selects stimulus presentation parameters, randomization procedures, and other aspects of design. Includes sample experiments: Muller-Lyer illusion, Precognition, Signal Detection and others. Instructor's guide, student guide.

Data Base Manager (Douglas Eamon). Menu-driven routines to allow entry and modification of data on disk files.

Statistical Techniques (Douglas Eamon). Microcomputer version of F. Rae's "Guide to Statistical Techniques in Psychology and Education." Links statistical analysis procedures to various designs and dependent measures.

Stand-alone Programs for Instruction in Psychology (Douglas Eamon). Programs designed to allow students to simulate experiments. Approach-avoidance conflicts, classical conditioning, attitude change, effect of hypothalamic lesions on eating, cortical localization of memory, concept formation, cognitive development, reaction time, operant conditioning and others.

COMPUTER SOFTWARE SOURCES

CONDUIT
P.O. Box 388
Iowa City, IA 52244

Human Relations Media
175 Tompkins Avenue
Pleasantville, NY 10570

Life Science Associates
One Fenimore Road
Bayport, NY 11705

Douglas B. Eamon
Department of Psychology
Albion College
Albion, MI 49224

Rosen Grandon Associates
7807 Whittier Street
Tampa, FL 33617

The Winchedon Group
3907 Lakota Road
P.O. Box 10114
Alexandria, VA 22310

Human Systems Dynamics
9249 Reseda Boulevard
Suite 107
Northridge, CA 91324

Dr. Joseph E. Steimmetz
College of Osteopathic
Medicine
Ohio University
Athens, OH 45701

Michael Levy
William J. Froming
Marcia Belcher
Department of Psychology
University of Florida
Gainesville, FL 32611

Instructional Software
420 Lombard Street
Albion, MI 49224

SELECTED REFERENCES

Bare, J. K. (1982). Microcomputers in the introductory laboratory. *Teaching of Psychology, 9,* 236-237.

Bassic, M. S., & Allen, J. P. (1976). TIPS: Individualization and economy for mass instruction. *Teaching Sociology, 3,* 185-190.

Benedict, J. O. (1979). CLASCON-SIM: A computer program to simulate experiments in classical conditioning. *Behavior Research Methods and Instrumentation, ll,* 603-604.

Butler, F. E. (1980). MicroSKED. *Behavior Research Methods and Instrumentation, 12,* 152-154.

Bray, R. M. (1981). Evaluation of the TIP computer management system in a social psychology course. *Teaching of Psychology, 8,* 139-142.

Castellan, N. J. (1980). The use of matrix manipulation programs in teaching statistical methods. *Behavior Research Methods and Instrumentation, 12,* 172-177.

Durett, H. J. (1980). Inexpensive plotters and digitizers for psychological research and instruction. *Behavior Research Methods and Instrumentation, 12,* 244-247.

Fischler, I. An on-line laboratory in cognition and perception. *Behavior Research Methods and Instrumentation, 12,* 116-119.

Keenan, J. M., & Keller, R. A. (1980). Teaching cognitive processes: Software for laboratory instruction in memory and cognition. *Behavior Research Methods and Instrumentation, 12,* 103-110.

Kelly, A. C. (1968). An experiment with TIPS: A computer-aided instructional system for undergraduate education. *American Economic Review, 58,* 446-457.

Levy, C. M. (1980). Getting an on-line departmental teaching laboratory on-line. *Behavior Research Methods and Instrumentation, 12,* 111-113.

Posner, M. I., & Osgood, G. W. (1980). Computers in the training of inquiry. *Behavior Research Methods and Instrumentation, 12,* 87-95.

Seltzer, R. A. (1971). Computer-assisted instruction--What it can and cannot do. *American Psychologist, 26,* 373-377.

White, K. D. (1980). An on-line laboratory in sensation and perception. *Behavior Research Methods and Instrumentation, 12*, 114-115.

PART II.

TEACHING THE INTRODUCTORY COURSE:
GENERAL INFORMATION AND RESOURCES

INSTRUCTIONAL METHODS

In this section we discuss four aspects of teaching: approaches to education, use of objectives, methods of instruction, and preparation for teaching. Each of these topics could justify chapter length discussion, therefore our presentation necessarily will be cursory. Nevertheless, we highlight important issues that should be considered prior to teaching the introductory course. MacLeod's (1971) questions for the beginning teacher of psychology serve as an organizational framework for this general discussion of instructional methods. When preparing for teaching there are certain questions the instructor must consider. "What is your purpose in teaching psychology? What kind of psychology are you teaching? To whom are you teaching it? How are you teaching it? How are you preparing yourself to teach it?" (MacLeod, 1971, p. 245). The answers to these questions will in large part determine how the instructor will organize his or her course. MacLeod originally posed these questions for the beginning teacher of psychology, but we believe that they have value for teachers at every level of experience. Moreover, we will consider the questions in the context of introductory psychology.

APPROACHES TO EDUCATION

MacLeod's first question is the most basic because it asks the teacher to consider why introductory psychology should be a part of the psychology curriculum. MacLeod casts his answer to the question in the mold of general education. He challenges psychology instructors to think of themselves first as members of the broad teaching community responsible for the general education of students, and second as a teacher of a specific discipline. This challenge may be easier to meet than one first imagines. Psychology has close ties with many biological and social sciences both historically and with respect to contemporary issues. Psychology itself is a diverse field and instructors of the introductory course must be prepared to lecture on such wide-ranging topics as nerve physiology, primate social behavior, and attribution theory. In fact, the introductory psychology teacher must be familiar with each of psychology's six orientations as identified by Mann (1982): Psychology as science, an applied field, a helping profession, a facilitator of self-development, as human wisdom, and as paradigm. These six orientations define the breadth of psychology and correspond to the reasons why students are attracted to psychology in the first place (Mann, 1982). Thus, a substantial case can be made for introductory psychology as a general education course.

Within the context of general education, then, MacLeod next asks instructors to consider what kind of psychology they are teaching. He suggests that instructors should emphasize problems that have historical significance, rather, we suppose, than highly specialized topics unique to a subfield of psychology or to current fads within the field. There are at least two aspects to the question of what kind of psychology to teach. One aspect concerns the topics selected for emphasis and the other aspect concerns one's approach to education.

Individual instructors will vary in what they consider to be the most important topics to emphasize in lecture or in class assignments. A developmental psychologist may give a developmental orientation to the introductory course, a physiological psychologist may emphasize the biological aspects of psychology, and a clinical psychology may give greater weight to applied topics than to basic research. Regardless of one's specialization within psychology, however, the teacher of introductory psychology must command a broad view of the discipline inasmuch as the introductory psychology course generally serves as a prerequisite for all subsequent courses in the psychology curriculum. Brown's (1980) survey of parents of students and students themselves enrolled in introductory psychology courses offers some interesting food for thought with respect to selection of topics. Respondents were asked to select 10 objectives from a list of 128 that they would like the introductory course to satisfy. Parents selected objectives related to biological psychology, learning and memory, personality, social psychology, and emotional behavior. In general, parents more than students expressed interest in achievement motivation, creativity, problem solving, and intelligence. In contrast, students more than parents were interested in topics of an experiential nature (sleep, dreaming, meditation), or topics involving human sexuality (stereotypes, sex differences, determinants of sexual arousal). Parents and students agreed that emphasis should be given to anxiety and punishment, but felt that relatively little time should be devoted to the history of psychology, sensory or perceptual processes, developmental psychology, psychotherapy, or comparative psychology. Combining parent and student "top 10" choices yields a sampling of topics that more than likely would correspond well with faculty opinion. While such surveys are informative in that they point out what nonpsychologists consider to be "relevant" topics, arguments have been made against using relevance as a criterion for determining course content.

In their analysis of trends in contemporary education, Furedy and Furedy (1982) propose that approaches to education can be placed along a continuum, the ends of which they label Socratic and Sophistic. Instruction at the Socratic end of the continuum emphasizes interest in subject matter, critical inquiry, objectivity, basic research, realism, and conflict. Instruction at the Sophistic end of the continuum emphasizes person orientation rather than subject-matter orientation, persuasion, subjectivity, applied research, and consensus. The Furedy's argue that contemporary psychology is dominated by the Sophistic approach, which incidentally, would embrace "relevance" as a criterion for topic selection. For example, a Sophistic textbook stresses the relevance of psychology to everyday life, is physically attractive, easy to read, and lax in scholarly referencing. In contrast, the Socratic text emphasizes the subject matter of psychology, its empirical findings, and theoretical controversies. Little concern is given to the text's physical appearance or to its reading level. Furedy and Furedy argue that the Sophistic influence on instruction and text writing also finds its way into the classroom in the form of student evaluation of professors.

Whereas one may be able to attribute improvements in the quality of classroom instruction to student evaluations of professors, the possibility exists that others may equate professional competence with student ratings, thereby ignoring other aspects of the professor's responsibilities such as those related to research or clinical supervision. Moreover, many forms used to evaluate professors give greater weight to the professor's enthusiasm, wit, and interest-in-student-learning than they do to the professor's knowledge of his or her subject matter, including its empirical findings, theoretical controversies, and methods of investigation.

Brown's survey data suggest that students will not respond well to courses that emphasize the bold facts of psychology. On the other hand, overemphasis on the relevance of psychology to everyday life fails to communicate the approaches and methods of psychology or its way of dealing with the historical problems of significance that MacLeod stresses. Thus it seems advisable for teachers to seek an approach to education that falls somewhere near the middle of the Socratic-Sophistic continuum.

According to Furedy and Furedy (1982) the proliferation of programs designed to teach faculty how to teach also can be attributed to the shift to the Sophistic approach to education. Although in many instances these programs may be, "....run by people who regard themselves as practicing a new profession rather than just helping faculty in a professional way" (Furedy & Furedy, 1982, p. 18). However, there also are many aspects of teacher training programs that have helped to improve the overall quality of instruction in colleges and universities including hints for writing learning objectives, preparing lectures, and assessing student performance.

LEARNING OBJECTIVES

MacLeod's third suggestion is that instructors consider who it is that they are teaching. Since the vast majority of students enrolled in the introductory psychology course will not major in psychology and may in fact never take another psychology course, MacLeod's suggestion that instruction should be oriented to the general student seems appropriate. Indeed, a frequent mistake made by many beginning instructors is that they set the level of their course instruction several steps higher than is appropriate for the background knowledge of the students enrolled in their class. One cannot deliver a graduate level lecture to college freshmen and expect much learning to take place. Thus, the instructor must determine precisely what information he or she hopes students will gain from the introductory level course. This, of course, is a question of course goals or objectives.

Goals and objectives are not the same. "A goal is a broad statement of the kind of performance, knowledge or attitude a student will eventually exhibit, in the long run, as a result of learning in school" (used with permission of Stephen Yelon). The goals for introductory psychology proposed by Walker and McKeachie (1967) are among the best that we have seen.

Goals for Introductory Psychology

1. Communicate elementary concepts
2. Communicate facts in support of concepts
3. Introduce the student to the full range of subject matter
4. Integrate course material
5. Communicate basic attitudes of the discipline
6. Communicate the intrinsic interest of the subject matter
7. Present the newest developments in the field
8. Provide individual guidance and monitoring
9. Develop selected intellectual skills
10. Provide a suitable identification model for the student

(Adapted from Walker, E. I. and McKeachie, W. J. 1967. *Some thoughts about teaching the beginning course in psychology.* Belmont, CA: Brooks/Cole.)

In contrast to these general goals, objectives are quite specific. "An objective is a description of the student's behavior at the end of a course. It contains the behavior he or she will exhibit, the conditions of testing and the standards for adequacy of performance. It may be cognitive, affective, or motoric. It may be simple or quite high level and complex" (Stephen L. Yelon, personal communication). The more detailed the course objectives the more likely it is that the teacher will have successfully integrated the teaching, learning, testing, and evaluation components of instruction. Objectives serve a number of useful functions: they indicate what it is that students must learn, they focus the teacher's preparation and selection of lecture topics, they guide the construction of test items, and provide a base for evaluation of the course by assessing how well students achieve the objectives. Stephen L. Yelon, a specialist in the area of learning and evaluation, summarizes the uses of objectives quite nicely:

Uses of Objectives

1. Objectives help decide if a student has learned.
2. Objectives help a teacher create test items.
3. Objectives are one of the ways a teacher can evaluate his or her course by seeing how many students in the course attain the objectives.
4. Objectives help a teacher select relevant concepts, principles, and skills to include in the course.
5. Objectives help a teacher select methods for presentation and materials to use.
6. Objectives help a teacher to communicate his or her intentions to the students.
7. Objectives help a teacher to communicate his or her intentions to colleagues, administrators, and community people.
8. Objectives help a teacher with curricula by cutting the trivia and overlap, filling the gaps, and guiding the pace of learning.
9. Objectives help organize complex teaching and training needs.
10. Objectives can help the teacher provide the evidence that he or she is working.

According to Yelon, a good objective relates logically to the performance goal, is appropriate for audience needs, is consistent with the department and/or one's personal philosophy, and specifies completely the conditions, behavior, criteria and lower limits of student performance. He recommends the following guidelines for deriving objectives:

1. Write general goal
   a) Derive from an analysis of subject matter
   b) Create out of philosophy
   c) Use data from needs assessment
   d) infer from present course materials
   e) infer from present text
2. Write performance requirements of a referent situation after the course (job, profession, next course, avocation, intellectual pursuit),
3. Write the closest testible simulation of the performance required in the referent situation as a course objective

(with permission of Stephen L. Yelon).

Thus, one of the instructor's goals in the introductory psychology course may be to have students understand something of the history of psychology. An objective related to this goal might be the following:

01-3 List and define the five historical schools or movements in the history of psychology. Your definitions should specify the subject matter, research goals, and research methods for each school (Student Study Guide, Chapter 1).

What functions does the objective serve? It informs the student that there are five historical schools in the history of psychology and that the instructor will expect the student to be able to define each school and to explain differences among the five schools with respect to three specific characteristics: subject matter, research goals, and research methods. The objective also reminds the instructor what it is that he or she expects students to learn, and therefore, dictates the type of test items to be used to measure learning. For example, to ask the student to trace the historical development of one of the schools, or to ask the student to link the historical schools to contemporary approaches in psychology would be inconsistent with the objective as stated above. On the other hand, the following test item would be consistent with the objective:

Which of the following schools of psychology showed the least interest in a person's psychological experience?

a. structuralism
b. Gestalt
c. behaviorism
d. psychoanalysis

(From Student Study Guide Self Test, Chapter 1)

Thus, learning objectives can help to balance the diversity of backgrounds students bring to the classroom, by providing specific guides for study. Writing objectives forces the instructor to directly consider what he or she expects students to learn. Once these decisions are made, student diversity becomes a less important issue because each student will be guided toward mastery by the same set of learning objectives. In a very real sense, this shifts the responsibility for performance outcome directly to the student, provided that the teacher has linked test items to learning objectives. Moreover, it is important to keep in mind that the benefits of learning objectives apply regardless of the particular instructional method used to present course material.

INSTRUCTIONAL METHODS

MacLeod's fourth question concerns selection of an instructional method for the course. He advises instructors to be flexible, to try various methods until one is found that matches the instructor's style, the teaching context, student characteristics, and subject requirements. In fact, two methods of instruction dominate college teaching: the lecture method and the contingency management method. In small classes, experiential methods can be used, although it is possible to blend components of experiential learning into each of the dominant methods through the use of classroom demonstrations and out-of-class projects. We first will consider the lecture method, then several contingency management methods, and with brief commentary on experiential methods.

Lecture method. The lecture method is the dominant instructional approach used in higher education today, just as it has been throughout the modern era of university education. Despite its popularity among instructors, the lecture method has received its fair share of abuse from students. For example, Charles Darwin, Samuel Johnson and Sir Richard Burton voiced little regard and much distain for lecturers at such distinguished universities as Oxford, Cambridge, and Edinburgh.

Studies comparing the lecture method with other instructional methods indicate that lectures are not more effective than alternative methods at stimulating thought or changing student attitudes, and are unpopular and inflexible (Howe, 1980). Why then, Howe asks, does the lecture method continue to dominate higher education? Howe (1980) suggests three reasons for the continued use of lecture to impart information to students. Lectures provide a social function by bringing together students who share a common purpose, provide a learning environment in which students are relatively free from distractions, and provide a ritual function in that lectures put learning on display. An additional reason for the continued use of the lecture, and perhaps a more important one, is that the lecture represents an efficient and cost-effective way to impart information to students. Obviously, this "justification" for the lecture method applies more to the large educational institution than to the small institution. For example, the task of teaching introductory psychology to 8,000 students per year, with individual classes enrolling 600 students, precludes selection of alternative methods for most instructors. Indeed, few large universities have the means to support the number of graduate teaching assistants required to conduct weekly discussion sections for the large introductory course, as was common practice in the 1960s. Thus, class size is a key constraint on one's choice of instructional method.

Silverstein (1982) offers one possible solution to the problem of large class size and the disadvantages of the lecture method. Silverstein teaches 1,200 students by combining two perspectives; the traditional lecture method for imparting skills and ideas, and the Feirean method which emphasizes the process of education and the avoidance of lecture. Silverstein's goals for the introductory course include improving students skills in reading, writing, and oral presentation. No curves are used to evaluate student performance and students are required to teach one another. Each student attends a formal one-hour lecture each week, and then participates in two one-hour long discussion sections of 15 to 20 students each. Each week students are given a reading assignment, a writing assignment, and an out-of-class project. This approach requires as many as 40 teaching assistants! Silverstein finds the cadre of assistants by recruiting advanced level undergraduate students. The student assistants are screened carefully. Once final selections are made, receive a training experience which prepares them for their role in the course. Frequent meetings with the instructor throughout the term assures quality control of the discussion sections. There is one aspect of this innovative variation of the lecture method that must be considered carefully before attempting to implement it. Specifically, this approach greatly increases the amount of time that the faculty member must invest in the introductory course. Although less time is spent on lectures, the time involved in monitoring teaching assistant performance and supervising all aspects of the testing, feedback, measurement, and evaluation components of the course may exceed the time one usually spends on lecture preparation.

There are ways, however, to enhance the effectiveness of the lecture without giving oneself over completely to the Sophistic side of the Socratic-Sophistic continuum. The starting point is to recognize that the lecture is an oral presentation that the teacher makes *to* the student: a one-way communication in which the teacher is the source of information and the student is the passive recipient of that information. Thus the instructor must find ways to impart information in a provocative and interesting fashion. One need experience no guilt in attempting to make lectures interesting!

Successful lectures require preparation! At minimum, one must prepare materials for new lectures or update old ones (reorganizing and integrating material where necessary), prepare lecture notes (strive for a happy medium between overly terse notes and full written lectures), rehearse the lecture (listening to a tape recording of one's lecture can be an invaluable and humbling experience), and write specific goals and objectives for the lecture (this will assist integration of material in the lecture). Table 9 provides a thorough outline of the steps involved in lecture preparation. Using the outline in Table 9 cannot guarantee a successful lecture, but it surely will move the instructor in the right direction. The beginning instructor must remember that the initial preparation for a course will require a great deal more time and effort than will subsequent preparations for the same course. However, taking the time to prepare good lectures initially will not only save time in the future but will more than likely produce a more rewarding learning experience for the students, and therefore a more enjoyable teaching experience for the instructor.

TABLE 9

Detailed Lecture Method Outline

	A. Preparatory Student Activity To increase the probability that students are prepared for class and that they will derive the greatest possible benefits, you can:
Study guides	1. pass out study guides which include self-evaluation questions, an outline of the lecture, difficult material;
Advanced reading and quiz	2. require readings related to the lecture before class with practice quizzes with some automatic feedback keyed to sources;
Glossary	3. provide a glossary of key items and concepts before class;
Recitation before	4. use recitation to prepare for lecture.
	B. Attention Getter To capture attention and provoke curiosity, grab attention with:
Case	1. an important case which will be solved with the new information;
Generalization	2. a strong generalization which contradicts common thought or brings up an issue;
Quote	3. a powerful quote;
Question	4. a series of questions which will be answered;
Puzzling action	5. a relevant action which is difficult to explain;
Recent event	6. ideas or actions students relate to, such as recent news item or a movie;
Puzzling demonstration	7. a demonstration which presents the theme or is difficult to explain;
Incongruous facts	8. a set of incongruous or paradoxical facts, a puzzle which will be understood with the information to come.

C. <u>Advanced Organizer</u>

To create a mental set, state what you will be talking about.

Goal

1. What the listener will be able to do outside of class based on his learning; the goal. (When considering the goals and objectives see if they are best suited for lecture.)

Why content

2. Why the knowledge is in the lecture--how information relates to student experiences, interests, values, beliefs, present or future activities

Objective

3. What the listener will be able to do with the knowledge gained by the end of class--the objective

Exam

4. What exam the material will be on and the form it will take

Recap

5. Recapitulate from previous lecture.

Outline

6. State (and possible hand out or write on board) an outline of all that you intend to say. State the major ideas in the broadest term.

Handouts

7. If the organization of your presentation is intricate, if there are very important lengthy quotes, diagrams, or tables which students must inspect closely, put these on handouts and give them to students at the beginning of class.

Key terms

8. Define and illustrate all key terms that you will be using even if students are supposed to know them already.

Progressive argument

9. Use a progressive argument occasionally; but provide a worthwhile conclusion and describe what you will be doing and label as you go.

D. <u>Information</u>

To communicate the information well, state each point clearly and for variation precede each point with a question.

<u>Content</u>

Point fits

1. Show where each point fits in your outline.

Limit content

2. Limit the content to be taught. Some say include about 7 chunks of information in about 35 minute lecture.

Essential ideas

3. Only include ideas and examples central to your major points.

Appropriate level of explanation

4. Explain each point at a level of difficulty appropriate to the group's background. Watch vocabulary and idioms.

State different ways to use handouts

5. If a point is particularly complex, state it in different ways using several examples and/or analogies. Handouts containing diagra-

matic or pictorial explanations of the point may also be especially helpful.

Follow with to know

6. Present all the ideas essential to your point before following up with content which is simply "nice to know."

Accurate illustration

7. State or show an example or demonstration which fits the attributes of your idea precisely.

Clever example

8. Choose the cleverest, most curious, most novel, most humorous, or most intellectual example.

Meaningful ideas

9. Relate ideas and examples to students' experience, future works, or interests. Refer to recent events, anecdotes, humorous events.

One example

10. Present at least one illustration for every idea.

Varied media for examples

11. Instead of only verbal examples, for increased attention, present some examples using varied media: film (an example of a skill well executed), a demonstration (a social psychological principle shown by duplicating Asch's experiment in class), slides (examples of various disease entities to be identified). (Collect examples which you can use even when you are not teaching; maintain a file of issues, cases, jokes, cartoons, in short, anything which will help you make your point in an interesting, precise, and memorable fashion.)

Restate point

12. Restate your point after each example.

<u>Presentation</u>

Use telegraphic notes

1. Unless you are quoting some authority, do not read your notes. Use telegraphic notes.

Vary stimulus

2. Vary the stimulus and mood, vary voice, volume, speed, the approach, the activity.

Speak audibly

3. Speak precisely and audibly.

Talk

4. Talk to students.

Eye contact

5. Maintain eye contact.

Provide cues

6. Cue attention.

Comfort

7. Provide for physical comfort.

Reduce distractions

8. Reduce distractions (objects, board, and mannerisms).

Time

9. Stay on time.

Provide full demonstration

10. When demonstrating:
    a. provide cues to look for and steps.
    b. show slowly.
    c. precede each move by a short cueing sentence.

Tutor or discuss within lecture

11. If you are better at discussion or tutoring than you are at lecturing, you may consider conducting a discussion or a tutorial within a lecture. Select a student or a dozen seats

which are designated as the tutor or the discussion group. Rotate students through these seats each class. Conduct a discussion with the twelve students, while the rest observe and listen or tutor one student.

E. Question Practice and Feedback

Call for response

1. You can: pose a problem, or state a case to be analyzed, or ask a question, or present an issue, and ask students to respond: individually (written response), or in pairs (comparing answers once they are done). or in small groups (4-6) in a stated amount of time (e.g., 1 minute, 5 minutes).

Active appropriate

2. Students' responses should include practice responseor use of information leading to attainment of the objective. (See detailed chart for the kind of responses desirable for different types of knowledge.)

Provide feedback

3. To provide knowledge of results and to reward those who have answered correctly, you should provide feedback consisting of the correct answer, or possible correct answers, or the characteristics of an acceptable answer by: stating the answer, showing the answer on an overhead, passing out the answer in a handout, having a student state the answer and verifying it.

Prompt and reinforce

4. Praise students for correct responses and provide prompts by reflecting or questioning wrong responses, rather than providing the answer.

Use efficient questions

5. Ask for questions, but to save time ask for the type of question you want which deals with the main idea.
   Inefficient way: Any questions?
   Efficient way: Do you have a question about the characteristics or sequence of steps in doing...

Transition

6. After this phase, state your next point--show how it relates to the last and do the rest as with the first.

F. Summary

Summarize
refer to next

Restate your main points, refer to the next lecture and conclude with a flourish as you began.

G. Assessment

1. To measure achievement:

Provide quiz

To reward students for paying attention during class, give a short quiz testing key ideas at the end. Provide answers then or have students confirm the answers as an assignment. There is no rule that says you must lecture for 50 minutes. More learning may take place in a ten minute quiz than in the 40 minute lecture which precedes it.

2. To measure attitude and lecture effectiveness:

P.C.Q.
   a. Use a post class questionnaire which asks for the best and worst of a class and which asks for specific questions. Answer the questions submitted by students at the beginning of the following class.

Debrief
   b. Hold a group discussion in which participants are encouraged to provide feedback on the presentation (e.g., what they learned, what new ideas were provoked, what they liked best, what they liked least, what improvements could be made, etc.)

(Reprinted with permission of Stephen L. Yelon, Michigan State University.)

Contingency management methods. Contingency management methods differ sharply from the traditional lecture method and represent its major competition as an instructional method in higher education. The lecture method is teacher-centered. Contingency management methods are student-centered; that is, the student assumes primary responsibility for seeking information, studying it, and demonstrating mastery of the information. Moreover, within limits, the student can control the pace at which learning occurs and the outcomes of the learning effort. Although many variations of contingency management are now in use, they all derive historically from F. S. Keller's original method (Keller, 1966, 1968), which generally is referred to as the Personalized System of Instruction (PSI). We will not attempt to describe all of the variations on Keller's theme, but rather will concentrate on common features of PSI methods. Then we will highlight three specific variations of PSI: Programmed Student Achievement (PA), Programmed Achievement Study System (PASS), and Teaching Information Processing System (TIPS).

There are many common features to PSI methods of instruction (Keller, 1966, 1968; Ryan, 1974). First, students are given specific and detailed learning objectives. Second, the information to be mastered is organized into small segments or units. For example, a book chapter might be subdivided into two smaller units for mastery testing. Third, formal lectures are not given. Rather, information is presented by written materials only. These materials could be the student's text and/or materials especially prepared by the instructor. Fourth, students must pass short unit mastery examinations in sequential order. In other words, students must pass each unit before they are permitted to study a new unit. Fifth, students must be allowed to take multiple tests on the same unit material. The objective is to have students pass a unit mastery test regardless of how many times the test must be taken. (In actual practice, instructors usually place limits on the number of retests that can be taken.) Note that the teacher's responsibility is to prepare quite a large number of tests with many alternate forms for each test. Usually the student must achieve high performance (90 - 100%) in order to pass a unit test. Sixth, because the student can control the rate of progress through the course (by passing unit examinations), PSI methods are referred to as self-paced methods of instruction. Finally, PSI methods require a large number of teaching assistants (proctors) who assume primary responsibility for preparing students for the unit mastery examinations. Proctors are available to students during scheduled times, administer the unit tests, provide immediate knowledge of results, and review test results with individual students. Usually the proctors are advanced level undergraduate students or sometimes are undergraduates at any level but who have passed the introductory course with an "A" grade.

The instructor has responsibilities other than preparation of unit examinations. It is the instructor's job to prepare course objectives, organize material into sequential units, prepare tests, arrange for feedback, and supervise proctors. Supervision of proctors begins with their selection. All applicants for a proctor position must be interviewed to determine if they clearly understand the time commitment that must be made and whether they can handle the responsibilities iinvolved when assisting in the instruction of their peers. After the initial interview and selection process, proctors must participate in training sessions designed to teach them how to perform their job and how to handle responsibilities and problems associated with PSI instruction. After the course begins, the instructor must continue to meet with proctors on a weekly basis to review procedures and trouble-shoot problems. Finally, most instructors schedule a few "lectures" which are given only after a certain number of unit mastery examinations have been passed. Attendance at these "lectures" is voluntary and they are not used to impart information directly related to unit mastery tests. The lectures can be used to present a special view of a topic area, to explain particularly difficult text material, or to discuss aspects of a topic that are not covered in the written material. Teachers who think that contingency management instruction will give them more free time than they would have using the lecture method are in error. In fact, contingent management methods probably require a greater time commitment than the lecture method.

PSI approaches to instruction are not problem-free. Perhaps the major complaint is that PSI contributes to grade inflation. Indeed, PSI methods typically produce a bimodal grade distribution, with higher percentages of A's, B's, and F's and smaller percentages of C's and D's than when the instructor uses a curve to evaluate student performance. When PSI methods are used, instructors and administrators must be prepared for the possibility that they will work; that is, that students will demonstrate mastery and strive to pass the number of tests that will earn a prescribed grade.

Student withdrawal is another problem with PSI methods. Because all aspects of the course have been succinctly spelled out to students, they will withdraw from the course if they are having difficulty with the initial unit tests. Another problem is generally referred to as procrastination or delayed student work (Semb, Glick & Spencer, 1979). Wesp and Ford (1982) varied the structure of paced testing in an effort to deal with the problem of proscrastination. They compared three levels of PSI in which students were given varying degrees of freedom in setting their own pacing schedules. They found that the rate at which students took unit examinations was inversely related to pacing flexibilty. As flexibility decreased, the rate of test taking increased. The highest rates occurred in the moderate flexible pacing condition. Based on these findings, Wesp and Ford suggest that the problem of procrastination may best be handled by teaching students time management and study-organization skills. These topics are well suited for the lecture component of the PSI method and can also be addressed by the proctors during scheduled class time.

Programmed Student Achievement (PA) is a variation of the PSI approach (Lamberth & Knight, 1974; Lamberth & Kosteski, 1979). PA is instructor paced, whereas PSI is student paced. PA allows students to take unlimited quizzes, but the first grade received by the student is the one that counts toward the achievement of mastery.

Typically, students must achieve 100% mastery before they are allowed to move to the next unit. If the student attains 80% on first testing and 100% on the second testing, the student's recorded performance level remains 80%. Moreover, the student must achieve 100% mastery prior to a deadline set by the instructor or else the final grade is reduced by 1 letter grade for each quiz that is not passed by the specified deadline. In contrast, most PSI approaches allow students to take an unlimited number of retests with the highest grade achieved on any of the tests counting toward the final grade. Thus, a student who meets criterion on the first test receives the same grade as the student who achieves criterion on the fourth retest.

Programmed Achievement Study System (PASS) is another variation of PSI (Haddad, Nation, & Williams, 1975). PASS is similar to PA in that one's score on the first administration of a unit test counts. However, it differs from PA in that bonus points can be earned on subsequent quizzes that are then added on to the score obtained on the first administration. Haddad et al. (1975) reasoned that if students are able to earn bonus points on retests, they will not feel threatened by negative consequences if examinations are retaken. In the PA system, the student must retake a quiz and attain 100% mastery if that criterion was not met on the first administration of the examination. But, regardless of the fact that 100% mastery is attained, no change occurs in the original score. In PASS the student is rewarded for attaining criterion mastery by having bonus points added to the original score.

Which method works best? To test this question, Lamberth and Kosteski (1979) randomly assigned students in the same class to PA and PASS methods. All students received information about the two methods before random assignment was done. To minimize bias, the classroom instructor was blind as to which students were assigned to which group. Unit mastery tests accounted for 70% of the student's grade, the remaining 30% was accounted for by the final examination. The final examination consisted of 51% new test items, and 49% test items taken from the unit examinations. Lamberth and Kosteski found no differences between PA and PASS groups on weekly examinations, the final examination, or in course grades. PA students scored slightly better than PASS students on old and new items of the final examination, but the difference was not statistically significant. The authors argue that PA has the advantage of not being as susceptible to charges of grade inflation as is the PASS method, and note that PSI is most open to grade inflation criticism because it is the only one of the three methods in which the student's highest grade counts. If grade inflation is an important factor for the instructor, the PA and PASS methods should be given preference to the PSI method.

A fourth contingency management method, Teaching Information Processing System (TIPS), is now in use in over 150 universities (Kelly, 1968, 1972). Recently, Arkes (1980) applied TIPS to the large introductory psychology class. TIPS differs significantly from PA, PASS, and PSI methods. Students take weekly unit quizzes and receive immediate feedback about their performance. However, students do not have to demonstrate mastery. Moreover, no proctors are involved and self-pacing is eliminated. Instead, after taking a unit quiz a computer provides the student with knowledge of results and then assigns readings tailor made to the errors made on the unit quizzes. The computer generated feedback sheets then are placed in mailboxes for student pickup. Student performance is determined by three examinations with all questions different from those contained on the unit quizzes. Throughout the course, Arkes recorded which feedback sheets were picked up, and then was able to link student effort on the weekly quizzes with their performance on the three examinations. Participation in the weekly quiz program was directly related to performance on the class examinations. For each feedback sheet that was picked up by students an additional 3.5 questions were answered correctly on the examinations. Students whose participation was high averaged slightly more than 10 more correct answers on the examinations compared to their cohort matched for high school class rank. Finally, TIPS tended to be of greater benefit to students in the lower third of their high school classes than to students in the upper two-thirds. Arkes suggests that students can benefit from contingency management methods without relying on self-pacing or unit quizzes. Interestingly enough, less than half of the feedback assignments were handed in by students, although many students reported doing the assignments as homework. Since the assignments didn't count, why hand them in!

The four contingency management methods described above are among the most popular behavioral approaches to teaching. However, many other variations are possible. Each method has its strengths and each has limitations; all are subjected to the general criticisms noted above. One of the strengths of contingency management approaches to classroom instruction is that these methods can and are being submitted to experimental testing. As Lamberth and Kosteski demonstrated, students can be randomly assigned to treatment conditions and steps can be taken to eliminate experimenter (teacher) bias. The Little, Brown package for PSYCHOLOGY can be easily adapted to any of these contingency management methods. Both students and instructors have specific learning objectives. The test bank contains items that are specifically linked to the learning objectives. Therefore, it should be a relatively simple procedure to generate a number of unit quizzes and if desired, to generate an independent set of test items for a final examination. Keep in mind, however, that contingency management methods require careful preparation and continued administrative involvement if they are to be successful.

Experiential methods. Experiential methods are person-oriented and process-oriented (Cooper, 1980). They emphasize development of individual self-awareness, awareness and sensitivity to others, and interpersonal communication. Formal examples include the encounter group and the T-group; less formal is the in-class discussion, as for example, led by a proctor or discussion section teaching assistant. In effect, experiential methods focus on Mann's "psychology as facilitator of self-development" orientation. Formal experiential methods rarely are used as the sole instructional method in introductory psychology. Informal experiential approaches, however, can be useful for certain class demonstrations in which students are asked to role play situations or act out simulations of experiments. Cooper suggests that experiential methods are well suited for demonstrating phenomena in social psychology, such as, "...interpersonal influence, conformity, leadership, decision making, power, communication networks, roles,....etc." (Cooper, 1980, p. 43). Several class demonstrations described in Part I of this manual are best performed with small groups. However, it may be the case that experiential methods are best applied to the introductory course in training sessions for proctors and/or teaching assistants.

PREPARATION FOR TEACHING

MacLeod's final question asks how instructors should prepare themselves for teaching. He emphasizes the importance of obtaining a broad education and of being personally involved in the search for understanding within the discipline, so that psychology has meaning to the instructor beyond the fact that it is a subject to be taught. It is interesting that so little time is spent in higher education preparing graduate students to be teachers (Williams & Richman, 1971). Over twenty years ago, Riesman and Jencks (1962) cryptically noted that, "...there are hardly any graduate schools that make a serious effort to induct graduate students into teaching, in contrast with throwing them as underpaid auxiliaries into large introductory classes to sink or swim, haze or be hazed (p. 101). Things have not changed much since the early 60s. While we clearly are not advocating an infusion of teaching methods courses into the graduate curriculum, it does seem advisable to expand efforts to teach graduate students effective teaching skills. Williams and Richman (1971) surveyed 150 department chairpersons and an additional 50 chairpersons from selected institutions and asked a variety of questions related to teaching. Eighty percent of the chairpersons from the general sample and 78% from the selected sample indicated that evidence of teaching skills was more important than evidence of research skills when making hiring decisions. Yet, 98% of the general sample and 89% of the select sample indicated that their graduate programs did not emphasize techniques of effective teaching. Respondents from both samples suggested that use of apprenticeship programs and the provision of good role models would be effective ways to instill effective teaching skills in graduate students. We agree, but ask just a bit more.

We suggest that all faculty responsible for supervising teaching assistants, whether they are graduate students teaching independent sections of a lecture course or undergraduates serving as proctors in a PSI course, develop a formal program for training assistants. One does not have to start from scratch! Many programs are available and can be adapted to suit one's particular needs. The following describes a workshop approach that was used to prepare graduate student assistants for teaching independent sections of a child psychology course. It was adapted from a workshop used for beginning teaching assistants in the Michigan State University Department of Sociology, and both programs were supported by the Michigan State University Educational Development Program. The workshop was held on the weekend just prior to the beginning of classes. The workshop was based on the general premise that instructors will, "...be able to teach better if they are familiar with the....literature dealing with learning, motivation, organization and presentation of subject matter, individual differences in learning abilities, group dynamics, and other materials related to classroom instruction" (Alexander & Davis, 1970).

MODEL WORKSHOP FOR TEACHING ASSISTANTS

General Workshop Objectives:

1. Teaching assistants will know the expectations attached to their position. They will become familiar with its formal and informal requirements, range of functions, and relation to faculty members.
2. Teaching assistants will become familiar with teaching techniques applicable to the classroom, and to the importance of interpersonal skills in handling the dynamics of the classroom situation.
3. Teaching assistants will know how to evaluate student performance. They will become familiar with the construction and grading of both structured and unstructed examination questions.
4. Teaching assistants will know what teaching resources are available to them in both the University and the community.

The workshop began on Friday evening. The objectives for this session were:

1. To acquaint teaching assistants with one another.
2. To explain the history and purpose of the workshop.

3. To have all participants identify in writing their goals and objectives for the workshop.
4. To have participants identify major problem areas associated with teaching independent sections of the course.
5. To provide an opportunity for participants to ask questions about the structure and rationale of the workshop.

The formal workshop began on Saturday. Responses to objective 4 above indicated that student concerns could be categorized into five problem areas: design of instruction, presentation of instruction, handling of interpersonal conflict, assessment of instruction, and development of content expertise. These five problem areas were reviewed briefly and it was decided that each would be discussed individually in the weekly meetings held during the term. Then the workshop proper began.

Session I: Formal Expectations the Instructor has for Teaching Assistants (9:00 - 9:30)

Objectives:

1. To answer the question: What is it that teaching assistants are expected to do?
2. To present the content of the Code of Teaching Responsibility, results of a questionnaire (sent to faculty) concerning expectations for teaching assistants, and data on department of origin of students taking the course.

Session II. Teaching Styles and Instructional Objectives (9:30 - 10:30)

Objectives:

1. Given one or more instructional objectives, be able to select those stated in performance terms.
2. Given a well written instructional objective, be able to identify the portion of it that defines minimum acceptable performance.
3. Given one or more performance items, be able to select those appropriate to the evaluation of the objectives.
4. To be able to define and cite advantages and disadvantages of each of the following instructional methods: formal lecture, lecture-discussion, personalized system of instruction.

Session III. The First Class (10:45 - 11:30)

Objectives:

1. To review tasks to be accomplished during the first class session.
2. To ease anxiety about their performance on the first day.
3. To discuss problems encountered in the classroom, particularly related to students dropping and adding the various sections of the course.

Session IV. Preparing and Delivering Lectures (1:00 - 1:45)

Objectives:

1. To list in writing the uses of lecture format.
2. To discuss and reinforce the importance of learning objectives.
3. To present and discuss techniques of preparing and delivering lectures.

Session V. Conducting Class Discussions (1:45 - 2:45)

Objectives:

1. To point out differences between lecturing, reading, and discussion groups.
2. To discuss methods of identifying material relevant for class discussion.

3. To identify what the teaching assistant can expect to have happen during class discussion.
4. To show how to prepare for class discussion.
5. To present some methods of discussing materials designated for class discussion.
6. To present methods of tailoring the mode of presentation to the subject matter.
7. To present methods of stimulating and initiating discussion.
8. To present possible problems and ways to cope with or solve them.

Session VI. Construction of Test Items (3:00 - 4:00)

Objectives:

1. To explore through discussion the functions of testing.
2. To illustrate the importance of matching learning objectives and expected test performances and to provide a step-by-step procedures for insuring that they do match.
3. To provide concrete procedures and examples of how to construct test items, both essay and objective items (multiple-choice, true-false, completion, matching).

Session VII. Evaluating Examinations (4:00 - 4:30)

Objectives:

1. To inform teaching assistants of the test scoring office and how to prepare materials for computer scoring.
2. To provide teaching assistants with methods for insuring consistency in examination grading.
3. To stimulate further teaching assistant thinking about constructive comments on student essay responses and term or project papers.
4. To initiate future teaching assistants into the realities of academic life: the consideration of ways of discovering and dealing with teaching.
5. To inform teaching assistants of the students' rights and responsibilities, including procedures for handling student grievances.

Session VIII. Review and Evaluation of the Workshop (4:30 - 5:00)

Objective:

1. To obtain constructive criticism of the workshop, including its strengths and weaknesses.
2. To identify topics requiring additional discussion or new discussion during weekly meetings of the teaching assistants and the supervising faculty member.

Each teaching assistant gave one lecture which was videotaped and then evaluated by the assistant and a member of the University's Learning and Evaluation Services staff. In addition, the supervising faculty member made in-class evaluations of two lectures for each assistant. One of these occurred early in the term and one toward the end of the term, and each was followed by a feedback session. (See the section below on Testing and Evaluation.)

The assistants' concerns about content expertise was dealt with in several ways: lecture notes, test items, and other instructional materials were solicited from the department faculty; teaching assistants were organized into small work groups to develop topical lecture guides; and a teaching resource area was established so that all materials could be readily available.

This training program proved to be quite successful. Administrative problems were minimal. Teaching assistants received good reviews from the students and made substantial improvements in their lecture style throughout the course of the year. Moreover, each of the assistants developed an exceptionally broad knowledge of developmental psychology and several subsequently volunteered to teach independent sections of introductory psychology in order to prepare for their comprehensive examinations.

Clearly, the benefits of this program outweighed the additional time commitment required by graduate students and faculty, and components of the program have become self-sustaining. Although we received much help from the professional staff of the Department of Learning and Evaluation Services, the group also drew heavily on its own resources. Our experience with this program suggests that efforts to teach teachers how to teach are no more reflective of Sophistic approaches to education, than they are of Socratic approaches (Furedy & Furedy, 1982). Programs like the one described above are consistent with the suggestion that the apprenticeship model may be the most effective way to introduce graduate students to techniques of effective teaching in as much as they depend on the initiative of individual faculty members rather than representing department-wide "methods" courses. Instructors seeking information about the teaching of psychology may find the reference list on page 197 a helpful starting place.

REFERENCES

Alexander, L. T., & Davis, R. H. (1970). "Developing a system training program for graduate teaching assistants." East Lansing: Educational Development Program.

Arkes, H. R. (1980). Teaching information processing system (TIPS): Evaluation in a large introductory psychology class. *Teaching of Psychology, 7*, 22-24.

Brown, L. T. (1980). What the consumer thinks is important in the introductory psychology course. *Teaching of Psychology, 7*, 215-217.

Cooper, C. L. (1980). Experiential methods. In J. Radford & D. Rose (Eds.), *The teaching of psychology* (pp. 33-50). New York: John Wiley.

Furedy, J. J., & Furedy, C. (1982). Socratic versus Sophistic strains in the teaching of undergraduate psychology: Implicit conflicts made explicit. *Teaching of Psychology, 9*, 14-20.

Haddad, N. F., Nation, J. R., & Williams, J. D. (1975). Programmed student achievement: A Hawthorne effect? *Research in Higher Education, 3*, 315-322.

Howe, M. J. A. (1980). Conventional methods. In J. Radford & D. Rose (Eds.), *The teaching of psychology* (pp. 19-32). New York: John Wiley.

Keller, F. S. (1966). A personal course in psychology. In R. Ulrich, T. Stachnik, & J. Mabry (Eds.), *Control of human behavior* (pp. 91-93). Glenview, IL: Scott, Foresman.

Keller, F. S. (1968). "Goodbye teacher...." *Journal of Applied Behavior Analysis, 1*, 79-89.

Kelly, A. C. (1968). An experiment with TIPS: A computer-aided instructional system for undergraduate education. *American Economic Review, 58,* 446-457.

Kelly, A. C. (1972). TIPS and technical changes in classroom instruction. *American Economic Review, 62,* 422-428.

Lamberth, J., Knight, J. M. (1974). An embarrassment of riches: Effectively teaching and motivating large introductory psychology sections. *Teaching of psychology, 1,* 16-20.

Lamberth, J., & Kosteski, D. (1979). Mastery teaching with and without positive incentives. *Teaching of Psychology, 6,* 71-74.

MacLeod, R. B. (1971). The teaching of psychology. *American Psychologist, 26,* 245-249.

Mann, R. D. (1982). The curriculum and context of psychology. *Teaching of Psychology, 9,* 9-14.

Riesman, D., Jencks, C. (1962). The viability of the American college. In N. Sanford (Ed.), *The American college.* New York: John Wiley.

Ryan, B. A. (1974). *PSI.* Washington, D.C.: American Psychological Association.

Semb, G., Glick, D. M., & Spencer, R. E. (1979). Student withdrawals and delayed work patterns in self-paced psychology courses. *Teaching of Psychology, 6,* 23-25.

Silverstein, B. (1982). Teaching a large lecture course in psychology: Turning defeat into victory. *Teaching of Psychology, 9,* 150-155.

Walker, E. I., & McKeachie, W. J. (1967). *Some thoughts about teaching the beginning course in psychology.* Belmont, CA: Brooks/Cole.

Wesp, R., & Ford, J. E. (1982). Flexible instructor pacing assists student progress in a PSI instruction. *Teaching of Psychology, 9,* 160-162.

Williams, J. E., & Richman, C. L. (1971). The graduate preparation of the college professor of psychology. *American Psychologist, 26,* 1000-1009.

TESTING AND EVALUATION

Evaluating student performance is an inescapable aspect of teaching. Regardless of the method of instruction, teachers must provide students with an indication of how well course content was mastered. Usually this is accomplished by testing. Testing and evaluation, though closely related, are not the same. Tests measure student performance, evaluation involves interpretation of test results. How well tests measure student performance depends on a variety of factors. Were test items properly constructed? Were test items derived from learning objectives? Was the test a valid measure of course content? Were students adequately prepared for the test? Were testing conditions amenable to optimal performance? Test files that accompany the current text were designed to provide a rich source of well-constructed test items, systematically linked to learning objectives. However, many instructors will want to supplement the test-item file with questions that are tailor-made to material covered in lectures. Therefore, in the first part of this section we discuss aspects of test item construction and test selection.

Evaluation of student performance involves interpretation of test data. For example, one class may use a self-paced approach with clearly spelled out learning objectives, unit mastery examinations, and predetermined evaluation criteria. In such classes, students may be informed on the first class day that a set number of unit mastery examinations, if passed, will result in a pre-determined grade. Another class may use a traditional lecture approach with the student performance measured by several midterm examinations and a final examination. However, the criteria for evaluation might not be set until all scores from examinations are summed, arranged in a distribution, and curved according to some fixed or arbitrary standard. Although the text material for each class may be the same and the questions drawn from the identical item pool, the methods of evaluation differ markedly. Regardless of the instructional model selected, it is good practice to determine how students are to be evaluated prior to the beginning of the course so that a clear description can be included in the course outline.

Evaluation is not restricted to student performance. Faculty performance also is evaluated. Indeed, graduate teaching assistants are evaluated both by students and by supervising faculty. In the second part of this section we discuss aspects of grading and evaluation and provide some sample materials that we have found to be useful in the evaluation of students, teaching assistants, and instructors.

OBJECTIVE TESTS

Several aspects of the total course must be considered when determining how to measure student performance. These aspects include the instructional model, class size, time constraints, and course objectives. Objective tests are preferred when the course is organized for self-paced instruction. Self-pacing generally requires frequent testing over small segments of the text material with options for repeat testing for each segment. Students must be able to receive immediate feedback about test performance in order to prepare for repeat testing if necessary, or to prepare for the next self-pace unit. Short objective tests are optimal for this instructional format.

Objective tests also are preferred when class enrollments are large. It is unlikely that instructors would choose to use essay examinations or term papers when class enrollments number in the hundreds. On the other hand, essay examinations and/or term papers may be the measurement techniques of choice for small enrollment classes. Objective tests, whether linked to self-paced instruction or to traditional lecture formats also facilitate rapid feedback of results. Regardless of length, such tests can be computer scored with feedback to students available overnight or at least within a day or two. Software packages exist which allow cumulative scoring of test results and grade assignment according to predetermined criteria. Finally, objective tests are easily integrated with learning objectives. Many convincing arguments have been made to support the learning virtues of "testing to objectives" (Ebel, 1973), but others point out potential abuses of such tactics (Exner, 1973). Perhaps if one keeps in mind that education is not reducible to behavioral objectives (Yellon & Weinstein, 1977), the advantages of objectives will surface as aides to educating, not as education itself.

If objective testing is selected to measure student performance, the instructor's next task is to choose the type of objective test items desired: options include multiple-choice, true-false, matching, and short-answer or completion questions. In fact, true-false and matching items are variations on the multiple-choice theme. Thus we will consider each of these before turning to the short-answer question.

Multiple choice questions. Multiple choice questions have several advantages which they share with other types of objective items. They are easily adapted for computer scoring and allow for rapid feedback to students about test results. Constructing good multiple-choice questions requires considerable time and effort, but will be an investment with great reward if the result is a more valid and reliable measuring instrument.

Each multiple-choice question contains three parts: a stem, a solution, and several distractors (Yellon & Weinstein, 1977). The stem should state the problem simply and clearly, with as much of the problem as possible contained in the stem itself:

Stem: Maria has noticed that the faster she reads her textbook, the less she can remember of what she has read. For her, at least, there is a ________ correlation between reading speed and amount learned? (from Student Study Guide, Chapter 1, item 20)

Students should be able to read the stem, determine an answer to the question, and then check to see if their answer is among the alternatives. The solution should be stated as clearly as possible. Each alternative should be a plausible answer without reference to other alternatives. Thus, in a real sense, the student can consider the stem and each of the alternatives separately as true-false items, eliminating the false items in search of the correct solution. Length of the solution and the distractors should be the same. If the length of alternatives deviates significantly, students may be cued to approach or avoid an answer merely on the basis of its discrepant length not because of its truth or falsity.

Discrepant Alternative Length:

Stem: Prior to 1960, autonomic nervous system responses were thought to be:

Distractor: (a) regulated by the pineal gland.
Solution: (b) involuntary.
Distractor: (c) operantly conditioned.
Discrepant Distractor: (d) beyond modification by any type of conditioning. (either classical or operant).

Preferred:

Stem: Prior to 1960, autonomic nervous system responses were thought to be:

Distractor: (a) regulated by the pineal glands.
Solution: (b) involuntary behaviors.
Distractor: (c) operantly conditioned.
Distractor: (d) learned behaviors.

Questions should be stated positively; try to avoid negatives. However, if the stem does contain a negative, underline it so the problem situation is clear to the student.

Negative Stem:

_______was not one of the structualists' elements of experience. (Student Study Guide, Chapter 1, p. 4)

Questions also should be grammatically consistent; that is, stem and distractors should match in grammatical form:

Grammatical Inconsistency:

The part of a multiple choice question that states the problem situation is called the:
a. solution.
b. distractors
c. alternatives.
d. stem.

In the example above, the question calls for a singular answer. Therefore, alternatives (b) and (c) can be eliminated because they are plural. Of course, the problem is easily corrected by simply rewording the stem:

Grammatical Consistency:

Which of the following correctly identifies the problem situation part of a multiple-choice question?
a. solution.
b. distractor.
c. alternative.
d. stem.

When developing distractors avoid "jargon" or "cute" alternatives. Students will be sufficiently anxious about the test and do not need to be "entertained" by the test items. Finally, the position of the solution among the distractors should vary randomly from one question to another. No pattern should characterize solution position as, for example, finding that the solution always is positioned as a first or second alternative.

There are two types of multiple choice question: those that stress facts and those that stress application. Examples of both are contained in the test file for *Psychology.*

Fact: The _____approach is also referred to as the stimulus-response approach.
a. psychobiological.
b. cognitive.
c. ethological.
d. behavioral. (Student Study Guide, Chapter 1, item 10.)

Applied: John no longer displays hostility and fear following brain surgery. The neurosurgeon probably removed association areas from the ______lobes of the cerebrum.
a. frontal.
b. occipital.
c. parietal.
d. temporal. (Student Study Guide, Chapter 2, item 4).

Most introductory psychology students will be in their first year of college and may have little experience with multiple choice questions. Including something like the following in the course outline, or as a separate handout, may give students a better test taking orientation than they otherwise would have.

TABLE 10

Taking the Multiple-Choice Examination

When taking a multiple-choice examination, your task is to select the best solution from among a variety of possible solutions. Following the suggestions below should help you to work your way through the test as efficiently and accurately as possible.

1. Check your test to be sure that all questions are in your set. Occasionally some pages are not reproduced well or are left out when the tests are assembled.
2. Skim through the examination to orient yourself to the questions being asked with respect to content covered by the questions.
3. Go through the test answering all questions for which you are certain you know the answer.
4. Go through the test again answering those questions you originally skipped. Keep the following points in mind for each question:
   a. eliminate possible solutions that seem to be obviously wrong,

b. give some weight to your first impression with respect to the correct solution.
c. change answers when you have a logical reason for doing so. This often leads to a change from an incorrect response to a correct one, but do not change answers on a whim. Often it is the case that your first choice is the right one.
d. correct solutions have been randomly distributed to alternative positions so do not waste time attempting to find a pattern for the location of the correct solution. No such pattern exists.

5. If you have any questions about the test items, simply raise your hand and one of the proctors will help you, short of supplying you with the answer to the test item.
6. Be sure to check your answer sheet to be certain that you have marked the correct space for each question. Once the tests and answer sheets are collected, it is not possible to give credit for a question that you knew, but marked incorrectly on the answer sheet.

True-false questions. The true-false question requires students to evaluate the truth value of a declarative sentence. True-false items should contain a single idea, stated in a manner that makes it clearly true or false. Avoid complex statements and negative statements. Include the source of a particular statement if there are different views on the topic. The following example from material discussed on page 470 of the text illustrates this point:

T F The first few years of life are the most important for the development of an individual's personality and character.

If part of the assignment included the section on "The Psychoanalytic Approach," it may assure that students will select True as the the answer. However, other material may lead a student to argue that the statement is false because it is stated inconclusively and does not take other approaches into account. Providing a frame of reference for the statement will help to eliminate confusion and reduce the number of heated debates between students and instructors with respect to what the question intended. A less ambiguous item would be:

T F According to Freud, the first few years of life are the most important for the development of the individual's personality and character.

Debate exists as to the balance between true and false statements in a true-false test. Considerable evidence indicates that false statements are more discriminating than are true statements. Ebel (1980) attempted to determine the extent to which knowledge of the proportion of false statements in a true-false test affected student performance. He administered a test containing 82 false statements and 41 true statements to students in an advanced undergraduate class. The test first was administered routinely, with the exception that students were told that they would be informed of the number of true and false statements contained on the test when they handed in their examinations. At that point they would be able to change their answers by recording changes on a second answer sheet. When the unchanged answers were scored, they indicated that students recognized false statements as false better than they recognized true statements as true. Students tended to change answers only for those questions which originally were difficult for them. However, the average number of answers changed was just slightly under 6. Overall, Ebel recommends that true-false tests can justifiably include a greater number of false statements than true statements--false statements are more discriminating than true ones, and the greater proportion of false items does not impair the validity of the test.

Matching. Matching, like true-false, is a form of multiple choice. In a matching item, there is a set of stems which are to be matched individually to a set of plausible solutions. The example in Table 11 is abridged from the Study Guide (Chapter 7) and is illustrated in a form useful for computer scoring with 10 response columns (A - J). Note that the number of solutions exceeds the number of stems. Generally, this is considered good form for matching items. Directions must indicate whether possible solutions can be used once, more than once, or perhaps may not match any stem at all. Gronlund (1968) takes a dim view of matching items because it is difficult to construct items in which each possible solution is plausible for each stem. If this conservative position is taken, matching items seldom would be used as measures of student performance.

TABLE 11

Sample Matching Items

(Adapted from Student Study Guide, Chapter 7)

Question Stems	Plausible Solutions
1. Jean Piaget	A. a prominant baby biographer
	B. mental operation involved in conservation
2. mesoderm	C. reflex response which can be modified by experience
3. visual tracking	D. mental ability which is the basis of social deception
4. reversibility	E. a sensory response which is present at birth
5. Lawrence Kohlberg	F. behavior in which sensory input and motor response are coordinated
6. sucking	G. he emphasized maturation more than experience
7. embryonic	H. period of prenatal development in which the nervous system is generated
8. Arnold Gesell	I. mental ability which is basic to categorization
	J. he formulated a six-stage theory of moral development
	K. embryonic tissue layer which becomes the bones, muscles, and circulatory system

Short answer questions (Completion). Short answer questions bridge the gap between objective and subjective approaches to measurement. In the short answer item, an objective stem presents a problem situation similar to a stem in a multiple-choice item. The student's task is to supply a missing word or words. The short-answer item can be used to test recall of specific information.

> According to Piaget, a child develops the ability to conserve during which stage of cognitive development?
>
> ________

Or, it can be used to measure the student's ability to analyze a problem or to integrate information in a more complex fashion.

> What aspect of cognitive development during the sensorimotor period is important to consider when studying the infant's attachment to caregivers? ______

Oftentimes short answer items are used more to guide student review of material than to measure student performance in a formal testing situation. The following short answer item is taken from Chapter 12 of the Study Guide and illustrates this point:

> The four ways psychologists have found to measure emotion are _____, _____, _____, and _____.

When combined with a programming key, this type of question can serve as an effective technique for testing one's comprehension of text material immediately after reading and/or studying a particular chapter.

When constructing the short-answer question, the space allocated for the answer should approximate the length of the word or words required. Moreover, the stem must be phrased carefully so that only one correct answer is possible. If too much space is allocated, many students may attempt to fill the space rather than answer succinctly. The short-answer item emphasizes recall memory, rather than recognition memory. The disadvantage of this requirement is that the material covered in introductory psychology is expansive and extraordinarily diverse--from brain physiology to perceived attractiveness--that using tests that emphasize recall are almost certain to produce lower achievement levels than are tests which emphasize recognition memory. All things considered, therefore, there seem to be far more advantages to multiple-choice items compared to any of the other types of objective test items for measuring student performance.

ESSAY EXAMINATIONS

Essay examinations are preferred as measures of student performance when class size is small, when course objectives emphasize synthesis and evaluation rather than mastery of bold fact, and when one wishes to encourage development of writing skills (Nunnally, 1959; Yelon & Weinstein, 1977). Essay examinations do require less time to prepare than do objective tests but savings in preparation time is offset by greatly increased grading time. On the other hand, care must be taken when preparing essay questions. Essay questions should be tied to course objectives, should indicate what points are to be discussed, should be stated in a fashion that encourages analysis and evaluation rather than presentation of detailed facts, and should allow students to address a topic broadly. Emphasis should be given to "why" "explain" "contrast" "criticize" "evaluate" questions rather than "who" "what" "why" and "list" questions.

> Explain why psychologists have concluded that prior experience with physiological arousal alters current interpretations of physiological arousal (Student Study Guide, Chapter 12).

After writing a question, answer it. That is, provide a model answer that can be used as a scoring key. Be sure to indicate how many points must be included in an answer in order for it to receive a specific grade for the item. In addition, one must determine the value of each question relative to the total examination, whether or not grammatical misconstructions and/or spelling errors will generate penalty points, and how much time must be allowed for each question and for the total test.

It is best not to allow choices; that is, have all students answer all questions. Permitting students to choose among several possible questions creates problems for grading and interferes with sampling of course content.

The instructor can reduce bias in grading by following several simple rules. When scoring the test, greater consistency is obtained when the answers to a particular question are scored for all students rather than scoring one student's entire examination before proceding to the next student's examination. Avoid inclusion of too many questions relative to the amount of time available to answer the questions. Students with poor penmanship and/or those who write slowly will be penalized by time constraints compared to students who write fast and have legible handwriting. Some evidence suggests that student gender also can bias instructor evaluation. Even many scientific journals have adopted a "blind" review process in part to eliminate negative attributions reviewers have for female authors. One way to avoid this problem in test scoring is to use a coding scheme to identify tests (e.g., student I.D. number). No names on tests please! Another solution is to have more than one person grade each test. If tests are scored by more than one examiner, points assigned to each question should be marked on a separate sheet of paper, not on the test itself. Thus, one grader's score will not bias the other grader. The two test scores can be matched later to determine reliability of item scoring (provided that all students have answered the same questions), grades can be assigned, and discrepancies between scorers resolved.

McKeachie (1978) suggests that essay tests are valuable not only as measurement tools, but also as educational instruments. He cites evidence showing that students study more efficiently for essay examinations than for objective tests. In addition, he notes that the essay gives students a chance to have their understanding of a concept checked by someone in the field. Therefore, it is essential to include written comments on the tests that are handed back to students. Finally, McKeachie suggests that the instructor is able to get a much clearer view of what students are learning from lecture and text when an essay examination is given.

FEEDBACK

Feedback is one of the most important and most neglected aspects of evaluation. Feedback provides the student with a chance to clear up any misconceptions about a particular subject and helps provide missing information when preparing for subsequent examinations.

On the day of the examination let students know when feedback will be provided. One method that is useful is to allow students to make notes on the test booklet. If they place their code number on the test booklet, then when answer sheets are handed back, each individual can review the test using their original test booklet and their scored answer sheet. Obviously, this practice is going to work best for small classes. In the case of multiple-choice examinations inform students that they cannot keep the test booklet *and explain why.* Once they understand how a test item bank is developed they often are more cooperative when asked to return the tests. They are also apt to give useful comments on how a particular question should be reworded to avoid ambiguities for future classes. Students should also be allowed to review tests during scheduled office hours if they have further questions.

Many instructors avoid reviewing test results in class in order to avoid bickering over each question. McKeachie (1978) offers two ways to deal with this problem. In the first, the instructor should determine which questions were answered incorrectly by many students. When reviewing these questions the instructor should read the item stem and all the alternatives. For each distractor the instructor should explain why it is incorrect. "This procedure gives you the 'jump' on the chronic criticizer. It is more difficult to maintain that a given choice is right under these circumstances than it would be if you had said nothing about the various alternatives and students could argue that the correct alternative was not completely correct." (McKeachie, 1978, p. 172).

The second way McKeachie suggests dealing with the chronic criticizer is to return tests and arrange students into small groups. Each group reviews the test noting the questions that remain ambiguous or unclear even after group discussion. The class, as a whole, then presents these questions to the instructor as the expert. This method, therefore limits the points being discussed to only those important to many students. As in the first approach, the instructor should have clear reasons for rejecting each distractor.

Finally, if during the feedback session it becomes clear that a question *is* ambiguous and more than one response may actually be correct, then scores should be changed.

GRADING

The criteria used for grading should be clearly stated on the course syllabus and discussed the first day of class. This helps the instructor remain objective in the grading process and minimizes complaints about grades once scores have been posted. The inexperienced instructor can check institutional and departmental norms to get a guideline for grading practices. Among the decisions to be made are:

1. Should grading be based on an absolute scale or on the curve? Decide the exact scale to be used and explain it during the first class session. For example, most students will not understand the standard score distribution and it is worth the time required to explain it on the first class day.
2. Will extra credit assignments be given so that students can raise a grade? If so, decide beforehand what the assignments will be, the amount they can contribute to a grade, and the dates when the assignments are to be completed.
3. Will make-up examinations be given? If so, be sure students understand what will be accepted as a valid reason for missing an examination. Most institutions have clear policies with respect to makeup examinations.

When posting examination and final grades, post by student number rather than by name. If letter grades are assigned to individual test scores it is best to be as rigorous on grading the exams as you plan to be when assigning a final grade. Keep in mind that the amount of student anxiety over grades is reduced when the requirements are clearly outlined and when they are able to evaluate their own progress throughout the course.

EVALUATION OF INSTRUCTOR PERFORMANCE

Evaluating the individual lecture. Instructors can improve their teaching skills by asking students to evaluate individual lectures. The Class Communication Questionnaire described in Table 12 has been used at Michigan State University and elsewhere and is a useful tool for obtaining feedback from students about individual lecture performance. These forms are useful when given early in the term, and then again late in the term. However, they can and should be used whenever the instructor wants feedback on a specific lecture topic. Remember to review the feedback thoughtfully and not defensively.

TABLE 12

Class Communication Questionnaire

Purpose: To obtain student opinions for improving instruction.

Do You Really Know How Things are Going in Your Class?

As you lecture, have you ever wondered whether you have gotten your point across to your students? Are you ever in doubt whether your examples are understood? If you are interested in improving your instruction and in helping your students to learn, you need answers to questions such as these--and the best place to obtain answers is from the students themselves. The class communication questionnaire (CCQ) is an excellent vehicle for obtaining information on how you are coming across in class. It is flexible and easy to use and can be adapted to your own particular requirements. Various forms of the CCQ have been successfully used by many instructors at Michigan State University and other colleges and universities.

Research studies indicate that feedback from students helps instructors improve their teaching skills. Most improvement occurs when the instructor places a positive value on student opinion and knows how to go about modifying his teaching procedures.

What is the CCQ?

The class communication questionnaire is a single sheet of paper containing a number of questions. An example of the CCQ is given below. The questions are stated in an open-minded format to allow students the widest latitude in answering and so as not to restrict the kind of information you receive. It is not necessary to include all the questions in the example. Questions 1 and 4 are most informative and should be used.

How to Use the Questionnaire

The CCQ is not an "evaluation" instrument. It is an instrument designed to collect the kind of information you need to improve your instruction. You might use it during the first few weeks after a term begins and once or twice during the term. Do not use it too frequently or you will "saturate" your students.

Pass out the CCQ at the beginning of the class period and inform your students of your purpose for using it. Ask them to turn it in at the end of the class period and remind them that the questionnaire is to be filled out anonymously. The information you receive will be both interesting and provocative.

How to Provide Feedback to Students

You must not fail to provide feedback to your students about their efforts. Students do not usually encounter an instructor who is interested in their reactions to a course, and they may have difficulty believing that you intend to use this information for constructive purposes. For this reason, the first time you use the CCQ you may receive some bizarre replies, written by students to "test the system." They only way to convince them that what they say will be taken seriously is to show them that you have read their comments and have made some decisions because of their suggestions. Thereafter, unconstructive comments rapidly disappear.

To provide feedback to your students, select representative responses to each of the questions on the CCQ and, at the next class meeting, read the responses you have selected and comment upon them.

1. Do not hesitate to include several responses to the first question, that is, examples of what the students said they liked about the class.

2. Select at least one suggested change that you believe would improve the course and that you are prepared to implement. Inform the students how you intend to implement the change.

3. Select at least one suggested change that cannot be implemented, for practical or other reasons, and tell the students the reasons.

Providing feedback to your students is essential to the effectiveness of the CCQ. Students want and need to know the opinions of other students so that they can check out their own perceptions. They appreciate a demonstration of instructor concern for their problems and welcome the opportunity to make constructive comments regarding the conduct of the course. When these procedures are followed, students will continue to give you valid and important information each time you ask them to fill out the questionnaire.

Interpreting the Information on the CCQ

Many of the comments students make will indicate clearly some needed modifications in your instruction. For example, you may discover that you speak too quickly or that you do not provide sufficient examples, or that you erase the board before your notes can be copied. However, some comments may indicate problems that are more difficult to alleviate. For example, many student comments refer to poorly organized subject matter. The reason for this may be that subject matter that is organized for a scholarly presentation to colleagues is not well organized for presentation to students and may actually interfere with their learning. If you would like assistance in interpreting student comments or in modifying your instruction appropriately, you may wish to seek some expert consultation.

Class Communication Questionnaire

1. What did you like about this class?

2. What did you like least about the class?

3. What would you like to see changed about this class?

4. What specific questions about the subject matter do you have?

(From: Davis, R. H., & Alexander, L. T. *Evaluating instruction. Guides for the improvement of instruction in higher education, #3.* Copyright 1977 by Michigan State University Board of Trustees. With permission.)

Another way to have one's teaching evaluated is to ask a colleague to attend one of your lectures and to provide feedback. Ideally, this should be a reciprocal arrangement. The advantage of this approach is that it allows one to discuss alternatives in lecture style with someone who has encountered the same situation. The Teacher Observation Record (Table 13) was developed at Michigan State University as an aide in evaluation of lecture style. In fact, the TOR was developed as a tool for evaluation of graduate teaching assistants in order to provide rather comprehensive feedback to them when delivering "invited" lectures or when teaching independent sections of a course. As we noted in the previous section, graduate education in psychology involves little formal preparation for teaching. We noted that one way to help graduate students develop teaching skills is to conduct training sessions. Another way is to evaluate their lectures. For the past five years we have been using the TOR for just that purpose. Early in the term the graduate assistant requests the supervising faculty member to evaluate a lecture. Note that the teaching assistant selects the lecture topic and sets the date for the observation. We use this practice because we want to evaluate the teaching assistant's best performance if possible. Later in the term a second observation occurs. After each observation the teaching assistant meets with the faculty member to evaluate the teaching performance. For experienced teaching assistants only one observation per term is made. Everyone involved in the program must understand that the intent of the observation is to provide constructive criticism, to help graduate students to develop good lecture techniques. The intent of the program is strengthened if the faculty supervisor reciprocates and has the teaching assistant observe his or her performance as well. With careful planning and good communication these observations can be extremely helpful to both graduate students and faculty. Hopefully in the final analysis, the undergraduate students in the introductory psychology classes will be the ultimate beneficiaries.

TABLE 13

Teacher Observation Record

Department of Psychology
Instructional Development Project

Instructor ____________

Observer __________

Date __________

<u>Method</u>

1. Teacher's speaking style (check all that apply).
   ( ) too fast
   ( ) too slow
   ( ) too loud
   ( ) too quiet
   ( ) overuse of a word/phrase (specify:
   ( ) good speaking style

2. Teacher's stance.
   ( ) stiff
   ( ) fidgety
   ( ) lethargic
   ( ) comfortable

3. Teacher's attitude
   ( ) nervous
   ( ) relaxed
   ( ) enthusiastic
   ( ) bored
   ( ) encouraging to students (receptive)
   ( ) other: ____________

4. Use of chalkboard or overhead projector
   ( ) good use
   ( ) too much time spent writing on board/projector
   ( ) too little use of board/projector

5. Use of examples
   ( ) good use of examples/illustrations
   ( ) too few examples/illustrations
   ( ) too many examples/illustrations
   ( ) poor examples/illustrations, specify: _________

6. Use of notes
   ( ) good use of notes--not distracting
   ( ) too much reliance on notes
   ( ) disorganized--should make more use of notes

7. Interaction with students
   ( ) participation/questions encouraged
   ( ) participation/questions discouraged

8. Reaction to questions
   ( ) positive--answer provided with interest, enthusiasm, no "put down"
   ( ) negative--students likely to have felt uncomfortable
   ( ) flustered--responded positively, but seemed somewhat uncomfortable

9. Student attitudes toward class
   ( ) interested--active involvement
   ( ) interested--passive involvement
   ( ) bored/disinterested
   ( ) lost, frustrated, irritated, angry, etc.
   ( ) other ______________

10. Classroom structure and atmosphere: check all that apply
   ( ) Formal classroom structure (stiff)
      ( ) high control (stifling)
      ( ) moderate control (flexible)
      ( ) low control (chaotic)

   ( ) Informal classroom structure (pleasant, relaxed)
      ( ) high control (stifling)
      ( ) moderate control (flexible)
      ( ) low control (chaotic)

<u>Content</u>

1. Facts presented
   ( ) accurate
   ( ) a minor misconception may have been generated: specify __________
   ( ) several misconceptions may have been generated: specify __________
   ( ) overgeneralized too much
   ( ) inaccurate in one or more ways

2. Organization
   ( ) excellent
   ( ) good
   ( ) average
   ( ) fair
   ( ) poor

3. Amount of information presented
   ( ) too much
   ( ) too little
   ( ) about right

4. Appeal of the lecture
   ( ) seemed interesting to almost everyone
   ( ) seemed interesting to only a few
   ( ) seemed to bore almost everyone

5. Use of motivators (e.g., a problem, current event, demonstration, etc.)
   ( ) effective
   ( ) superfluous
   ( ) confusing
   ( ) did not use (were not needed)
   ( ) did not use (would have helped)
   ( ) used a unique motivator (specify and bring to the attention of other instructors)

6. Level of lecture material
   ( ) above current student knowledge
   ( ) at current student knowledge
   ( ) below current student knowledge

<u>Summary</u>

1. Overall rating of the lecture
   ( ) excellent
   ( ) good
   ( ) average
   ( ) fair
   ( ) poor

2. Major reasons for the above rating:

3. Cite instructor's major assets.

4. Cite instructor's major liabilities.

5. Specific recommendations for improvement.

Individual lectures are evaluated to provide information to instructors about how well students and/or colleagues perceive their teaching. Although reliability and validity data for instructor rating forms are practically nonexistent, we still advocate their use. Some investigators have found modest reliability whereas others have found the rating forms to be extremely poor measuring instruments. We are convinced, however, that information provided by these forms can be extremely useful to all instructors. In the end, it is the use to which the instructor puts these data that is important, not the reliability or validity of the instruments. (Most instruments have at least face validity.) If the instructor ignores student feedback, it matters little what form the feedback is in. If, on the other hand, the instructor does pay attention to student feedback, we suspect that instructors will learn a great deal about their teaching.

COURSE EVALUATIONS

Course evaluations serve a broader set of purposes than do evaluations of individual lectures. They are used to provide feedback to the instructor with respect to the course as a whole. They also are frequently used as part of the criteria for deciding promotions and for determining salary increases. Students often use the class results to communicate opinions about faculty to their peers, although in many institutions students do not have direct access to the data. Course evaluations are usually given toward the end of the term. The instructor should check at his or her particular institution to see if a standard form is available and the particular institutional rules regulating its use. Or, one might wish to use a form similar to that developed by Professor Charles Hanley at Michigan State University (see Table 14).

TABLE 14

Experimental Course Evaluation

Course __________

Instructor __________

This is a questionnaire about your reaction to the course. Your response may provide you with catharsis, give you a chance to say something good, or let you communicate your thought about course improvement.

To use the questionnaire, SEPARATE YOUR REACTION TO THE INSTRUCTOR FROM YOUR REACTION TO THE SUBJECT MATTER.

1. The Instructor. Imagine that you have $100 to distribute as bonuses among the instructors you've had this quarter (semester). You can give all of it or only part of it to any instructor and return all or part of it to the University, as you prefer.

   How much would you allot to the instructor of this course? ______

   How much would you allot to your other instructors? ______

   How many other instructors do you have this term? ______

   How much would you return to the University? ______

2. The Subject Matter. Suppose you had a second $100 to divide among the Departments or Schools offering the courses you now are taking. Again, you can give all or part of it for any course or return all or part of it to the University.

   How much would you assign to the Department of Psychology for offering the subject matter of this course? ______

How much would you allot to your other courses? ______

How much would you return to the University? ______

3. Improvement. What is *the single most important thing* that would have to be different for you to increase the amount you would spend for this course or this instructor?

4. What was the *single best thing* in the course or instructor that motivated you to give as much as you did?

(Reprinted with permission of Charles Hanley.)

REFERENCES

Ebel, R. L. (1980). The feasibility of using more false than true test items. *Academic Psychology Bulletin, 2*, 53-57.

Ebel, R. L. (1973). Evaluation and educational objectives. *Journal of Educational Measurement, 10*, 273-279.

Exner, R. M. (1973). Behavioral objectives and educational decisions. *Educational Technology, 13*, 17-33.

Gronlund, N. E. (1968). *Constructing achievement tests.* Englewood Cliffs, NJ: Prentice-Hall.

McKeachie, W. (1978). *Teaching tips: A guidebook for the beginning college teacher.* Lexington, MA: D. C. Heath and Co.

Nunnally, J. C., Jr. (1959). *Tests and measurements: Assessment and prediction.* New York: McGraw-Hill.

Yelon, S. L., & Weinstein, G. W. (1977). *A teacher's world: Psychology in the classroom.* New York: McGraw-Hill.

TEACHING RESOURCES

BIBLIOGRAPHY ON TEACHING

Anderson, R. J. (1970). Stability of student interest in general psychology. *American Psychologist, 25*, 630-632.

Apply, M. H. (Ed.) (1970). The place of psychology in the university. *American Psychologist, 25*, 387-468.

Badia, P., Harsh, J., & Stutts, C. (1978). An assessment of methods of instruction and measures of ability. *Journal of Personalized Instruction, 3*, 69-75.

Bare, J. K. (1982). The introductory psychology course in the Eighties. *Teaching of Psychology, 9*, 42-45.

Barker, L. L. (1971). *Listening behavior.* Englewood Cliffs, NJ: Prentice Hall.

Barzun, J. (1945). *Teacher in America.* Boston, MA: Little, Brown & Co.

Bondy, A. S. (1978). Effects of reviewing multiple-choice tests on specific versus general learning. *Teaching of Psychology, 5*, 144-146.

Brandt, L. W. (1970). American psychology. *American Psychologist, 25*, 1091-1093.

Brown, G., Charrington, D. H., & Cohen, L. (1975). *Experiments in the social sciences.* New York: Harper & Row.

Bruner, J. S. (1968). *Toward a theory of instruction.* New York: W. W. Norton & Co.

Caldwell, E. C., Bissonnettee, K., Klishis, M. J., Ripley, M., Farudi, P. P., Hochstetter, G. T., & Radiker, J. E. (1978). Mastery: The essential essential in PSI. *Teaching of Psychology, 5*, 59-65.

Centra, J. A. (1952). *Strategies for improving college teaching.* Washington, D.C.: American Association of Higher Education.

Chandler, T. A. (1978). The questionable status of student evaluations of teaching. *Teaching of Psychology, 5*, 150-152.

Cole, D. L. (1982). Psychology as a liberating art. *Teaching of Psychology, 9*, 23-26.

Costin, F. (1978). Do student ratings of college teachers predict student achievement? *Teaching of Psychology, 5*, 86-88.

Costin, F. (1982). Some thoughts on general education and the teaching of undergraduate psychology. *Teaching of Psychology, 9*, 26-28.

Dambrot, F. (1980). Test-item order and academic ability, or should you shuffle the test-item deck? *Teaching of Psychology, 7*, 94-96.

Daniel, R. S. (1970). Teaching psychology in the community and junior colleges. *American Psychologist, 25*, 537-543.

DesLauriers, M. P., Hohn, R. L., & Clark, G. M. (1980). Learner characteristics and performance effects in a self-paced instruction for community college students. *Teaching of Psychology, 7*, 161-163.

Deutsch, A. M., & Byers, E. S. (1978). Improving college teaching: A handbook for the new instructor. *JSAS Catalog of Selected Documents in Psychology, 8*, 20 (MS# 1656).

Flanagan, J. C. (1973). Education: How and for what. *American Psychologist, 28*, 551-556.

Frankel, C. (1968). *Education and the barricades.* W. W. Norton.

Furedy, J. J., & Furedy, C. (1982). Socratic versus Sophistic strains in the teaching of undergraduate psychology: Implicit conflicts made explicit. *Teaching of Psychology, 9*, 14-20.

Gardiner, J., & Kaminska, Z. (1975). *First experiments in psychology.* London: Methuen.

Gronlund, N. E. (1970). *Stating behavioral objectives for classroom instruction.* New York: Macmillan.

Haskett, G. J. (1973). Research and early education: Relations among classroom laboratories and society. *American Psychologist, 28*, 248-256.

Hebb, D. O. (1974). What psychology is about. *American Psychologist, 29*, 71-79.

Jacobs, L. W. (1980). Instructional techniques in the introductory statistics course: The first class meeting. *Teaching of Psychology, 7*, 241-242.

Johnson, D. F., & Mihal, W. L. (1973). Performance of blacks and whites in computerized vs. manual testing environments. *American Psychologist, 28*, 694-699.

Johnson, T. M., & Pennypacker, H. W. (1971). A behavior approach to college teaching. *American Psychologist, 26*, 219-244.

Jung, J., & Bailey, J. H. (1976). *Contemporary psychology experiments: Adaptations for laboratory.* New York: John Wiley & Sons.

Keller, F. S. (1968). "Goodbye teacher...." *Journal of Applied Behavioral Analysis, 1,* 79-89.

Keller, F. S. (1966). A personal course in psychology. In R. Ulrich, T. Stachnik, & J. Mabry (Eds.), *Control of human behavior.* Glenview, IL: Scott, Foresman, Inc.

Keller, F. S. (1969). A programmed system of instruction. *Educational Technology Monographs, 2,* (1).

Knox, W. J. (1970). Obtaining a Ph.D. in psychology. *American Psychologist, 25,* 1026-1032.

Lattell, L. A. (1978). A workshop for new graduate student teachers of undergraduate psychology courses. *Teaching of Psychology,* 5, 208-209.

Mack, D., & McCaffer, R. (1978). Computerized random item selection and quiz production for mastery testing. *Teaching of Psychology,* 5, 98.

MacLeod, R. B. (1971). The teaching of psychology. *American Psychologist, 26,* 235-249.

Mann, R. D. (1982). The curriculum and context of psychology. *Teaching of Psychology, 9,* 9-14.

McCollom, I. N. (1971). Psychological thrillers: Psychology books students read when given freedom of choice. *American Psychologist, 26,* 921-927.

McGovern, G. (1970). The child and the American future. *American Psychologist, 25,* 157-160.

McGovern, L. P. (1978). The executive monkeys: Fact and fiction in introductory psychology texts. *Teaching of Psychology,* 5, 36-37.

McGraw, M. B. (1970). Major challenges for students of infancy and early childhood. *American Psychologist, 25,* 754-756.

McKeachie, W. J. (1969). *Teaching tips: A guidebook for the beginning teacher.* Lexington, MA: D. C. Heath.

McKeachie, W. J., Lin, Y-G., Moffett, M. M., & Dougherty, M. (1978). Effective teaching: Facilitative vs. directive style. *Teaching of Psychology,* 5, 193-194.

McKenzie, S., & Cangemi, J. P. (1978). What new students in introduction to psychology really want to learn: A survey. *Journal of Instructional Psychology,* 5, 5-7.

McKinney, F. (1980). Undergraduate psychology and self help. *Teaching of Psychology,* 7, 103-104.

McMichael, J. S., & Corey, J. R. (1969). Contingency management in an introductory psychology course produces better learning. *Journal of Applied Behavior Analysis,* 2, 79-83.

Morrow, R. (1976). *What every TA should know.* Berkeley, CA: University of California Press.

Mosher, R. L., & Sprinthall, N. A. (1970). Psychology education in the secondary schools. *American Psychologist, 25*, 911-924.

Nation, J. R., & Bourgeois, A. E. (1978). PASS, an alternative method of teaching introductory psychology. *Research in Higher Education, 8*, 273-282.

Nazzaro, J. R. (1974). The two-year college instructor: A profile. *American Psychologist, 29*, 554-557.

Nowlis, V., Clark, K. E., & Rock, M. (1968). *The graduate student as teacher.* Washington, D.C.: American Council on Education.

Oettinger, A. G. (1969). *Run, computer, run.* Cambridge, MA: Harvard University Press.

Palkovitz, R. J., & Lore, R. K. (1980). Note taking and note review: Why students fail questions based on lecture material. *Teaching of Psychology, 7*, 159-161.

Polsky, S. E. (1978). Student evaluation of college instructors: Preferred teacher roles and student personality type. *Dissertation Abstractions International, 39B*, 960.

Popham, W. J., & Baker, E. L. (1970). *Establishing instructional goals.* Englewood Cliffs, NJ: Prentice-Hall.

Resnick, J. H., & Schwartz, T. (1973). Ethical standards as an independent variable in psychological research. *American Psychologist, 28*, 134-139.

Robin, A. L., & Cook, D. A. (1978). Training proctors for personalized instruction. *Teaching of Psychology, 5*, 9-13.

Rogers, C. (1966). *Freedom to learn.* New York: Charles E. Merrill, Co.

Rose, D., & Radford, J. (Eds.). (1980). *The teaching of psychology.* New York: John Wiley & Sons.

Ruble, R. (1978). A dozen helpful books for psychology teachers. *Improving College and University Teaching, 26*, 79-80.

Seemay, J. (1973). On supervising student research. *American Psychologist, 28*, 900-906.

Skinner, B. F. (1968). *The teaching of teaching.* New York: Appleton-Century-Crofts.

Smith, F. (1975). *Comprehension and learning: A conceptual framework for teachers.* New York: Holt, Rinehart & Winston.

Spiegel, D., & Keith-Spiegel, P. (1970). Assignment of publication credits: Ethics and practices of psychologists. *American Psychologist, 25*, 738-747.

Sunberg, C., Malott, R., Ober, B., & Wysocki, T. (1978). An examination of the effects of remediation on student performance in a PSI psychology course. *Journal of Personalized Instruction, 3*, 93-97.

Swenson, E. V. (1982). Faculty adaptation to changes in undergraduate psychology education during the Eighties. *Teaching of Psychology, 9*, 59-62.

Terman, M. (1978). Personalizing the large enrollment course. *Teaching of Psychology, 5*, 72-75.

Turner, R. H. (1968). *Promoting worthwhile discussions in the classroom.* Chicago: Science Research Associates.

Tyler, F. B. (1970). Shaping of the science. *American Psychologist, 25*, 219-226.

Walker, E. L. (1963). Utilizing student motivation for mastering content in psychology. In G. K. Smith (Ed.), *Current issues in higher education.* Washington, D.C.: American Association for Higher Education.

Wexler, M. (1976). The behavioral sciences in medical education. *American Psychologist, 31*, 275-283.

Winzenz, D., & Winzenz, M. (1978). Individualized readings for introductory psychology. *Teaching of Psychology, 5*, 159-160.

Woods, P. J. (Ed.). (1973). *Sourcebook on the teaching of psychology.* Roanoke, VA: Scholars Press.

Yamamoto, K. (1975). *Individuality: The unique learner.* Chicago: Charles E. Merrill.

FILM SUPPLIERS

ACI Films, Inc.
35 West 45th Street
New York, NY 10036

Alternatives on Film
P.O. Box 22141
San Francisco, CA 94122

American Broadcast Company TV
1330 Avenue of the Americas
New York, NY 10019

Appleton-Century-Crofts
400 Park Avenue South
New York, NY 10016

Audio Film Center
34 MacQuiston Parkway South
Mt. Vernon, NY 10550

Audio Visual Instruction
Gill Coliseum 133
Corvallis, OR 97331

Bailey Film Associates
2211 Michigan Avenue
Santa Monica, CA 90404

BFA Educational Media
2211 Michigan Avenue
Santa Monica, CA 90404

Biomed Arts Association
350 Parnassus Avenue
Suite 905
San Francisco, CA 94117

Brandon Films, Inc.
221 West 57th Street
New York, NY 10019

Campus Film Distributors Corp.
20 East 46th Street
New York, NY 10017

Canadian Film Institute
1762 Carling Avenue
Ottawa, Canada

Carousel Films, Inc.
1501 Broadway
New York, NY 10036

Churchill Films
662 North Robertson Blvd.
Los Angeles, CA 90069

College Film Center
332 South Michigan Avenue
Chicago, IL 60604

Contemporary/McGraw-Hill Films
Trade Order Service
Distribution Center
Princeton Road
Hightstown, NJ 08520

Coronet Films
65 East South Water Street
Chicago, IL 60601

CRM-McGraw-Hill Films
110 Fifteenth Street
Del Mar, CA 92014

Encyclopedia Britannica Films, Inc.
Educational Corporation
1150 Wilmette Avenue
Wilmette, IL 60091

Filmakers Library
133 East 58th Street
Suite 703 A
New York, NY 10022

Films, Inc.
5625 Hollywood Blvd.
Los Angeles, CA 90028

Harcourt, Brace, Jovanovich, Inc.
757 Third Avenue
New York, NY 10017

Harper and Row Media
2350 Virginia Avenue
Hagerstown, MD 21740

Indiana University
Audio-Visual Center
Circulation Department
Bloomington, IN 47401

Instructional Television Services
Brigham Young University
Provo, UT 84602

International Film Bureau
332 S. Michigan Avenue
Chicago, IL 60604

J. Gary Mitchell Film Co.
2000 Bridgeway
Sausalito, CA 94965

John Wiley & Sons, Inc.
Educational Services Department
605 Third Avenue
New York, NY 10016

Learning Corporation of America
1350 Avenue of the Americas
New York, NY 10019

Lippincott Company
Division of Higher Education
East Washington Square
Philadelphia, PA 19105

McGraw-Hill Book Company
Text-Film Division
330 West 42nd Street
New York, NY 10036

Media Guild
P.O. Box 881
Solana Beach, CA 92075

Mental Health Training Film Program
58 Fernwood Road
Boston, MA 02115

National Audio-Visual Center
Washington, D.C. 20409

National Film Board of Canada
1251 Avenue of the Americas
New York, NY 10016

NBC Videotape
WNET
304 West 50th Street
New York, NY 10019

NET Film Service
Audio-Visual Center
Indiana University
Bloomington, IN 47401

New York University Film Library
26 Washington Place
New York, NY 10003

Perennial Education
P.O. Box 855
Highland Park, IL 60035

Psychological Cinema Register
Pennsylvania State University
University Park, PA 16802

Psychological Films
189 N. Wheeler Street
Orange, CA 92669

Pyramid Films
P.O. Box 1048
Santa Monica, CA 90406

Research Press
Box 31772
Champaign, IL 61820

Time-Life Films
Multimedia Division
43 West 16th Street
New York, NY 10011

University of California
Extension Media Center
2223 Fulton Street
Berkeley, CA 94720

INSTRUCTIONAL MATERIALS FROM THE AMERICAN PSYCHOLOGICAL ASSOCIATION

The following resources have been prepared under the auspices of the American Psychological Association (APA) and are available from:

American Psychological Association
Order Department
1200 Seventeenth Street, N.W.
Washington, D.C. 20036

Teaching of Psychology. Division 2 (Division on the Teaching of Psychology) publishes the journal *Teaching of Psychology* (originally "Teaching of Psychology Newsletter). The journal includes articles on all aspects of teaching and, in our opinion, should be steady reading for all teachers of psychology. Inquiries about Division 2 and about the journal should be addressed to the editor: Robert S. Daniel, Editor, Department of Psychology, McAlester Hall, University of Missouri, Columbia, MO 65211.

Benjamin, L. N., Jr., & Lowman, K. D. (Eds.). (1981). *Activities handbook for the teaching of psychology, (244 pp.).*

Ethical Principles in the conduct of research with human participants. (1982). APA, (88 pp.).

Ethical Principle of Psychologists. (1981). APA, (11 pp.).

Fretz, B. E., & Stang, D. J. (Eds.). (1980). *Preparing for graduate study: Not for seniors only.* APA, (96 pp.).

Johnson, M., & Wertheimer, M. (Eds.). (1979). *Psychology teacher's research book: First course.* APA, (224 pp.).

Kulik, J. A. (1973). *Undergraduate education in psychology.* APA.

Maas, J. B., & Kleiber, D. A. (Eds.). (1976). *Directory of teaching innovations in psychology.* APA.

Program on the teaching of psychology in the secondary school: Final report. (1970). APA.

Psychology as a health care profession. (1979). APA, (20 pp.)

Reed, J. G., & Baxter, P. M. (1983). *Library use: A handbook for psychology.* APA, (128 pp.).

Ryan, B. A. (1974). *PSI: Keller's personalized system of instruction: An appraisal.* APA.

Standards for educational and psychological tests. (1974). APA, (76 pp.).

Standards for providers of psychological services. (1979). APA, (16 pp.).

Thesaurus of psychological index terms (3rd ed.). (1982). APA, (362 pp.).

Woods, P. J. (Ed.). (1979). *The psychology major: Training and employment strategies.* APA, (331 pp.).